CW00821596

SOLDIER OF
THE RAJ

SOLDIER OF THE RAJ

WILLIAM MAGAN

MICHAEL RUSSELL

© W. M. T. Magan 2002

The right of W. M. T. Magan to be identified
as the author of this work has been asserted by him
in accordance with the Copyright, Designs
and Patents Act, 1988

First published in Great Britain 2002
by Michael Russell (Publishing) Ltd
Wilby Hall, Wilby, Norwich NR16 2JP

Typeset in Sabon by Waveney Typesetters,
Wymondham, Norfolk
Printed and bound in Great Britain
by Biddles Ltd, Guildford and King's Lynn

Maps by J. D. Cartographics

All rights reserved
ISBN 0 85955 275 6

Contents

Acknowledgements

I am grateful to Maxine, my wife, and to Nancy Christopherson, for their help in editing the text.

I
Sandhurst

I was brought up as a boy in Ireland in what was an unusual family. My mother, a fine horsewoman, daughter of a famous Master of Hounds in Ireland and of his starched upper-class English wife, had to elope to wed her Irishman, Shaen Magan, descendant of a long line of Irish chieftains and landowners, who was not considered good enough for her by her mother. I was born in 1908. My father was a notable shot and a most entertaining raconteur. We walked miles of Irish bogs together out shooting, while I carried his increasingly heavy bags of game. Perhaps that gave me a taste for walking in wild places. Later, as a young man, as this book recounts, I was very fortunate. I was adventurous and inquisitive, and I had the opportunities to go to places where other white men had seldom, if ever, been and to have experiences which they had never had.

I was educated in England. It was my father's friend Johnny O'Rourke who told me about life in the Indian Cavalry, and because of him that I decided, at the age of fifteen, to become an Indian Cavalryman too. I joined the Royal Military College, Camberley – Sandhurst – in January 1927, and assumed my first military rank, Gentleman Cadet (G.C.) Magan. I was posted to No. 4 Company ('Lovely Four') in the east wing of the Old Building.

Sandhurst was not just another form of school or university. We were paid members of His Majesty's Armed Forces. I think our pay was four shillings (20p) a day, but we never saw it. It was taken off us, even though the fees were high, and set against such things as messing and laundry.

I travelled overnight from Ireland with a neighbour from Carlow who was joining at the same time as myself. When we arrived in the morning we were each allotted a reasonably spacious bed-sitting room and allowed to settle in and unpack. But that was the end of leisure. Next morning, we had our first parade. We had no uniform, but were issued with what was known as 'canvas drill', which consisted of rather full, baggy brown drill trousers which could be worn over other clothes, and a loose jacket of the same material, shaped like a Mao Tse-tung jacket. That was our uniform for the first few weeks, while our proper uniforms, for which we had been measured during the first day or two, were being made by the local tailor and the bootmaker was making our boots. We later wore canvas drill for musketry, so as not to get our uniforms dirty when we lay on the ground on the ranges.

The first parade was taken by the Company Sergeant-Major, Sergeant-Major Brittain, of the Coldstream Guards – a holy terror who later became nationally well known as the epitome of a Guards drill sergeant. His No. 2 was a sergeant from a line regiment, a somewhat beery individual whose name I have forgotten. Brittain never used his name – not in public at any rate; he called him 'Colour-Sergeant', which sounded, when barked across the parade ground, like 'Colour-Sarn'. 'No. 3 from the left of the rear rank, Mr X, idle; take his name, Colour-Sarn.' The Colour-Sergeant was the recording angel who took notes of our misdemeanours, but we learnt to wheedle him with horse-racing tips.

If you could stand the first six weeks at Sandhurst, you could stand anything. We were chased from morning till night. In particular, we were drilled unendingly into parade ground automatons, with unremitting square-bashing and arms drill. Brittain was a genius. You couldn't like him, and he certainly didn't set out to be liked, but you had to admire his skill. His timing was always 100% perfect. He must have been one of the best drill sergeants the Army has ever had. When he had brought us up to standard, some of us would occasionally take an opportunity to watch the Guards drilling in London – the changing of the guard, for instance. We thought they were rotten compared to us. In fact our only serious competitors seemed to be C. B. Cochran's chorus girls, who could knock spots off the Guards with their timing and synchrony.

We had to polish the most important items of our kit – our belt, our chinstrap, and our best parade boots. We spent hours getting what was known as a 'surface', mirror bright, in which you could almost see your face. Anything less than that was 'idle'. But there were also in the Company some old retired soldiers who acted as batmen. They were covered in tattoos, and had strange tales of service in India, Egypt, Burma and so on, with not a little lip-licking over the girls they'd left behind them. They cleaned our other boots, did some button polishing and other refinements.

One of them, a barmy creature, started off our day. 'Wake up, wake up,' he would bellow down the corridors, 'show a leg, show a leg. The sun's burning out your eyeballs.'

Up and dressed, we would assemble on the company steps facing the parade ground, on which Brittain would be standing, with the Colour Sergeant hovering somewhere about. Brittain called out the right marker and placed him, and then yelled at us: 'No. 4 Company juniors, get fell in!'

We would rush clattering down the steps in our nailed boots, almost certainly to be halted by a roar of 'Get fell out again. 'Orrible! Get a move on!' Back we would go up the steps, and then Brittain again: 'Now! I want to see you move! Wait for it! Now!' Then a further scream: 'Get fell in!'

Somebody always caught it. 'Colour-Sarn: Mr Y, idle. Take his name.' We were always addressed as 'Mister' by the NCO instructors, which in no way softened the strafing we got. (We had a peer of the realm in our Company. He was 'Mister' as well – 'Mr Lord X.') For our part, we addressed the NCO instructors as 'Staff', though this didn't apply to the senior NCO, the Regimental Sergeant Major. He addressed us on parade and said: 'I call you "Sir". You call me "Sir". The only difference is that you mean it and I don't.'

The Adjutant was Captain F. A. M. ('Boy') Browning, Grenadier Guards, later Lieutenant-General Sir Frederick Browning, DSO (and married to Daphne Du Maurier). He had been an Olympic hurdler. Like Sergeant-Major Brittain, he was a holy terror on parade – and off it if need be – but he could also unbend and be friendly. On Saturday mornings the whole College paraded together, including the College band – veterans from regimental bands, excellent hand-picked musicians – and Browning drilled us from his white horse. We always drilled on the main parade ground in front of the Old Building, and he would be down by the lake, 100 yards or more away. He had a splendid voice, and the eye of a hawk.

'Battalion – slope arms! No. 18 from the left of the rear rank of 3 Company, idle. Take his name.'

He was often hovering about the parade ground at other times, and there is a story that he came up unseen behind a squad one day and said to one of the cadets from behind: 'Keep your left elbow in, Smith'; and Smith promptly fainted.

When we got our uniform and various items of equipment, there was scope for a refinement of the chasing we were getting. Our programmes of work were so arranged that we had to change our clothes as often as possible between work periods. Thus drill would be followed by riding which would be followed by PT which would be followed by musketry which would be followed by a classroom lecture. For each we would have to be differently clad. That meant a dash to our rooms, and a very quick change – and we had to be immaculately turned out or we were 'idle' – and back on parade *in time*. Almost the worst of all offences was to be late for anything. I can still hear the clatter of boots as fifty Gentlemen Cadets rushed up the stone steps and along the stone flagged corridors to their rooms, their rifles banging on the floor or against the walls in the general stampede.

The handsome grounds at Sandhurst cover a large area. To get to our various parades we sometimes marched, but mostly we went on bicycles – to the stables for riding, to the ranges for musketry. And we went further afield into the surrounding country for 'map-making and field sketching'. I once set up my mapping easel and board in the middle of a railway line and only just managed to whip them out of the path of an oncoming train. Meanwhile the Hartford Bridge Flats and the Ely 'Pip H' public house, two familiar landmarks on those bicycling excursions, became a part of one's earliest military vocabulary. We did not cycle haphazardly. We had cycle drill, and cycled in formation. In 4 Company we developed a team of trick cyclists and we put on a public display which started with the main doors of the Old Building being flung open, and the participants pouring out through them on their bicycles and down the stone steps at top speed and onto the parade ground, where the rest of the display took place.

Bicycle parades were under the command of one of ourselves, according to our rank as an NCO. It was practice in command and, on the whole, we took it seriously enough, but every now and again a little levity might creep in. I recall one occasion when someone was taking his first parade, who we knew was going to find it hard to keep a straight face and act the stern NCO. He fell us in, straightened up the two ranks, then, in a very smart and well-simulated authoritative voice, shouted at us: 'From the right – number!'

We were ready for it, and went off as smart as a machine-gun: 'One, two, three, four, five, six, seven, eight, nine, ten, knave, queen, king, ace.' The poor man was quite unable to come the flinty NCO over us, and doubled up laughing. Fortunately neither Brittain nor any officers were anywhere near. After that we behaved ourselves.

The Sandhurst course lasted eighteen months, divided into three terms. There were two terms a year – January to July, and September to December. First term cadets were known as 'juniors', second term we were 'intermediaries', third term we were 'seniors'. There were four companies, Nos. 1, 3, 4 and 5. There was no No. 2 Company. 1 and 3 were in the New Building, 4 and 5 were in the Old Building. The companies, each about 150 strong, were divided into four platoons each. Our No. 4 Company commander was Major Frankie Chalmers, DSO, MC, The Black Watch. He was very aloof and we seldom saw him. I certainly didn't get to know him personally. My first platoon commander was Captain Fitzmaurice, DSO, Royal Tank Corps, an exceedingly nice man whom I was to meet again later in India.

In addition to all our physical parades and work, we did a lot of military academic classroom work, such subjects as strategy and tactics, military history, military law. We also each had to do two purely academic subjects. I chose history and economics. My economics don was a very good professor named Priestley, a brother of J. B. Priestley. I was lucky, too with my history don, 'Pansy' Richards, a member of the Army Education Corps. There was no set history curriculum. On the first day Richards came round the class and asked each of us what period we would like to study. I wanted to try something more exotic than the usual school fare of English history spiced with a little European Continental history, and I said to Richards that I would like to study the history of ancient Mexico.

His eyes lit up. 'You couldn't have chosen anything more interesting,' he said, and put me straight on to Prescott. It was a decision I had no reason to regret.

The only game I played seriously was rugger, but I nevertheless played a lot of other games. We started a club in 4 Company called 'The Weasels', which had a smart chocolate-coloured tie with a pale blue stripe. It had only one rule. Members must be prepared to play any game whatsoever, against any opponent, and at any time unless they were already committed to some other appointment on behalf of the Company or the College. Thus I would find myself playing soccer or hockey or cricket against school teams, clubs and so on.

I was also in the Sandhurst revolver four – only four out of 600 cadets – and I could possibly have been in the rifle eight, had it not clashed with cricket and revolver fixtures. Some of the refinements and techniques of shooting can be taught, but I think it is largely a gift.

One of our annual Rugby football fixtures was against the French Military College, St Cyr. The match was played in alternate years either at home or away. I had the good fortune to be included in the team for an 'away' year, and we went to Paris and stayed at St Cyr, where we were fêted for the inside of a week. We also took a fencing team.

We were, of course, very interested in the way St Cyr was run. It was very different from Sandhurst. Despite the French Revolution, there was a distinct class difference between the cavalry and the infantry, which did not exist at Sandhurst. There was also an extraordinary office among the cadets. One of the cadets, without rank, or rather with only the rank of 'private', was chosen, elected or appointed, I know not how, to be the 'father' of the college, with the title 'Père Système'. To him either individual or collective cadet problems were taken in the first instance. He was a sort of ombudsman and, even more than that, had to try to be guide, philosopher and friend both to the cadets and to authority.

The cadet who held the post at the time of our visit was an extraordinarily impressive person, and the impression lasts with me to this day. He wasn't a commanding soldier; quite different – a gentle, pastoral sort of man of unshakeable inner strength and, one would suppose, wisdom; a man of the golden mean. It seemed a remarkable piece of French perception.

We went for a ride in the Bois de Boulogne generously mounted on the best of their beautifully trained horses. They also mounted us – at least those of us who wanted to take part – for a steeplechase; and we were allowed to take part too, alongside units of the French Army and a contingent of St Cyr cadets, in a review for the President of France.

In between we visited the Citroën motor-car factory and were treated to a glass of champagne in the board room by M. Citroën himself. Another day it was off to tea at the British Embassy with the Ambassador, Lord Crewe, and his wife, followed by a marvellous two-piano recital. We were taken to the Casino de Paris and, more soberly, Napoleon's tomb. We also paraded in uniform and laid a wreath on the tomb of the Unknown Soldier under the Arc de Triomphe. Afterwards, when we were allowed to mingle with the crowd, I saw a girl who had been at school with my sister Mollie and had stayed with us in Ireland, and who was then at a Parisian finishing school. She and I had a chat. Next day our photo appeared in one of the English papers noting inaccurately that 'the Sandhurst cadets visiting Paris are losing no time improving the *entente cordiale*'.

And then there was the purpose of the visit, the rugger match.

Unfortunately, we were a much stronger team than the French. It was rather embarrassing to defeat such generous hosts by a rather wide margin. But, although we were no more than budding 'brutal and licentious' soldiers, we were not without our own rough kind of diplomatic instincts and sensibilities. Towards the end of the game, the French captain, a delightful, gentlemanly man named Hubert, picked up the ball under his own goalposts, and the Sandhurst side, as if on some subliminal command, prostrated itself under his feet in feigned tackles all down the field without impeding his progress in the least, enabling him to score a spectacular try between our posts. The honour of France was saved, and we joined warmly in the congratulations. Our fencing team, I should add, had meanwhile been routed.

At the end of our stay, we were paraded before the College Commandant, General Colin, and made honorary cadets of St Cyr and given the red and white plume to wear in our caps. The French had given us a marvellous time, and their cadets could not have been more welcoming and hospitable. It is the only time that I have ever cleaned my teeth in champagne.

We were much more free at Sandhurst than at school. So long as we were not required to be in the College for some specific purpose, we could leave it at any time we liked, but we had to be back by a given time. We had to 'warn out' if we were going to be out for dinner on Saturdays or Sundays. Other days, we had to dine in mess. But on Saturdays and Sundays we had to be in by 11 p.m. and we had to report back on arrival. To be late was an almost capital crime. I recall some hair-raising drives back in the fog.

Discipline was very strict, and no excuses were accepted. We just had to get used to living in that sort of a milieu and soon learnt to accommodate ourselves to it. I think, nevertheless, that the authorities had a problem – the range of punishments available to them was very small. They couldn't fine us. We had no money: they had already collared it all. They couldn't put us in prison. They couldn't tie us to a gun wheel and flog us. There really were only two punishments available: 'restrictions', so called, and being 'sent down' and dropping a term. The latter was so harsh, and hard on possibly hard-up parents, who would thus lose a term's fees, that it was very sparingly used. Moreover, it would almost certainly jeopardise a cadet's chances of entry into the regiment of his choice. I recall only one case. So, it had to be 'restrictions' for all offences; except that there was one other minor punishment known as a 'puttee parade', which took place after dinner.

Dinner was a civilised meal held at a set time and for which we dressed in our blue patrol uniforms. One night a week – known as 'band night' – the College band played. 4 and 5 Companies messed together and after dinner we went to our rooms, at leisure to read or write or pursue our academic studies. But anyone with a puttee parade had to change out of his blue patrols back into khaki uniform and full equipment including rifle. He was then paraded, clattering, in the stone corridor and given a very hard and intensive perhaps twenty minutes or so of double mark-time, press-ups and so on. They were called 'puttee parades' because our nether uniform garments were plus-four shaped trousers with puttees below. Rolling your puttees onto your legs – and often needing to do it very quickly – so that the folds were equally spaced was an acquired art. To be unequally spaced was – it surely goes without saying – 'idle'.

'Restrictions' meant confined to barracks. The maximum that could be awarded was fifty-six days. The minimum was probably three days. Restrictions were very irksome – I escaped them, as indeed did most of us. On restrictions you had always to be in uniform. You could never change into mufti, and you had to be in your Company's rooms in the College unless you were either on parade or taking part in an organised game. A bugler toured the College grounds at unspecified times and blew the 'restrictions call'. All those on restrictions then had to go to the company parade ground at the double, in uniform and immaculate, where they were inspected and the roll call was taken.

One man in 4 Company of my term, Tony Crofton-Atkins, who later in life got into much more serious trouble, was habitually on restrictions. There was a bad moment when a peppery colonel relative proposed to visit him at Sandhurst one weekend and take him out to tea. Panic in the Crofton-Atkins camp. What was he to do? He dared not confess that he was on fifty-six days' restrictions.

We held a council of war and came up with a solution. Two or three of us would hang about in the Company building in uniform and be ready to meet the relative before he could start asking questions of anyone else. We would tell him that, very unfortunately, Tony would be unable to go out to tea because he had been put on fire picket duty, and it was such an important assignment that he did not like to ask to be excused it. However, we would take him along to Tony's room and provide some refreshment. If and when the restrictions bugle went, we would then rush about the building shouting, 'Turn out the fire picket.' The other people on restrictions of course had to be told of the plan.

In due course the relative arrived and was told this cock and bull story. We took him to Tony's room, brought the refreshments, and then withdrew. Some time later, inevitably, the restrictions bugle went, and we really got into action. We rushed round the corridors yelling, 'Turn out the fire picket. Turn out the fire picket.' I hammered on Tony's door, put my head in and said 'Excuse me, sir' to the colonel, and then, 'Come on, Tony, double up. Haven't you heard the fire picket call?' So out came Tony and, with the other poor malefactors, poured down the steps and onto the parade ground for the restrictions parade, roll call and inspection.

After that, those of us who could claim not to be on actual picket duty took the peppery relative for a tour of the grounds and got him off the premises as expeditiously as we could. But the wicked do at times flourish like a green bay tree, and Tony collected an extra large tip in recognition of the self-sacrificing sense of duty which had moved him to carry out his fire picket role rather than go out to tea. 'Duty before pleasure', we said, epitomised Tony.

My friend Douglas Leslie and I had an escapade. I am unclear about the organisation of the racing world but Douglas's father, Colonel Leslie, was a racecourse official – a stipendiary steward. Perhaps that stimulated some interest in racing among Douglas's circle, or perhaps it was just one of the varieties of wild oats with which we were experimenting at the time. At all events, we used to study form and have small bets, and we used to go to race meetings. So we were familiar with all the well-known racecourse figures, down to the tipster in African finery with his cry of 'I got a horse! I got a horse!'

We did our homework diligently. We didn't lose money, nor did we make enough to tempt us beyond our very slender means. We took a racing tipster's weekly sheet published by a man who called himself 'The Watcher – The man with a hundred eyes'. I remember he had one wonder horse, named Appelle, that was always going to do the devil and all, but invariably ran well down the course. However, we did not blindly follow the Watcher's tips. They were top-up information. We went by a study of horses' breeding and form; of trainers, of jockeys and so on.

We had just enough success with our selections to encourage us to try to cash in on them by becoming tipsters ourselves. Douglas Leslie and I planned to try it out one Saturday afternoon at Alexandra Park ('Ally Pally'), then one of the London racecourses. We reckoned we had to be suitably clothed, so we borrowed, or bought, from 'Ma' Hart, the pawnbroker lady in Camberley, some very loud checks. To disguise these, we smuggled ourselves out of the College well wrapped in raincoats.

Having arrived at Ally Pally, we had a few minutes' cold feet and then peeled off the raincoats, revealed ourselves in the full glory of our awful checks, stuck our umbrellas in the ground – it had been raining – and started shouting our agreed patter: 'We're Mr Worcester, the man from the North; the man with the information; all the winners for a shilling!'

We soon had a large crowd round us, but didn't sell many cards – although, as it turned out, we had five winners out of the seven races. We decided not to persist too long, however, because one of the old tipsters, a man well known on the racecourses in those days as 'The Captain', was decent enough to give us the hint that we would be in trouble with the rest of the fraternity, a tough lot who wouldn't take kindly to competition from us. He also offered to take us to the Derby with him because he said he had never seen anyone draw a crowd quicker – an offer we had to decline.

A lot of people amused themselves going racing on a Saturday afternoon, and we had had to take the risk that someone from Sandhurst might be there and we might be spotted. So, as soon as we got back to the College, and had discarded our loud clothes, I went up to the officers' mess and had a word with the mess steward, asking him to let me know if he heard any talk among the officers about a certain Mr Worcester. 'Oh,' he said, 'I just heard some talk about a Mr Worcester racing this afternoon.'

I returned to Douglas Leslie in a state of some despondency. 'We're sunk,' I said, 'the officers already know something about this.'

For the next few days we went about in considerable trepidation, wondering if, and when, and how, the axe would fall. We were both corporals, and at least we must expect to be reduced to the ranks. Then the moment came. Leslie and Magan were ordered to attend Company Office next morning at 11 o'clock, to see the Company Commander.

By then we had a new Sergeant-Major. He was nothing like Brittain's weight, or gifted with his authority, but he tried to assume it with a barking, confrontational briskness. He fell us in in the passage in front of the Company Office door.

'Now, Mr Leslie, Mr Magan, the Company Commander wants to see you both together. When he's ready, I'll open the office door, call you to attention, right turn, quick march, left turn. Right turn, halt, when you're inside. You'll then be standing in front of his desk. Salute smartly and say nothing. He'll do all the talking. I shall withdraw. Got that?'

'Yes, Staff.'

'Right, stand easy.'

'Standing easy' it wasn't. I don't remember many more uncomfortable minutes than the five we spent waiting outside that Company Office door.

Company Sergeant-Major Fenn came out of his office.

'Stand at ease. Shun!'

Then all the left turn, right turn business, and we were standing in front of the large desk behind which Major Frankie Chalmers was sitting. He was not very imposing, and rather portly. That he was gallant his DSO and MC made plain; and he wore an old-fashioned moustache with pointed ends. He constantly twirled the right one with his right hand, and occasionally gave the left one a little attention by brushing it up with his left hand. He always wore uniform during the working hours of the day, and was smartly turned out in Black Watch trews, a well-fitting khaki jacket, and buttons and Sam Browne belt so well polished that even we hypercritical cadets could not fault them.

When we had come to a halt, he leant back, tipping his chair against the wall behind him, and looked us up and down hard as though searching for any additional idle misdemeanours in our turnout. Then he began twirling his moustache, let his chair down again, and sat naturally at his desk. There were some papers on it which he looked at and turned over once or twice. Then he looked at us again, cleared his throat and, in his rather fruity voice, spoke for the first time. He may or may not ordinarily have been a man of few words, but on this occasion he was brief and to the point.

'It has come to my notice', he said, 'that you have both been showing a rather unusual amount of initiative recently. I am therefore promoting you both to sergeant, and I expect you to show a comparable degree of responsibility. That is all. Thank you. Good morning.'

With the smartest possible salutes and about-turns, we let ourselves out of that office with as much alacrity as we decently could. Sergeant-Major Fenn was there to meet us. He couldn't believe his ears when we told him what had happened. Our friends in the Company were likewise surprised to see that we still had our corporals' stripes, and incredulous when we told them that tomorrow they would have to address us respectfully as 'Sergeant'.

When we first arrived at Sandhurst, we were given a talk in a lecture hall by the College padre, a nice fatherly Irishman of a type very well known to me. It was not a moralising lecture, and he did not push religion at us. He was concerned to make only one point. He said we had reached the time in life when we had enough freedom to make our own choices, and one of the temptations that would be there, and would very likely even be pushed at us, or recommended to us by others, would be women. He urged us to resist it. I do not remember his arguments in detail. But I do recall him underlining the health hazards – venereal disease in its various forms, its disgrace and irreparable damage to health, and I recall him saying that the 'enthusiastic amateurs' – his words – were even more dangerous than the professionals.

While I was at Sandhurst, quite apart from the padre's staid warning, it was an environment where most healthy young men were probably more concerned to get their rugger colours. I was, however, once exposed to this world of doubtful morality. There was a famous, or infamous, night-club in London, 'The Forty-Three', run by a no less famous night-club proprietress, Kate Meyrick, the wife, or widow, of a doctor, who was in frequent enough trouble with the police to capture the tabloid press headlines. One of my friends insisted on taking me. He said it was marvellous. I was rather scared in case the police happened to raid it while we were there.

Kate Meyrick was a presentable woman with a strong personality. She had a following of influential people, though their influence perhaps stemmed more from rank and wealth rather than any particular attainments or achievements. She married two of her three daughters to peers. She was there the evening I was taken there, and I was introduced to her.

My recollection is that the club was in a basement. It was small and crowded, with people sitting at tables with drinks, and there was a small dance floor. The atmosphere was full of smoke; and there were the girls. They were young and good-looking and concerned to be agreeable. Their prime function was to be decoys for visiting men's pockets. When a 'guest' selected one as a dance partner, he had to offer her a drink. She invariably chose champagne. Probably the girls got a percentage on the number of bottles of champagne they could contrive to have ordered in an evening. At any rate I was delighted to be relieved of the assault on my resources, not to mention my anxiety about the police, when eventually we got out into the cold, fresh air of the London streets.

There was not much drinking at Sandhurst. People were too busy, too sensible, too hard up no doubt, and too concerned about their future career. I do not recall anyone being in trouble on a drink charge.

However, we all smoked. I smoked only Turkish cigarettes, because they had a seeming elegance which appealed to me. I enjoyed the way they burnt, and I enjoyed the smell. But I smoked them sparingly.

Much to my surprise, I acquired a wonderful girl-friend. Having been brought up with three sisters, I found that the school friends they brought home for holidays were merely a constant presence in the daily round, without ever a touch of romance. I really genuinely believed that I didn't want any more girls in my life, and certainly regarded myself as invulnerable to anything so seemingly absurd as a close entanglement. But then it happened, that mysterious rapport.

She was of my own Irish background. We were almost exactly the same age – she three months younger than I. She was exceptionally lively and the greatest possible fun, everybody's darling. I fell for her hopelessly on our first encounter, but I cannot think why she was so taken with me when there were so many more eligible fish around. We were parted when I went to India on leaving Sandhurst. She married a few years later, and died all too young. I have ever since kept a little signed picture of her which she gave me. I wonder what happened to the little keepsake that I gave to her. Her name was Noreen Villiers-Stuart.

For a dozen years after I met her, I never again had anything like a close association with a girl. The unencumbered bachelor life of a young soldier suited me too well. I didn't want entanglements. I liked to think my policy was 'attentive but aloof'.

One thing from Sandhurst still haunts me – the Last Post. George, one of the old retired buglers in the band, used to cycle round the grounds of the College at ten o'clock at night and, from various vantage points, sound the Last Post. The bugle, blown by a really sensitive bugler, is a beautiful, if limited, instrument, and George blew it like an angel. I would lie in bed and listen to it, every note crystal silver clear, first quite close, then, after a pause, as he cycled on, further away, and, at length, in the far distance, up towards the Staff College, the last note a long drawn-out diminuendo into the darkness of the night – the memory recalled over and over again as I have heard it sounded through the years over fallen comrades and men at arms. And to that I should add that there is no more beautiful memorial to the fallen officers of the British Army than the College chapel at Sandhurst.

The most memorable parade for all of us at Sandhurst was the last – the Passing Out Parade, at the end of which the senior term, who were passing out, marched up the steps of the Old Building and disappeared through its wide doors, followed by the Adjutant on his white charger.

One term at Sandhurst the monarch himself, King George V, took the salute at the Passing Out Parade. He was a stickler for military propriety, so every care was taken to ensure that he should find nothing wrong, and he didn't. When he was inspecting the ranks, accompanied by the Commandant, Major-General Girdwood, he stopped quite close to where I was and pointed to an undistinguished cadet whom I knew, and asked the Commandant his name. Why he should have wanted to know his name is hard to imagine. I felt a momentary embarrassment because I could not conceive that the General could possibly know. However, General Girdwood answered without hesitation and answered correctly. How did he know? Did he recognise all 600 cadets? He seldom encountered us individually, indeed one might say never unless we were prominent at some activity or other, which that cadet was not. Was it a bit of luck? One of life's unsolved mysteries.

I had a good memory, and therefore had no difficulty in cramming for exams, so I passed out of Sandhurst high, with no worrries about not being accepted for my chosen arm of the service, the Indian Cavalry. To be sure of a place in the Indian Army it was necessary to pass out in the first 35 out of the 150 who were being commissioned at the same time.

My report for my intermediate term survives. Although my exam marks placed me 14th out of 158 candidates, my Company Commander, Frankie Chalmers, in his very civilised and educated handwriting, described my 'Ability' as 'Average', so he was not overstating the case.

Conduct:	Very good.
Characteristics:	Has worked very hard and shown determination. He has a good influence in the Company and is developing satisfactorily as expected.
Commandant's Remarks (Major-General Girdwood):	Very satisfactory.

I have never enjoyed myself more than I did at Sandhurst. I particularly enjoyed the amateur theatricals. I staged a pantomime, in which I condescended to give David Niven a small part – rather parsimonious casting as it subsequently turned out. But as my recollections are largely of the fun and perhaps of incidents antipathetic to authority, the report may underline the fact that we took our training to be officers very seriously.

2
India: The 60th Rifles

I was commissioned on 30 August 1928. My commission is unusual in that it was not signed by the monarch, but by his consort, Queen Mary, during a period of Regency when King George V was unable to perform any royal duties on account of serious illness.

A fortnight later, on Friday 14 September 1928, I sailed for India on the troopship *Neuralia*. All the Indian Army cadets of my term at Sandhurst were on board, and some other people whom I knew as well. We took the normal sea route to India for those days, through the Mediterranean, the Suez Canal and the Red Sea. There were, of course, no air services to India at that time.

We 'coaled' at Gibraltar and, after we sailed, it took twelve hours to clean the ship of coal dust. At Port Said, where we coaled again, the whole tonnage of coal came aboard in baskets on women's heads. While the coaling was going on, we were treated to the gully-gully men and their remarkable sleight of hand, and also to the aquatic skills of the boys who dived for coins. And we were allowed ashore for a short visit to Simon Artz, to buy the odd souvenir, send postcards home, stretch our legs, and learn to avoid the touts offering less savoury wares.

On deck at night, in the bright starlight, leaning on the rail above the low throb of the engines as the ship glided between the high palm-lined banks of the Suez Canal was, for one who had never been east before, quite magical.

In the Red Sea we had a following wind. There were no fans and no air-conditioning in the cabins. All we had were 'wind-scoops' for the portholes which, with a following wind, were useless. None of us had ever before experienced such heat. There were four of us in our cabin, and we had a very nice Goanese cabin steward, Fernandes. One morning in the middle of the Red Sea, our early morning mug of 'gunfire' was brought by another man, de Souza. I asked where Fernandes was. 'Did you notice', he replied, 'that the ship stopped about half-an-hour ago?' 'Yes,' I said, 'I did.' 'Well,' de Souza said, 'they were burying Fernandes at sea. He died suddenly last night.'

We docked at Karachi on 5 October 1928, after a voyage of exactly three weeks, and I have a very strong first impression on landing in India of seeing an Indian soldier, a sentry, in beautifully ironed and starched uniform, everything spick and span and mirror polished. It was a promising omen. Looking at my own crumpled uniform, after the three weeks' voyage, I couldn't help reflecting – and the thought often recurred in the long years of service that were to follow – 'You're a better man than I am, Gunga Din.'

From Karachi, I went by train – it was an excruciatingly hot journey at first through the Sind Desert – to Lucknow in the then United Provinces, where I was due to do a year's attachment to the King's Royal Rifle Corps – KRRC – 60th Rifles, preparatory to joining the Indian Army. At some wayside meal I encountered for the first time a staple diet of India, some very unappetising fried brinjal – a small courgette.

The 60th were good enough to meet me at the imposing Lucknow railway station, in the person of Captain 'Puffin' Owen, a dapper Wykehamist, who I believe was killed a dozen years later when the 60th were defending Calais against the Germans at the time of Dunkirk.

At the time when I joined the 60th, officers who had elected to serve in the Indian Army spent their first year in India with a British battalion. We could thus get acclimatised, learn something about India, and learn Hindustani, also known as Urdu. This is a language that evolved in the Mogul armies in India in the sixteenth and seventeenth centuries, being a mixture of Persian and Hindi. The full name of the language is an example of that mixture – *Zaban-i-Urdu*. *Zaban-i* is Persian, meaning literally 'tongue of ...', while *Urdu* is a Hindi word meaning 'camp'; and it still was just that, the language we all talked in the Indian Army, though it was also much more widely spoken in India. Urdu was the first language, or mother-tongue, of very few of our soldiers in the Indian Army. Just as our first language was English, so theirs was the local language of their own part of India – for instance Punjabi for those who came from the Punjab – but, with some exceptions, in the Army we all spoke 'the tongue of the camp', Urdu or Hindustani. Notable exceptions were Gurkhali, spoken in Gurkha regiments, and Pushtu, spoken in Pathan units.

It was my immense good fortune to be posted to the 60th Rifles. Brought up as I had been in the wild Irish countryside, I was well in tune with the independent hardihood of the riflemen's traditions and, as a prospective cavalryman, I was equally at home with the quick thinking and decision-making that riflemen needed to develop in their original role as very independent forward skirmishing troops.

I was posted to 'C' Company and given command of No. 10 Platoon. I would have gone to the ends of the earth with those riflemen, who remain as fresh in my mind today as they were seventy years ago. I had a wonderful understanding with them, and I hope and believe that together we made a first-rate unit. They taught me a lot about soldiering. Many years later I learnt that when my year's attachment was at an end and it was time for me to go, a deputation had gone from the platoon to the CO to urge that our team should not be broken up, and that I should stay on and not go to the Indian Army.

'C' Company commander was Major Geoffrey Ashburner, but he was home in England on leave and the senior officer was the second-in-command, Captain Willie Osborne, who was ten years older than me. Soon after I joined the company, Willie Osborne took ten days' leave to Bombay to meet a girl off a ship from England who had come to India to marry him. They were married next day and had ten days' honeymoon. Willie asked me to look after his bungalow while he was away, which I did, and I had everything in good order for them on their return. Willie's new wife, Phyllis, was a beautiful and in every way exceptional girl. She and I were exactly the same age. We saw a lot of each other and a very close rapport grew up between us. Indeed, we came to love each other very dearly – and quite innocently.

Some time after I left the 60th and joined the Indian Cavalry, the Regiment was posted home to Aldershot and, when I got home on leave three and a half years later, I went there and called on Phyllis. She was delighted to see me, and we sat talking in her drawing room. While we were there, someone who had known me in India came in, and she said: 'Look whom I've got here.'

I returned to India after my leave and did not get home again for another five years. I then went to Aldershot again to see Phyllis, but did not find her. I made inquiries about her and was told that she had gone mad and was in a lunatic asylum – it was one of my life's most dreadful shocks.

Within a week or so of my arrival in Lucknow, the Battalion held some sort of open-day shooting competition. I went down to the ranges after breakfast and my Company Sergeant-Major immediately collared me. He took a few annas off me, told me he had entered me for a rifle-shooting match, gave me a .303 rifle I had never seen before, and a clip of five rounds of ammunition, and politely told me to get on with it in a tone that suggested, 'And don't let me down.'

Thereupon I lay down to fire my first shot in India. It was also the first time I had experienced the difficulty of aiming through the shimmering heat coming off the hot parched ground. However, I would try not to disgrace myself, or the Sergeant-Major, or my new found home in 'C' Company and my platoon. I took as careful and steady aim as I could, and squeezed the trigger gently – regulation fashion. The target was immediately hauled down into the butt. I could not think why, as I still had four rounds to go. Then a flag went up, and there was a shout of applause. Company Sergeant-Major Wilkinson, happy now to claim me openly as his protégé, clapped me on the back and perhaps barely refrained from saying, 'Good lad.' (I was only twenty; he a formidable father-figure.) I had scored a 'spot bull' – drilled a hole clean through the middle of a little spot stuck onto the centre of the bull's-eye, and I scooped the pool, which I thought it only seemly to hand to the CSM for Company sports purposes. I refrained from confessing that I had never even heard of a spot bull.

Those were still the days when a rifle battalion moved on its feet. Practice route-marches were supposed to keep us in good marching trim. They were an awful bore, and chore, and everybody hated them. We were short of officers, and it often seemed to fall to me to take charge. Route-marches took place first thing in the morning, but it soon got hot once the sun was up, with the temperature rising into the eighties and nineties even in October. It was also very dusty.

Having endured one or two of those marches, I hit on an idea. I think we had to do so many miles, so I worked out a special route with an *arrière-pensée* which I kept to myself. I told the CSM the evening before that I would lead the march. It would be the prescribed distance, but would be unusual. So, next morning, I marched them to the ruins of the old British Residency. Having got there, we fell out, and I asked the Company to sit round me in a semi-circle, and I told them stirring and interesting tales – or as stirring and interesting as I could make them – of the siege of the Residency during the Indian Mutiny. This was voted a good route-march painkiller, so I mugged up the history of every corner of Lucknow for future occasions, as well as other local information – Indian customs, religions, farming methods, and much else that could be seen and illustrated locally. I recall, in particular, the day I took them to Hodson's grave in the Martinière Garden. I told them about him, and I think we were all moved when I read out the inscription on his grave: 'Here lies all that could die of William Stephen Raikes Hodson.' I fear that some of the men who were there that day were destined to earn no less an epitaph at Calais in May 1940, along with others of my friends in the 60th. And I was not to know that I would one day be a member of the regiment Hodson raised to stem the Mutiny, and which bears his name to this day, even among our Indian successors.

One duty that seemed to fall to me rather often was the weekly trip to the bank to draw the regimental pay. Fortunately I was good at mental arithmetic because I had to count the money and was personally responsible for ensuring there was no mistake in the sum drawn. In those days a rifleman's pay was two shillings (10p) a day, less deductions for this and that. The bank was no more than two or three miles from our lines, but banks in India were so situated as to be principally for the convenience of the mercantile classes: that meant in, or very near, the teeming native cities with their noise and bustle, brightly coloured clothes, strange music, sacred cattle, goats and pi-dogs, countless booths selling everything under the sun, and a pervasive mixture of smells of fruit and spices, incense and perfumes.

I would travel by *tonga*, a hired pony-trap rather like a small and very poor cousin of a dog-cart. The driver sat in front and rattled his whip on the tailboard to spur the pony on, and the passengers – myself and my armed rifleman escort – sat behind. There was a hood to keep the sun off, and we proceeded to the bank in a succession of walks, trots and canters, and to the jingle of pony bells all the way. But the comfort or discomfort of such missions depended largely on the season of the year. In the hot weather the heat was infernal and appalling. In the monsoon season it was a merciless sweaty heat giving rise to the exceedingly disagreeable itching inflammation known as prickly heat. But in winter in many parts of India the weather is beautiful; warm sunny days and balmy nights; there can be no better climate in the world.

One freak of weather which occurred from time to time was a dust storm. There was a bad one while I was in Lucknow. It lasted several days. The wind blew inexorably. The air was darkened and thick with dust as fine as talcum powder. It got into everything – our food, our drink, our clothes, our eyes, our ears. It was a major task to clean the lines and get everything shipshape again.

A great pleasure round Lucknow was small game shooting. Many of us shot, but my most constant shooting companion was Tommy Trotter who had been at Sandhurst with me. He bought a rattly old motor-bike and sidecar and at weekends we used to set off in it for our shoots – mostly duck and snipe – which could be up to fifty miles away. How we piled ourselves, two guns, bedding rolls, food – and quite a lot of game on the homeward journey – into that contraption, I can no longer imagine. We never shot more than could be eaten.

We slept out. To bed down beside an Indian *jheel* (shallow, reedy lake) on a bright cloudless tropical night, and to go to sleep listening to the flocks of wigeon whispering to each other on the water was an unforgettable experience. One night, however, I see from some old diary notes, Tommy woke up to see a jackal standing over me.

'The handiest missile was a tin of Bartlett pears which the jackal had received in the ribs.'

And this little extract from my notes perhaps gives a whiff of the flavour of the Indian rural life that surrounded us on our shoots.

Tommy and I had been out shooting since dawn, and had returned to our bivouac for breakfast. The note goes on:

> While we were eating, an old man rushed into the camp and made for a small boy who had been watching us wide-eyed. A long chase followed in and out of the trees, the small boy squealing with fright, the old man cursing with rage. At length the boy was caught and dealt with. His crime was that he had found it much more interesting to watch us than his cow, which had thereupon gorged itself on the old man's crops.

Big-game hunting was still an acceptable – and dangerous – form of sport. Tommy Trotter took some Himalayan leave during the summer, and managed to shoot a black bear and a red bear. One of the 60th sub-alterns, by contrast, Joe Wingfield, perhaps anticipating the ecologist lobby of half-a-century later, instead of shooting bears returned from a Himalayan leave with a tame – well, fairly tame – black bear cub.

Colonel Tilden-Wright, commanding the 3rd Hussars, lived in the next bungalow. Returning one hot evening in the dark after polo, and after a stop for refreshment at the Gymkhana Club, he threw off his clothes without bothering to get a light – there was no electricity – and stepped into the cold bath that his servant had prepared for him. Unfortunately Joe's bear had had the same idea of a cooling wallow, and was already in the bath. Pandemonium! A naked colonel, a very wet bear, and a demented hue and cry of native servants. And a diplomatic incident between the 60th and the 3rd Hussars.

In contrast to our outdoor, physical and often pretty tough life, either in our military work and training, or of our own choosing, shooting and so on, was our very civilised mess life. The mess was well furnished, with interesting pictures and historic regimental trophies. That side of an officer's regimental life was perhaps epitomised by guest nights.

Before dinner we always bathed, shaved and changed, and we wore mess kit every night except Saturdays and Sundays when we wore dinner jackets. Because the climate was warm, and at times of year very hot indeed, the dining-room French windows onto the deep verandah were always open, and beyond was the garden where the band played on guest nights. I have a very particular recollection of one of the bandsmen, Corporal Noakes, an outstanding musician, playing the 'Posthorn Gallop' on a silver horn. After dinner the Bandmaster came to the dinner table and joined the Commanding Officer for a glass of port, and then returned to the band; and the officers moved out onto the verandah, with their port and liqueurs, their coffee and cigars, to enjoy the remainder of the programme.

It sounds an elegant and comfortable life, and so it was in spots. But there was plenty of discomfort as well. An Indian garrison was no place for softies; but that was seen to be no reason for not maintaining high standards of civilised conduct and dress. There were the familiar jokes about an Englishman always changing into his dinner jacket even under the trees and creepers in the heart of the jungle because his sense of decorum insisted that he be properly dressed for dinner wherever he might be.

But to return to our active regimental life. In my time there was not a single motorised vehicle in the Battalion, and I doubt that there would have been a man who would have known how to drive one. Field officers (majors and above) rode chargers – as military riding horses were always called – at the head of their companies or units. Everyone else marched. Our baggage was carried on AT (Army Transport) carts, lightweight vehicles drawn by two mules harnessed to a central shaft. We all got used to handling mules. They are creatures of character, with a satanic sense of humour, ever on the lookout to land you a sharp and unexpected kick.

Half the Battalion at a time spent half the hot weather in the 'hills' at a small military hill station called Kailana (some 7,000 feet up). During the march up from the plains, on a downhill bit of road into one of the many valleys, the mules of two AT carts, which were part of my responsibility, seized some trivial excuse, such as a fluttering bird, to bolt. I had gone ahead to reconnoitre something or other, when I heard the rattle of the carts – they had iron-shod wheels – and the sound of the galloping hooves coming down the hill behind me. I scrambled out of the way, and they shot past me, round the next of many bends, and out of sight. There was nothing I could do, and I had to resign myself to the awful pile-up which I knew I would find some-where lower down. However, a mile or two below was an Octroi post (local Customs) with a barrier across the road. They had got there intact and pulled up safe and sound and were nibbling the thin dry grass by the road verge. I'm sure they were laughing their heads off – you always know when mules are having a devilish good laugh. I was so relieved that I injudiciously went to pat them, and only just avoided an absolutely fizzing kick.

On the last morning's march up to Kailana, Ken Collen and I (he had joined the Battalion six months after me) went ahead of the marching column to make some arrangements for the troops' arrival. It was a beautiful Himalayan April day of bright sunshine, not a cloud in the sky. It was a champagne climate at 6,000–7,000 feet. In shorts and a khaki shirt, we were neither too hot nor too cold. All about us were wonders that we had never seen before: rhododendron trees the size of oaks, golden eagles and equally magnificent lammergeyers – the bone-smashing eagle – with a wingspan of up to ten feet, cruising low over-head, their slipstream drumming through their feathers, and the lovely athletic langur monkeys.

At length, about noon, we topped the final ridge and were stopped dead in our tracks by the breathtaking view. The valley fell away steeply for thousands of feet below us, and there, fifty miles away to the north, gleaming white against the deep cobalt blue of the sky, were the eternal Himalayan snows stretching as far as the eye could see, from distant horizon to distant horizon, in an unbroken line – 100 miles? 200 miles? It doesn't matter. Surely the world's most wonderful natural spectacle.

'What a marvellous sight!' Ken said.

'Yes,' I replied, 'and I shan't rest till I've seen them from the far side.'

I was destined at the end of my year with the 60th Rifles to join the 12th Frontier Force Cavalry (Sam Browne's). That arrangement had come about because Major Johnny O'Rourke, who had first fired my enthu-siasm, had been second-in-command, and had both recommended the regiment to me and me to the regiment. However, they needed to see me before the arrangement was confirmed. They were stationed in Rawalpindi in the Punjab, 650 miles north west of Lucknow. A month or so after we arrived in Kailana, I decided to go and see them.

After a stifling hot journey by train, I reached Rawalpindi early in the morning where I was met and taken to the 12th Cavalry mess. The Commanding Officer, or Commandant as we called our COs in the Indian Cavalry, Lieutenant Colonel Jack Gannon, was there, and three other British officers. I spent a few days with them, and could not have been treated in a more friendly or hospitable way. They lent me horses, so at least I was able to show that I could ride, which I had of course learnt to do as a boy in Ireland. They took me to the lines and introduced me to the Indian officers, and I was able to parade a little of the language I had been learning. They showed me how everything was organised. To see 600 perfectly trained and immaculately groomed horses, all looked after with unremitting care, was in itself quite an exciting experience. I went on the morning parades, saw all the mounted training and drills that were going on, and I was allowed to try my hand at some of them. There were also some social functions in the evenings in which I was included.

Colonel Jack Gannon was very relaxed and put me entirely at my ease. He said they were very pleased I was joining them; he could assure me that I would thoroughly enjoy the life of an Indian Cavalryman, and he gave me some fatherly advice about money. So I returned to my pleasurable life with the 60th in Kailana, with the warm feeling that I was going to find another very agreeable home from home when my time came to leave them.

Back then in the Kailana hill station, I continued to gather new experience of life in the Army and in India.

One bright Himalayan full-moon night, there was a sergeants' dance to which I was invited. The Himalayas have not yet got worn down and are therefore very steep; it is hard to find suitable spots for buildings. We had a whole mountain complex to ourselves, much of which was still forest because it was too steep to use. The Black Watch had just such another mountain a mile or two away. There was no one else in Kailana except some ancillary services, medical and so on. Because of those conditions, the sergeants' mess had been located 1,000 feet above the officers' mess. But that was nothing to us. We went up and down the *khud*-side (as the hillsides are called in India) like mountain goats.

At one point during the dance a sergeant invited me into the bar for a drink. What would I have?

'A lemon squash, please, sergeant.'

'Oh come, sir, one of these little things will do you no harm.'

I had experimented in a small way with alcohol, but I didn't like it and it didn't seem to like me. Apart from that, it seemed an unrewarding way of getting rid of one's money.

The little bottle the sergeant generously gave me was a 'MacEwen's Nip' – a five star beer. To me it tasted filthy, and I swallowed it quickly like medicine, whereupon my attentive host plied me with another, and perhaps with a third. I began to feel alarmingly light-headed. I explained that I had a dance date, and went out onto the mountainside in the bright moonlight and lay under a bush with my feet pointing down the valley and my head up the hill, with the night sky above me gyrating in sickening revolutions.

I remember that I was in white summer mess-kit, and had to brush off bits of dry leaf and twig when at last I recovered and returned to my hosts. It was a tremendous relief to slip the 1,000 feet down the *khud* to my bed. So be wary, young officers, of the hospitality of kindly sergeants. They probably have stronger heads than you.

In India death never seemed far away, although most of us survived. We did not have all the prophylactic medicines there are today, there were no antibiotics, and no sulphonamide drugs.

One day, in Kailana, I was asked to take a message across to the next mountain to an officer in the Black Watch. He was a senior captain in his mid-thirties. I was warned to be very careful of him. He had, I was told, lost his young wife the year before and hadn't got over it. He was morose in the extreme, highly unreasonable, and would be likely to resent my intrusion.

With misgivings, therefore, I set off. When I got to his bungalow, I was shown into his sitting-room by his servant. The fading female touch in the family *lares* and *penates* was palpable.

When the owner came into the room, he greeted me unsmilingly and asked me to be seated. I delivered my now long-forgotten message, which he accepted civilly enough. Then, as he didn't seem disposed to turn me out at once, I ventured upon a little conversation, which turned into a quiet and friendly talk of perhaps half an hour.

I had seen a fishing rod as I came into the house. I felt he needed to be taken out of himself, so I asked him if he would like to come and have a day's fishing with me – just he and I; a quiet day. It seemed awful cheek – a second lieutenant to an officer of another regiment, fifteen years his senior. I promised him a good basket of mahseer; I thought he was almost tempted. But he declined. 'Not yet,' he said. I took my leave. I thought it hard that he had to live there on that rather lonely, distant, foreign mountain, with his young wife's grave hardly a hundred yards away.

We all played a lot of games, soccer and hockey mostly, with the men but, when we returned from Kailana to Lucknow in the monsoon of 1929, I started, for the first time in the Regiment, a rugger team.

Monsoon rugger has its own peculiar flavour. The temperature is between 95°F and 100°F, and the wet-bulb is very high, causing excessive perspiration. There may be upwards of three inches of rain in a day. The ground nevertheless remains bone hard, but with an inch of very wet mud on top so that the game becomes largely a mud-lark for the scrum. One rifleman had the misfortune to break a leg – the only broken limb I ever remember in rugger.

One day Desmond Buxton, who was a captain a dozen years older than myself, came into the mess just before lunch, and said to me, 'You'd better hurry up.' I asked why.

'You bought a polo pony yesterday, didn't you?'

I admitted it.

'Well, I've put you down for two chukkas of polo this afternoon.'

I protested that I did not even know which way up to hold a polo stick.

'Never mind. Always start at the deep end.'

Desmond was a man of seasoned wisdom, and was no doubt right. I do not recall that anything untoward happened at my polo debut, and thereafter I played regularly.

While I was in Lucknow, we were honoured by a visit from a famous English lady tennis-player – Miss Ryan. She wondered, obviously very doubtfully, whether there was anyone in the place good enough to give her some practice. She was recommended to try the club 'marker' – i.e. pro-cum-groundsman.

He was a Hindu whose appearance was the absolute negation of athleticism. Small and a little plump, he wore a *dhoti* down to his knees and invariably a white shirt with tails hanging out fore and aft. He had unbuttoned, voluminous shirtsleeves flapping about his wrists. A blue, sleeveless waistcoat completed his tennis kit, apart from bare feet and a very unstable turban, which always seemed to be on the point of falling off and needed constant nudging back onto his head. He held the tennis racquet halfway down the handle.

His main business in life – his profession, it might be said – was to provide practice for club members. To that end, what he had to do was to keep returning the ball so that they could play another stroke. It was not for him to win points, but only to make a playable return. He must have been one of the world's greatest geniuses at keeping the ball in play.

Miss Ryan, a powerful woman, began serving him what to any other opponent would have been certain aces, and pounding the ball into every corner of the court. Shirt-tails flying, shirtsleeves flapping, turban wildly and precariously askew, his grip getting ever shorter on the handle of the racquet, the marker, with unremitting diligence and zeal, sped about the court with the speed and agility of a weasel, scraping the ball up from however seemingly impossible an angle and sending it corkscrewing back to Miss Ryan, thus dutifully discharging his professional office of giving the Lady Sahib a chance of another shot. Far from appreciating this typically loyal sense of Indian duty, Miss Ryan became frantic at her inability to get the ball past him; and the more frustrated and frantic she became, the more erratic grew her tennis until, in the end, in utter desperation, she inflicted a crushing defeat upon herself. She lost 6–2, 6–2, 6–1, or something of that order.

I think we often suppose that conditions were harsher in the past. That is not my experience. I believe that, even though we marched, while the modern soldier is mechanically transported, training is much harder today than it was in those days, and the modern soldier is liable to have to endure much more sustained discomfort, if we except the trench warfare of the First World War.

Perhaps, too, it is supposed that we now live in a more democratic age in which officers and men are closer to each other than in the past. That may be so, but I wonder. From the earliest days, the role of the rifleman involved an essential intimacy in battle between officers and men. Let me conclude then by quoting from a letter I received from a rifleman after I had left the Regiment, and which reflects the relationship between a platoon commander of those days and his soldiers seventy years ago. I must apologise for the rather flattering reference to myself. I have not known what to do about it. But I have been advised to leave it in in order to retain the full flavour of the letter which reflects the *politesse* of a rifleman of those days when writing to an officer he knows well.

6842800 Rfn. Carr F.
'C' Coy 1st Batt; K.R.R.C.
Outram Bks
Lucknow U.P.

7.11.29

Dear Sir,

Please excuse me writing to you, but I can assure you that it is a pleasure to keep some knowledge of you in the platoon, and having got your photo which Sgt. Green asked me to send to you I thought it a fine line of communication to open from.

Well Sir, we are now on the annual Coy: Training and some jolly fine mess ups have been made to date, but I suppose that things will finish trumps and we will be as fit as we were when under your command.

Dear Sir we have now got Mr. Barnett and Capt. Ashburner back with us and also an officer who is attached, and what with Mr. Scot-Makdougal we are pretty full up, although it is often heard in the platoon and in the Coy: generally 'I wish Mr. Magan were here' but I might say Sir, nobody wishes it more than Sgt: Green and myself.

Well Sir the old platoon is keeping its head above water as regards sport they are in the fourth round of the 'Platoon Hockey' and last night played a draw 2–2 with the 'Employed' at football which if they win will put them in the fourth round of that also.

I don't think I can say more till I know how you take these few lines, only that the whole platoon join with me in wishing you all the very best of luck in your new regiment. Hoping to hear from you soon.

I am Sir,
Yours Obediently
Rfn. F. Carr

If that letter reveals something, I hope, more than anything, that it mirrors my own affection for the soldiers of No. 10 Platoon, and the fact that in those far off days men and officers were very close to each other. Some of the riflemen were much older, and very much more experienced, than myself. Two of them had been decorated for gallantry in the First World War with Military Medals. Yet they helped and supported me in every possible way, and they never used my youth or my inexperience to take the mickey out of me. They had generous hearts, and I valued their friendliness, and was happy and proud to serve with them. The photograph to which Rifleman Carr refers was a group photograph we had taken of the platoon before I left.

It was on a warm afternoon, 10 October 1929, that I waved good-bye, as my train pulled out of Lucknow railway station, to the party of 60th Riflemen – officers and men – who had been kind enough to come to see me off to the north of India. Thus, to my deep regret, my time with the 60th had come to an end.

3
Joining Sam Browne's Cavalry

At the time of which I am writing, India stretched from the eastern frontier of Afghanistan to the northern frontier of Burma, and contained what are now Pakistan and Bangladesh, and it is in that sense that I shall be referring to India, not to the truncated country that it is today.

Rawalpindi was in the northern Punjab, only 100 miles from the mountains of the North West Frontier. *Punjab* is corrupt Persian for *Panch-Ab*, meaning Five Waters, or Five Rivers, the famous five rivers of the province – the Indus, the Jhelum, the Chenab, the Ravi and the Sutlej – but although it is a riverine area, much of it is rugged and hilly. That was the country for which I was now destined. It would be a harsh contrast to the parklike region around Lucknow with its open fields dotted with groves of village trees. That was the great plain of the Ganges of which the Gumpti river which flows through Lucknow is a tributary. I was also facing the contrast of leaving a battalion of British infantry to join a *risala* – Hindustani for a regiment of Indian cavalry.

After travelling all night, I reached Rawalpindi early on the morning of 11 October 1929, and was met at the station and taken to the 12th Cavalry mess, where I had been given a bed-sitting room in the mess building. There were only three officers present with the Regiment when I joined. It was not infrequently the case in the Indian Army that regiments were short of British officers (BOs). There might be twenty or so British officers on the strength but, with officers on leave, or courses, and on other appointments, that could be reduced to a bare handful.

I knew my way about, because of the courtesy visit which I had paid to the Regiment during my year with the 60th Rifles; so, after a bath and breakfast and settling myself in, I went to the lines to report officially to the acting Commandant – Colonel Gannon being on leave. His office chair was occupied by the next most senior officer present, Captain Algy Melville.

Northern Command Headquarters were in Rawalpindi and, being short of staff, had temporarily borrowed Algy to fill a staff captain's appointment – the sort of pen-pushing job that was anathema to him. The general commanding Northern Command, the audacious but uncertain-tempered General Sir Robert (Bob) Cassels, walking one morning along the passage on the way to his office, passed Algy's office door which was ajar and heard him, in a loud voice, say to the British sergeant clerk: 'I don't want to know what the bloody thing's about, sergeant; just show me where to sign it.' Such can be the paradoxes of life that Algy, having been returned with alacrity to regimental duty, found himself in temporary command of the Regiment.

I hadn't met him until I stepped into the Commandant's office, saluted him smartly, and reported my arrival. He greeted me without much fuss and then, without even inviting me to sit down for perhaps a little fatherly chat (he had been through the First War and was some fifteen years my senior), he said: 'You'd better get along to 'C' Squadron lines. You're commanding 'C' Squadron.'

'What do I do when I get there?' I asked.

'You'll find out,' he said. Then he added: 'Come round and have a drink this evening, and meet my wife.'

And that was all the initial instruction I got. Later we got to know each other well and became close friends. Perhaps Desmond Buxton of the 60th would have approved – 'Chuck him in at the deep end'; but it seems outrageous. I was twenty-one, without any cavalry experience, and – without even a formal introduction – I was to walk into 'C' Squadron lines and take command of 100 men and 120 horses, and to do it in a foreign language. The truth is that, bored with peacetime soldiering, Algy was only time-serving, and two or three years later he retired and lived the life of leisure with his wife which they could well afford.

I did take command of 'C' Squadron of the 12th Frontier Force Cavalry that day but, before I come to that, I must describe the way in which my arrival in the Squadron would be seen by the Indian officers and men in it. That derived from the character and characteristics of the Regiment, which in turn derived from its history.

Throughout centuries of history every invader of India had come by the same route – over the passes of the North West Frontier mountains. But the development in Western Europe in the fifteenth century of the three-masted ship brought about the conquest of the oceans and opened a new route from the West to India, the sea route.

In the seventeenth century the British obtained three coastal trading posts, widely separated, in the southern part of India: at Calcutta in

Bengal; at Madras, further south on the east coast; and at Bombay, on the west coast. In course of time the guards who were needed to protect those trading posts grew, as the importance of the settlements themselves grew, into three separate armies under British command, manned by 'native soldiers', as they were then styled: the Bengal Army, the Madras Army and the Bombay Army, and reinforced by some British regiments.

By the mid-eighteenth century the Mogul Empire, which had never succeeded in establishing suzerainty over the whole of India, was in decline, leaving a vacuum of very unsettled conditions in its wake, a vacuum which the British, for the sake of peace and tranquillity, found themselves constrained to fill. It was principally the Bengal Army which pushed north-westwards until, by 1843, with the conquest and annexation of Sind by the Bombay Army, all India south and east of the Punjab was in British hands, or occupied by submissive princes in friendly treaty with the British.

The Punjab remained an independent Sikh kingdom under the remarkable Ranjit Singh, 'The Lion of the Punjab', and continued its independence for a few years after his death in 1839 until, in 1845, his ambitious and unstable successors attacked the British. That led to two wars against the Sikhs in which they were defeated in 1845 and 1848, whereafter the British annexed the Punjab.

Britain now ruled the whole of India up to the north-west mountain barrier, and it was this barrier which posed a major new problem. Its defence was needed against the warlike frontier tribes, against a possible hostile Afghanistan, against possible Russian intrigues, indeed against anyone who might have it in mind to use the historic invasion route to India through the north-west passes.

The answer was to establish a fourth army, the 'Punjab Irregular Frontier Force' ('Piffers'). In addition to infantry, it contained four regiments of cavalry, one of which was raised in 1849 by Lieutenant Sam Browne – later General Sir Sam Browne, VC, KCB – and called 2nd Punjab Irregular Cavalry. This, after a number of Indian Army reorganisations, had become Sam Browne's Cavalry (12th Frontier Force) – the regiment I had now joined.

The word 'Irregular', used in the earliest title of the Regiment, is of crucial importance, because it determined the Regiment's character. In short it was a *sillidar* regiment. The word '*sillidar*' is a corruption of two words, one Arabic, '*selah*' (arms), the other Persian, '*bardar*' (a bearer), thus meaning a 'bearer of arms'. There were two types of cavalry, one, Regular cavalry, equipped and mounted by the government, known as *bargirs*; and the other Irregular cavalry, in which the men provided their own horses, weapons and equipment, in other words they came *bearing their own arms* – sillidars. They were, of course, all volunteers. Unlike the Russian empire, there never was a conscript in the Indian Army even when, in time of war, it numbered millions.

The sillidar system had evolved in India long before the coming of the British, and went on evolving until it was finally abolished in 1921; but, insofar as it influenced and moulded the character of Sam Browne's Cavalry, its main features were these. To join a regiment, an Indian soldier had to be a man of substance, able to afford a horse good enough to serve as a cavalry mount. He had also to bring with him to the regiment his own equipment, a sword, and perhaps a lance, a tent, and all other accoutrements except his firearm and ammunition, which were provided by the government. He also had to arrange for a pony, shared with another man, on which to carry their baggage, and a syce, who was both groom and servant. Sillidars had to provide their own uniform, and were responsible for feeding themselves, their syces and their horses.

All this determined the sort of man who became an Indian soldier. He was necessarily a countryman, and a man of some substance: in fact at least a small yeoman farmer. Some men of greater substance, 'sirdars', would join and become leaders, 'Indian officers'. Thus Indian officers in the more modern Indian Cavalry continued to be known generically and collectively as sirdars.

There was no need for recruiting drives. There were more volunteers than regimental vacancies. Why did men join? They were paid, but that was not the main attraction. They had enough substance already not to be under any dire necessity to earn more. The reason for their joining is summed up in the Urdu word *izzat* – honour. To be a trained fighting man, to belong to a celebrated regiment, was to be a member of an honourable calling. To ride home into your village, if it was near enough, on your leaves and furloughs, on your own horse, dressed in distinctive scarlet regimental dress, and followed by your syce – your servant – with your pack animal, was to be, and to feel yourself to be, and to be recognised as being, someone of significance, perhaps even a battle-hardened warrior.

Because horses grow old and become unserviceable, because arms may deteriorate, accoutrements wear out, and there may be unexpected breakages, losses and so on, provision had to be made for those eventualities. To that end, the men made monthly deposits of money with the regiment to provide funds for replacements when needed. The regiments thus became financial institutions responsible in course of time for very large sums of money belonging to the members of the regiment. Some of it the regiment invested at interest; some it lent back to the men at interest; some it used commercially, for instance for large-scale farming to produce cheaper food for the men and fodder for the horses. Even in my own time we did some farming.

Officers and men were thus not only partners in a fighting unit, but also in a business enterprise, in which the men had considerable sums of money invested. That called for close co-operation in the running of the business, and that was provided by a weekly durbar for all ranks, under the chairmanship of the Commandant, at which every man had the absolute right to make any point or suggestion that he might wish to make. That was a matter of considerable importance to every individual because, when the time came for him to take his discharge, he had the right to take with him all that he had brought into the regiment as well as the accumulation of pay and funds in his regimental account. But it was of even more importance in determining the character of the regiment, in that the joint interest in the financial welfare of the regiment was an additional bond between British officers, Indian officers and men. And, more than that, the weekly durbar was an occasion when any question affecting the regiment could be raised: military matters, service conditions and so on. The sillidar regiments were therefore in all aspects of their life very close knit, being a brotherhood in arms amounting almost to veritable families; and, to everyone in them, the paramount interest of their life and service was the honour, prestige and well-being of the regiment.

Until well into the twentieth century Indians did not look upon India as a country, as their homeland. It was a continent too vast and too diverse for that. This was brought home to us in my own time when the Regiment was posted to the south of India where we were among small, very dark Dravidian people, whose languages none of us in the Regiment, British or Indian, could speak. We, on the other hand, British officers and our north country Indian men alike, were all Aryans, and looked much more like each other than any of us looked like the Dravidians of the south. Thus Indians tended to think of their homeland as the distinctive area from which they came.

Perhaps only the British, and a handful of radical oppositional nationalist politicians, saw India as a single entity – a view that was to be proved wrong by the breaking away of Pakistan, and the later independence of Bangladesh. The present Government of India must remain constantly vigilant against the possibility of such breakaway tendencies among her many distinct and different communities, regions and languages. If India were to break up it would be largely on a linguistic basis.

In most Indian regiments the men were recruited from a number of different communities and different localities. In Sam Browne's Cavalry we recruited from three different communities – from the Punjab Mussulmans and Sikhs, and Hindus (Dogras) hill men. We, the British, were not seen to be foreigners. We were another community, the *sahib log* from our own, albeit oversea, province, known as *wilayat*. *Wilayat* is derived from an Arabic word, used in Urdu, and indeed meaning a province. The word *wilayat* is corrupted in Hindi to *bilayati*, which is corrupted again in English to Blighty. Perhaps, also, in a country used to the caste system, there was nothing surprising in an officer caste emanating from *wilayat*.

We all had three loyalties which we recognised openly. One to our own home and whatever we might regard as our homeland. One to a common, important, but somewhat distant, point of loyalty – the king, the monarch, whose salt we had all eaten. No one can teach Indians anything about loyalty; there are no more loyal people in the world once they have 'eaten your salt'. The third point of loyalty, and of enormous significance to us all, was our Regiment. We strove for it, lived for it, and were ready to die for it. Its excelling good name and reputation meant everything to us, to all of us, Indians and British alike.

Sam Browne's Cavalry, guarding the marches of India along the North West Frontier, as was its *raison d'être* and its duty, was virtually on active service for seventy years, from 1849, when it was raised, until the outbreak of the First World War. It protected the prosperous westernmost plains of India from the fierce marauding Pathan tribes, who descended at times upon them in great hordes from the rugged hinterland of largely barren mountains lying between India and the Afghan border. Indian and British members of the Regiment had therefore, over many years, lived, worked and fought together in the closest possible association with each other on the Frontier, communicating and conversing with each other in Urdu, a language foreign to them all. There could also be wider duties as, for instance, when the Bengal

Army revolt took place in 1857 and Sam Browne's Cavalry sent a squadron to help quell the revolt, first in Delhi and then at Agra.

In my time, and earlier, the British officers, like our Indian soldiers, were not primarily mercenaries. We did it, of course, to earn our living. We were paid, but not much. The principal reason why we did it was because we enjoyed it. We also thought it useful, or we would not have done it. I suppose, too – without wanting to seem too high-sounding – that we, as with the Indian members of our regiments, regarded it as an honourable calling. It was, after all, not so long before that it was indeed regarded as so honourable a calling that officers were prepared to lay out considerable sums of money to buy their commissions, and had thereafter largely to finance themselves. Even in my time in the Cavalry, at least some private income was considered desirable. There was the advantage in all this for both officers and men that, if you are doing something not because you must, but because you want to do it, then you are likely to do it as well as you can.

Because, for our Indian soldiers, it was so honourable a calling to be a member of such a regiment, it became a family regiment in a literal sense. Sons and grandsons from the same Indian families followed fathers and grandfathers into its ranks. Moreover sons and grandsons of British officers did likewise.

That then, in outline, is the character of Sam Browne's Cavalry of whose 'C' Squadron I was told to go and take command. Although I did not realise it at the time, I was to come to understand later how I would have appeared to them – not as some inexperienced young inter-loper. The relationship was quite different from that.

The British officers were regarded as the *manbap* – mother and father – of the Regiment. They stood between the Regiment and the outer world. They were the ultimate guardians of its integrity and its welfare. They led it in war and peace. They were to the Regiment the equivalent of the paternal family on a large feudal estate. Although, therefore, I was totally unaware of the fact, my joining the Regiment was not just the arrival of a raw, young and inexperienced officer. It was, on the contrary, the equivalent of a younger son taking his place, and shouldering some of the responsibility, in running the family estates.

I am sure that I had been reading about, and studying, the Indian Army before I joined, but I had to experience the Regiment to discover its true nature. Because of the sort of men of some substance whom we recruited, it can truly be said that British officers, Indian officers, Indian men were, in general, people whose attitudes were founded on, and who were motivated by, a high degree of self-respect. There was virtually no crime or misbehaviour among Indian troops. A man's most precious possession was his honour. Should he stain it, he could never again hold up his head in his tribe, his village or his family. Thus in the Indian Army there was no corps of military police, and no need for one. They were exemplary soldiers with whom to share one's life. They were gentlemen.

Furthermore, it never occurred to me to suppose that our men were other than strictly moral. They married young, and I never had any reason to believe that they were other than faithful husbands. There was never a case of venereal disease in the Regiment. Indeed, I cannot imagine a man going back to his village with that stigma upon him. It is perhaps not a matter for wonder that leaders in some parts of the so-called Third World gravely doubt the influence of Western social values.

Philip Mason, the well-known writer on India, who was not a soldier but a member of the Indian Civil Service, in his excellent book on the Indian Army, *A Matter of Honour*, has this to say of the Indian soldier:

> The Indian Army was kept small for financial reasons. Low taxes meant a small army ... 150,000 to a population of 350 million. That meant picking men who could easily be trained to be good soldiers, men who understood before they came to the colours the concepts of military honour; courage, fidelity to comrades, pride in a man's body and his skill at arms, pride in himself and his regiment, his caste and his clan.

The relationship of British officer and Indian soldier was something that grew both from the Indian social scene and from the British. On the Indian side, there was a deep and ancient tradition of allegiance to a superior, with the obligation of protection on the one side and devoted service on the other. Closely linked with this were the twin ideas of fidelity to the salt one has eaten and the treachery of ingratitude to the salt. It was not hard for the recruit, coming from his village at eighteen or nineteen, to transfer this traditional allegiance to a sympathetic British officer or to the idea of the regiment. And, if handled with understanding, the allegiance would become a passionate devotion.

The following lines were written many years ago by a British officer serving with the Indian Cavalry (Hodson's Horse), and they hang to this day in Hodson's Horse officers' mess:

Lord make me worthy
   of the men I serve;
Worthy of their loyalty
   and devotion to duty;
Their wondrous willingness
   and ready laughter;
Their great humility
   that asks so little,
And gives so much,
So readily, without complaint.
Grant them their simple wishes, Lord,
   and bless them please,
For in this world,
No better soldiers breathe than these.

And a visit not long ago to India, at the invitation of Hodson's Horse, left me in no doubt that the Indian Army maintains its traditions and its character to this day.

4
'C' Squadron

I made my debut with 'C' Squadron at evening 'stables' – that part of the day's routine when the horses got their final grooming and final feed.

I do not recall feeling much anxiety at taking over the Squadron. I was conscious of three things. First that, for instance on route-marches, I had for short spells commanded 'C' Company of the 60th Rifles. To command 100 men did not therefore cause me much misgiving. Second, that I had a great deal to learn, and must make no secret of the fact, but just get on and do it with whatever advice and assistance I could get from anyone and everyone. Third, that I was nevertheless responsible, and must be sure that I discharged my responsibility to the full, for the well-being and good management of the Squadron. In the words of the American President Truman, I was conscious that 'the buck stops here'.

The men of 'C' Squadron were Dogras, people of Rajput origin who inhabit some of the valleys of the western Himalayan foothills. Most Dogras are Hindus, though some are Muslims. Those we recruited were Hindus from the Kangra Valley in the Himalayan foothills. They are elegant, handsome, gentle and gentlemanly people of impeccable good manners and behaviour, and marvellously brave and staunch soldiers.

On arrival in the horse lines, I was greeted by the senior Indian officer, Risaldar Hazura Singh. Indian officers received their commissions from the Viceroy of India and were known as Viceroy's Commissioned Officers (VCOs). The senior non-commissioned officer (NCO) rank was the equivalent of sergeant – *defadar* in the Indian Cavalry. There were no warrant officers, so the Indian officers filled the gap in the military hierarchy which in the British Army is filled by the warrant officers. But it is important to recognise that Indian officers were officers. They were not senior warrant officers. There were three ranks of 'Indian officer' in the Cavalry. Jemadar was the lowest, then risaldar, and in each regiment there was one risaldar major. The British officers and Indian officers treated each other with conspicuous courtesy, each addressing the other as 'Sahib'.

British officers had all had a formal English education, had passed
the Civil Service Commissioners Exam into Sandhurst or Woolwich,
and done the eighteen months' course there; or had been commissioned
from a university, having succeeded in a degree course. There were very
few university entrants. It was at that time harder to get into Sandhurst
or Woolwich than into Oxford or Cambridge; though none were very
difficult. To get into Woolwich it was necessary to be a fairly competent
mathematician. Sandhurst and the universities were no serious problem. At all events, British officers were formally educated, hand-picked
by selection, and specially trained.

Indian officers came into the Regiment as lads from Indian villages,
usually from families with a tradition of military service. They all
started as the equivalent of private soldiers – sowars, or jawans, in the
Cavalry – and worked their way up through the various ranks. They
had only such education as was available at a village school. But they
were very intelligent, very well mannered and dignified people, and they
responded well and quickly to the additional education and training
they received in the Regiment. The word *sowar* means a horseman. The
word *jawan* means a youth. 'Sowar' was used formally: for 'Send a man
to Brigade HQ with this message', it would be 'Send a sowar ...' For
'How are the chaps getting on at hockey?' it would be 'How are the
jawans getting on ...?'

The men who eventually received commissions from the Viceroy and
became Indian officers were the cream of this intake of valorous and
reliable warrior material from the Punjab villages. All our men were
long-service men, serving twenty years or more, so we really were a
professional army.

The Indian officers served under the British officers. British officers
commanded the squadrons. Indian officers commanded the 'troops'
(cavalry equivalent of platoons) within the squadrons, but it was traditional in the Indian Army that they were given a very great deal of
authority and responsibility, and they were very ready, willing and able
to take it, and to do it in a very relaxed way. I do not recall Indian officers ever being worried. Concerned, yes; but not worried. Some Indians received King's Commissions, and then had exactly the same status
as British officers. Some came through Sandhurst at that time as well-
educated young men and some were promoted from the ranks of
Viceroy's commissioned Indian officers; we had two such in Sam
Browne's Cavalry, Captain Mohammed Ayub Khan, a Mohammedan,
and Captain Autar Singh, a Sikh.

The most senior Indian officer in a cavalry regiment was the risaldar major, who was the Colonel's right hand man among the Indians. He was his confidant and adviser on all matters affecting those aspects of the lives of the soldiers that had particular Indian implications, such as religious or caste matters, village home influences and pressures, and a host of other things. We, the British in India, however long we were there, were well aware, as the years went by, of the limitations of our knowledge of India, about Indians and, in particular, about what might be going on in Indian minds. We were crucially reliant, therefore, on the constant flow of advice and comment which we received from the senior Indians who shared our tasks and with whom we worked intimately. That was the case not only in the Indian Army but also in all the other Indian services.

Risaldars, of whom there was at least one and sometimes two in each squadron, were in the same position of adviser and confidant to the squadron leader – as squadron commanders were known – as was the risaldar major to the CO. Thus, when Risaldar Hazura Singh and I greeted each other with respect on that my first evening in the Regiment, it came quite naturally to him both to accept my status as a British, King's commissioned, officer; and to act as my mentor in all that I ought to know about the squadron.

He walked me round the horse lines, where the men were grooming, and introduced me to the non-commissioned officers as we went. It would be time enough to get to know the men individually later. Like me, he was in an acting capacity, as the senior Indian officer in the squadron, Risaldar Bidhi Chand, was away.

Risaldar Hazura Singh was a sealed pattern Dogra. He was tall and slightly built, as straight as a ramrod, and with a notable moustache. Like all Dogras, who do not have the ebullience of, for instance, Sikhs, he was quiet and reticent. He had an air of patrician benevolence; and he spoke in a cultured way, with quiet authority, and he also had a delicious sense of humour. What we all felt for him was a deep respect. It would have been impossible to imagine him doing an unworthy thing, or having an unworthy thought. I have never known any man whom I admired, respected or liked more. There was, I think, between us that chemistry which brings two people exceptionally close together. I think, too, that I recognised in him the product of ancient and cultural refinement, and philosophical certainty, millennia older that Christianity, which did something to cause me to re-think my own values. He was in his forties, more than twice my age, old enough to be my father, and enormously more experienced, and had seen active service in the First World War Mesopotamian Campaign against the Turks. But that did not cause any barrier between us. I learnt much from him, just from being with him, and by his example, but as from an intimate rather than from a teacher. He was an elegant figure, a person of great dignity and a battle-hardened warrior.

When his time came to retire, he told me that he was going to add one or two Western comforts to the normal placid lifestyle of his hill village. In the seasons of pleasant weather, he proposed to sit outside with his eyes shaded by a large Australian sombrero hat, and his soul composed by the odd puff at a European-style pipe.

Two things Hazura Singh did for me that first evening: he nominated an orderly for me, and introduced me to him, and he selected a horse for me – a charger – until such time as I had bought my own. There was still a touch of the sillidar about the British officers, as they had to provide themselves with two chargers and with all their own equipment, including their arms.

The orderly chosen for me was an elderly sowar not far off retirement age. I have no doubt he was selected so that he could be 'my guide, philosopher and friend'. He knew all the ropes backwards. He was an exceptionally nice man, and served me very well, and helped me immeasurably. When he retired, I was given someone much younger.

Having broken the ice with Risaldar Hazura Singh, the squadron and the other Indian officers that first evening, I was ready to take my place in the day-to-day goings on of the Regiment. I was thus on parade with everyone else first thing at dawn next morning on my charger which my orderly had brought to the mess for me in due time.

Our horses in the Cavalry had two functions. Their primary function was that they were our vehicles. They got us to the battleground. Thereafter we were most likely to fight with our firearms on foot or, more likely, on our bellies. Their other function was as mobile vehicles of war. We could fight on horseback with swords (sabres) or spears (lances) or pistols.

Having been through the intensive Sandhurst course and done my year with the 60th Rifles, I already had a significant knowledge and experience of soldiering. What I now had to learn in addition was all the lore connected with the use of horses as the cavalryman's vehicle; how to fight on horseback; and how to get along with Indian troops. So, whatever I may have done that first morning on parade with Sam

Browne's Cavalry, one thing is certain. I would have been studying, from the things that were going on, the gaps in my own knowledge and experience that needed to be filled; and concerning myself with how best I might set about filling them. That, of course, was not all left to me and to chance. The more senior people ensured that I wasn't neglected and my own Indian officers went out of their way to be helpful.

It has always been the principle in the British and Indian Armies that the men are not asked to do anything that the officers cannot do – and indeed try to do better. So every officer, in some form or other, does all the training that a recruit does, and acquires all the skills that he acquires. And so I voluntarily joined the recruits for some of my training with them. I learnt, and practised to perfection, all that was known about how to fight on horseback – at full gallop, if necessary – with a sabre. We were a sabre regiment. We were not lancers, and didn't fight with spears. But we were a champion tent-pegging regiment, and so we learnt to use and, if necessary, fight with a lance as well.

A problem in the use of a cavalryman's horse as a vehicle was the disposal, and dispersal, of the horses once the men were dismounted. Where were they to go? Who was to look after them? If you had too many men doing that job, you would deplete your fighting force. The answers were that you must find dispersed cover for your horses, cover from the air as well as from the ground, if you can, and not more than one man must be used to hold four horses – and more than that if possible. A man with four horses might have to gallop for cover, and there might be obstacles on the way. So our recruits were practised until they became skilled at that sort of thing, and it was not long before I learnt to gallop down a line of jumps riding one horse and leading three others, with their heads held tight to me. We added refinements to that sort of exercise by, for instance, doing it bare-backed.

I loved drill, both infantry and cavalry drill. The two most satisfying drills are the solemn infantry slow march and the thrilling cavalry gallop past the saluting base on some ceremonial occasion. The squadron commander would swing his squadron into line at a gallop, and make sure it was a straight line as the squadron passed the reviewing officer or official. Cavalrymen had also to be expert at certain foot and arms drills, particularly for ceremonial purposes such as guard mounting.

In addition to our parade ground work, physical training, gymnastics, musketry, range-shooting and schoolroom work, we had also to leave the barrack lines and get out into the surrounding country to practise and perfect our tactical skills. For our camps – squadron and regimental – we went further afield and extended our training. Furthermore, in India, particularly in a teeming city like Rawalpindi, there was always the possibility of communal differences leading to rioting, in which case the police often needed military assistance in crowd control. Our 'role in aid of the civil power', as it was known, was therefore something else that we had to practise in urban conditions, and something in which we had to perfect our techniques. It was something in which, too, we had to know the law and be particularly concerned not to be lured into any excessive use of force. In my early letters home I expressed enormous admiration for the Indian police, and especially for their bravery.

Our concern always was that we should be fully trained and ready at all times to perform any duty that might be required of us. To that end we did not, and did not need to, work very hard. We trained our own recruits and our horses but, once we were trained, it was mainly a matter of keeping up the standard.

We were proud of our professional competence and readiness. It was no doubt also salutary to contemplate that, if we wanted to stay alive, we must at all times be 100% ready to face the wily and battle-worthy North West Frontier tribesmen, when called upon to do so. We trained our own recruits and our horses, and were concerned always that we should be fully trained. That said, once we were trained it was merely a matter of keeping ourselves topped up. So we didn't actually need to work very hard.

In effect, we worked mornings only. First parade was usually at, or soon after, dawn. Then, with a break for breakfast, we worked till lunch time. That ended the formal regimental day's work. It used to be said that we did half a day's work for half a day's pay. The afternoons were mainly given up to recreation, though there might be a siesta in the very hot weather in some places. We played polo three days a week, and other afternoons we probably schooled our horses and ponies. Squash, golf and tennis were available in most stations and most of us played hockey with the men. Recruit training continued in the evenings (it got dark early, about 6 p.m.), there was training for athletics and for competitions of one kind and another; and various duties around the lines such as evening stables. There was a racecourse next to our lines in Rawalpindi, and we took some part in horse racing; there was also the club to go to for those who wanted some extra-regimental association and company. But the time between dark and dinner was perhaps more often taken up with letter-writing, catching up with paperwork, planning exercises for our troops, working for promotion exams, or perhaps the Staff College, and language learning.

There was also a very active social life. There was a dance every Saturday night at the club. Dinner parties were frequent, and married people were very generous with their invitations to young bachelors like myself. Sunday lunches were another social event – the traditional dish being curry – and from time to time people would arrange picnics. Although there were no formal parades on Saturdays and Sundays, except guard-mounting, it was traditional to go for a ride before breakfast, the best part of the day in India, before it got hot. Another mess tradition, after the morning ride on Sunday, was mulligatawny soup for breakfast – described in the dictionary as 'an Indian soup with meat and strongly flavoured with curry'. More graphically, in the southern Indian Tamil people's language the word means 'pepper-water'.

Very early on, I took over the voluntary office of Mess Secretary, and it was one which, in one form or another, I occupied whenever I could throughout my forty years of service. Even later on, as a brigadier, I volunteered for the job in a senior officers' mess in the Middle East and, later on still, I was for fifteen years the chairman of one of the Ministry of Defence canteen committees. I enjoyed the business and financial work involved.

Thursday was, like Saturday and Sunday, a holiday. When I first went to India, and before there was any air-mail, the sea-mail to England went only once a week on the weekly P & O liner from Bombay. I think the ship arrived and sailed at weekends. Thursday, at all events, was mail writing day. Up-country we had received our English mail and there was still time to reply and catch the outgoing mail steamer.

At weekends I fished and shot as much as I could. Little or no fishing or small-game shooting was preserved in British India, so we could go where we liked. Neither fishing nor shooting were very good round Rawalpindi, but there were a couple of small rivers where I fished for mahseer, and I used to shoot some partridge and duck, all good additions to our mess pot.

5
Some Colleagues and Characters

Not long after my arrival in the Regiment, the Commandant, Lieutenant Colonel Jack Gannon, returned from leave. He was a gifted, easy man of equable temperament, a former county cricketer, a high handicap polo player, and a good penman who published a book of delightful vignettes of life in India. He and his wife were very kind to me.

About the same time, my substantive squadron commander, Major Ian Gordon-Hall – always known as 'Wrukie' (or 'Wrookie') – returned from an attachment to the Indian Signal Corps and took over the squadron; and I became his squadron officer – second in command. He was a war veteran, and I learnt a lot from him.

These two, and Major D. C. Branfoot, the senior squadron leader who commanded 'A' Squadron, the Sikh squadron, were the three British officers who most influenced me, and with all of whom I became very close. I was also much influenced by some of the Indian officers.

The senior Indian officer was the Risaldar Major, Gurbakhsh Singh, a Sikh, an extremely active, intelligent man of inexhaustible vitality. We lived in the saddle and covered a good deal of ground on our various exercises, but, wherever you were, it would be surprising if Gurbakhsh Singh did not put in an appearance and stir things up a bit.

One morning when I was out in the country doing some training with 'C' Squadron, I saw Gurbakhsh Singh looming up on the horizon at a smart trot with his orderly. He came up to me. My squadron was dismounted and the horses were hidden in *nullahs* (deep ditches) behind cactus clumps (the word *nullah* covers anything from a substantial valley or ravine to a small dry or wet watercourse).

'Salaam, sahib,' he greeted me. 'How are you?'

'Salaam, Risaldar Major sahib. Well, thanks; and how are you?'

'Well, thanks. And what training are you giving your squadron this morning, sahib?'

'I am practising them, Risaldar Major sahib, in taking cover quickly.'

'If you don't mind me saying so, sahib, you are wasting your time, and theirs. When you go to war, the first enemy bullet will teach them that!'

And bidding me an impishly polite farewell, he rode off to deliver a piece of his mind to someone else – British officer, Indian officer, or whoever else happened to cross his path, even perhaps the Brigade Commander.

Although formally addressed by us British officers as 'Risaldar Major sahib', he was also affectionately known as 'Gearbox'. A lot of the things we British liked doing appealed to him, so he played polo vigorously, went hunting when there was any to be had, rode in point-to-point races, and came shooting with us. It enlivens me even now to recall his effervescent spirit and endlessly bubbling enjoyment of life. He invigorated all of us in the Regiment. I learnt not long ago of his death at a great age.

Important in the hierarchy of Indian officers was the Woordie Major (the Jemadar Adjutant). When I joined Sam Browne's Cavalry, that appointment was held by Jemadar Muzaffar Khan, a Punjabi Mohammedan (PM). He was, in effect, the deputy to the Adjutant, at that time Captain David Gregson, who was himself a most dedicated and meticulous trainer of our recruits.

Muzaffar Khan was a large, strong man with a correspondingly strong voice, and a man of very positive personality. He had something of the sergeant-major about him. He was vigilant, and strict, but without ever overstepping the boundary line between that and harshness. Like a good sergeant-major, he could do everything better than anyone else. Thus, if someone was performing some task incorrectly, he would not stop at pointing out that they were wrong, and correcting them orally, he would demonstrate how to do it, with a performance that would not only be manifestly right but so expert as to be virtually inimitable. He and David Gregson, the Adjutant, produced between them a tier of magnificent instructors who, under their constant guidance and watchfulness, turned us out a continuous stream of excellently well-trained recruits.

Whether in uniform or in mufti, Muzaffar Khan was always an imposing figure, impeccably turned out. My fondest recollections of him are tent-pegging. Going full gallop, like a ferociously concentrated thunderbolt, the tail of the puggaree flying behind him, he would draw the peg as clean as a whistle every time, to the accompanying roars of the crowd. Later he became the senior risaldar of 'B' Squadron, the Mohammedan squadron, and was selected one year to go to England as one of the annual four Indian Officer Orderlies to the King.

Tent-pegging is a very ancient Indian sport, and a very exciting spectacle. A peg, about four inches wide, wired top and bottom to stop it splitting when the lance strikes it, is hammered into the ground. The rider gallops full gallop down a ride 150 yards long or so (with spectators on either side). He carries a lance and as he gallops leans far out of his saddle to the right so that his eye and lance point and the peg are all in line. The purpose is to drive the lance point into the peg and lift it high into the air. He does not thrust or plunge his lance into the peg. As he gallops he gradually lowers the lance point, and the momentum of the horse, galloping at thirty miles an hour, is sufficient to drive it through the peg.

A tent-pegging team consists of eight men mounted on eight well-trained horses. Each man takes it in turn to gallop for his peg. To lift the peg scores four points. The team has three turns, and the highest possible score is ninety-six points. We all took our hand at tent-pegging, but our Indian soldiers, with their dash, their instinct for the spectacular, their wonderful eye and supple wrists, excelled.

Another Indian officer with whom I came to be very closely associated was Jemadar, as he then was, Kanshi Singh. Like Risaldar Hazura Singh, he was a Dogra – a hill Hindu. When I was commanding the Headquarters Squadron of Sam Browne's Cavalry in 1936, he was with me as a risaldar. In the Headquarters Squadron we had all three classes of men whom we recruited, Sikhs, Dogras and Punjabi Mussulmans. The squadron included the regimental machine-guns and regimental signallers.

Kanshi Singh was a lightly built, very neat man, calm and courteous and an elegant horseman. But he was resolute, and he had a very clear mind. He knew exactly the results he wanted to achieve in the squadron, and he reached his goals without any fuss. He exercised his authority in a quiet, straightforward manner, but he was capable of dealing with difficulties by clever and tactful manipulation. His prime concern, without which the squadron could not reach its full effectiveness, was harmonious relationships between the three communities. And in that field he scored a minor triumph.

It was our custom, if the Regiment moved out of barracks to go to war, or on any major expedition – say to help quell a riot – or for extensive military manoeuvres, for each of the three sabre squadrons to shout their communal battle cry three times each. Squadrons being about a hundred strong, a hundred Sikh squadron voices could stir the soul with their repeated cry of 'Sath sri Akal' – 'Long live the Sikhs'. The origin of these battle cries was no doubt to strike terror into the hearts of the enemy. And the PMs' and Dogras' battle cries were a worthy match for the Sikhs.

However, when it came to the Headquarters Squadron, we had only between thirty and forty of each community, so the battle cries were relatively thin and unimpressive. I therefore discussed with Kanshi Singh whether we might try to get the whole squadron to shout all three battle cries, one after the other. He was all for it, so we contrived it; and as we next moved out of barracks on some manoeuvre, each of the other three squadrons had shouted their cry and were awaiting the puny echoes from Headquarters Squadron, when we astonished them with a resounding roar of each of the three community cries. It had never been done before.

For all his gentle demeanour, Kanshi Singh was a battle-hardened veteran. He had fought in France and in Mesopotamia in the First World War, and on the North West Frontier, and was widely respected not only for his personal qualities but also for his long experience and profound knowledge of regimental soldiering. He was one of those who was deeply disturbed by all the talk in the 1930s of possible Indian independence and the almost unthinkable prospect of British officers disappearing, and their long and fruitful comradeship with Indian soldiers coming to an end. He told me that when he first went to France in the First World War, the French thought the Indian soldiers must be savages because they appeared to eat the prunings in the orchards. Indians clean their teeth with twigs.

I must allow at least a passing thought, too, for our many humble and self-effacing, but pricelessly useful, regimental followers: our numerous grooms (syces), our farriers, our armourers, saddlers, *darzis* (tailors), *bhistis* (water-carriers), *dhobis* (washermen), cooks, sweepers, to say nothing of devoted, and usually very long-serving, officers' mess servants, and perhaps others whom I overlook, just as I am afraid we used to take their faithful service for granted. Then, in a category of their own, were the religious leaders of each denomination.

When Algy Melville returned to India from Mesopotamia after the First World War, he let it be known in the bazaar that he needed a bearer. A number turned up for interview. Algy looked at their 'chits' – testimonials from former masters. One elderly man came forward and Algy asked for his chits. He held out a single piece of paper. 'Is that all?' asked Algy. 'Have you only one chit?'

'Yes, sahib.'

'Well, that's no good,' said Algy, and went to dismiss him.

'But please read it, sahib.'

It was quite short, and went something like this: 'It is with profound sorrow that the end of my service in India causes me to part from Mohammed Baksh who has been my faithful friend and constant companion through thick and thin for thirty-seven years.'

It goes without saying that that was enough to get him the job, and years later, when Algy retired, Mohammed Baksh also decided to take his rest after half-a-century or so of faithful service in which he only had two masters. Such master and man relationships seem nowadays anachronistic, and perhaps they are; but surely, for all of us, service is the essence of a rewarding life. Master and man are simply serving at different levels, and with acknowledged strong obligations to serve each other. In our Army community they were more often than not bonded by a deep affection and would even have laid down their lives for each other. Besides, not everyone wanted the master's role. They sought no more than sheltered employment under a good master to whom they could have the satisfaction of giving loyal and devoted service.

Just such another man was Yusuf, our mess *abdar* (butler). I think I am right in saying that he had one master only, in that he devoted the whole of his working life to our mess. He was a charming man, always cheerful, always willing, exceptionally courteous, highly efficient, the soul of reliability, and with a delicious sense of humour. He was also very discreet. We once had a well-to-do Sapper officer living with us. When he came in from his work at lunchtime, he always asked Yusuf for a tankard of beer. Only Yusuf knew that the 'beer' was a bottle of champagne. As mess secretary doing the accounts, I naturally discovered it myself. Yusuf befriended not only all of us in the Regiment, but also our scores of visitors over the years. I have no doubt that he got lifelong satisfaction from fulfilling his strong Indian sense of duty.

6

Risalpur and Rawalpindi, 1930

In mid-April 1930 I went to Risalpur, in the North West Frontier Province, to join a British cavalry regiment, the 15th/19th Hussars, for a three months' attachment – it was part of our training. It was an agreeable experience, but I do not know in what way it was supposed to benefit us as budding Indian cavalrymen. My two companions had both had been at Sandhurst with me, and I knew them well. With one or two newly joined 15th/19th subalterns, we spent a certain amount of time in the riding school under a superb horseman, Bob Leaf, but all these refinements of horsemanship, and horsemastership, we could as well have acquired in our own regiments. Fortunately we were not left long to ponder the usefulness or otherwise of the attachment as we soon found ourselves involved in a frontier war.

All the political talk and agitation at that time about independence for India suggested to the tribesmen that the British were losing our grip, and that the plains of India were becoming a soft target. That was, however, very far from the case; our defence plans were excellent and up-to-date.

The 15th/19th Hussars were immediately ordered to the combat zone to counter the strong Afridi tribe, leaving only a skeleton staff to look after the lines in Risalpur. We three attached Indian Cavalry officers were not needed to take command of the 15th/19th troops, but we joined in all such auxiliary jobs between the lines and the Regiment as were required – escorting convoys and so on. It was very hot, and very dusty. I was often very confused about what was going on: I discovered the truth of that well-known military phenomenon, the 'fog of war'.

I had other experiences. Attacks on our part of the North West Frontier that hot weather were not limited to tribesmen. We had to deal with two other enemies. The first was locusts. Only someone who has actually witnessed the devastating onslaught of extensive swarms of locusts could believe in the possibility of such a scourge. They are large insects, much larger than grasshoppers, several inches long, and they come in millions, packed tight over a large area. Those that invaded us that hot weather were in the 'hopper' stage, most of them not yet flying. They were hopping, all in the same direction, shoulder to shoulder over a wide area. They climbed everything that had any leaf on it, stripping trees, bushes and plants of all leaves, flowers and buds in minutes. We dealt with them by digging a trench in their path and filling it with water where available, or else with burning grass, and driving the locusts into it to drown or burn.

The other enemy that summer was cholera. People were dead in hours, but some sort of short-term prophylactic had by then been formulated and we were able to get everyone in the cantonment, British and Indian, inoculated within two or three days and made safe. It must have been a grim business in India before they had this inoculation, for it used to wipe out a whole area in a few days. The British cemeteries in India are eloquent of the effects of cholera.

Against the Afridis themselves we suffered very few casualties. On our worst day we lost one man killed, and two wounded. The Afridis suffered much heavier casualties before clearing off back to the mountains.

I have mentioned that we were trained to fight on horseback with sword and lance. This may sound anachronistic even seventy years ago in the days of rifles, machine-guns, artillery and even some tanks and armoured cars, but we would hardly have gone on with such training had we had reason to regard it as entirely useless. For instance, the Poona Horse caught a lot of Afridis in the open and got in a charge with two squadrons. They were unfortunate to get slowed down for a few moments by some thick crops and heavy going, and lost one Indian officer and three men, and had five more wounded. However, they soon got galloping again and went home with the sword. They picked up nine Afridis killed by sword thrusts, and must have wounded a considerable number more.

That was less than a dozen years after the First World War. The shadows of the Second were not yet upon us. Horses were still not inappropriate for the sort of operations we had to carry out, though I am sure that none of us who had given any thought to the matter would have supposed them appropriate to a modern European war. We still had very little mechanisation in the Army in India, with no mechanical vehicles in the Regiment. Our baggage was carried on camels. There were very few private motor-cars. I think our CO, Jack Gannon, had one; one of our King's Commissioned Indian officers who was a well-to-do landowner, Captain Mohammed Ayub Khan, had one, and possibly Algy Melville and his wife. The rest of us got about on bicycles and horses. When I went any distance fishing or shooting at weekends, I would go by train and take my bicycle with me to the station nearest to the area I proposed to visit.

My letters throughout the hot weather of 1930 are full of comments on the state of unrest among the tribes on the North West Frontier. Indeed it looked as though we might be facing a major tribal confrontation in the latter part of 1930, and our mess had to accommodate another ten officers belonging to the additional infantry brigade which had been sent to reinforce our area. It was a problem that was to continue for some years, but one that we were well able to contain, even though with some hard fighting at times.

I returned from the Frontier to Sam Browne's Cavalry in Rawalpindi in the middle of July 1930, at the end of the hottest part of the hot weather. A day or two after my return someone asked me at lunch what I was doing that evening. I said I thought I might play squash with a Gunner friend, Henry Hamilton. 'He's dead,' came the reply. 'He died suddenly last week – cerebral malaria.'

It was one of those scars on the soul that never altogether heal.

Now they were slightly concerned about me. I had lost two stone in weight – though it was to turn out not to have been entirely due to the hot weather – and I was immediately ordered to take a month's leave in the hills. I protested that as the monsoon was starting and I had made no leave plans, it would be pointless and boring to sit in the rain in the hills for a month. Nevertheless I decided to take ten days' leave at a hill station named Khanspur, which was shared by my friends in the 15th/19th Hussars with the 9th Lancers from Sialkot. What we called 'the hills' in India were the nethermost ranges of the Himalayas, at 6,000 to 9,000 feet. Khanspur itself was 8,000 feet up, with a beautiful cool fresh climate at that time of the year.

There were only three 15/19th officers at Khanspur, and they were good enough to take me into their mess. One of them was Robert Dorrien-Smith, about my age and a keen naturalist (a member of the well-known family of Tresco Abbey, Isles of Scilly, and sadly to be killed – the same day as one of his brothers – in France in 1940). He and I walked and climbed while he collected plants for Tresco Abbey and butterflies for himself. One day we climbed a mountain from which we had a magnificent view of India, the Frontier and Afghanistan. We could see across the plains to Peshawar in the North West Frontier Province, and to the Safed Koh (White Mountain) in Afghanistan, a

distance of 200 miles from where we were. We could follow the course
of the Indus river across the plains, and clear to the north were the
snows. Altogether we had a range of views over something like 400
miles.

The hot weather did not begin to peter out in Rawalpindi until mid-
September. It was good for our health to get out of it when we could,
and I managed to get away to the hills again for another ten days in
September. I went with David Gregson, our adjutant, who like me was
a fisherman and a keen shot, and we chose the Batrasi Forest, where we
settled into the forest rest-house. It was not high, only about 4,000 feet,
but high enough to be nice and cool at that time of year.

Our idea was to fish the local Khaghan river, about four miles away
and in a valley 1,500 feet below. We went down the evening we arrived
to have a look at it, and it seemed just right. The water was coming
down fast, with a lot of colour in it, and was not cold – a fast torrent
with alternate rapids and pools, and very deep. But then it rained hard
that night and kept it up almost continuously for three days. In the
higher mountains it snowed every night and thawed in the day with the
result that, for the rest of our time there, the river was a tearing flood.
The flood water was the colour of tomato soup. The local people think
it wonderful and come for miles to drink it, for its supposed properties
for cleaning the liver and kidneys; and one man told me of a blind
woman who came and stayed by the river, and bathed her eyes in it, and
gradually her sight returned.

At a village on the river called Ghari Habibullah we found all the
lads swimming. They seemed very strong swimmers. They plunged into
the terrifying torrent, all foam and rapids, and struck out for the far
bank, about fifty yards away, but would be carried perhaps 200 yards
downstream before they reached the far side. The small boys learn to
swim with *khaddu* – gourds – tied onto their stomachs, or one under
each arm, to keep them afloat.

We organised a race across the river and back with a prize for the
winner. They had to start at a certain point, swim to the far shore, and
the first one back to the starting point was the winner: fleetness of foot
on the far bank counted considerably.

The son of the khan of Ghari Habibullah came to see us and asked if
we would like a day's chukor (red-legged partridge) shooting. So that
was arranged. The chukor come down out the hills at dusk into the
cornfields in the valleys to feed, and at crack of dawn start back again
up the hill, then find a comfortable spot a couple of thousand feet up

where they settle down for the day. The best time to shoot is as soon as it is light enough to see; so we started off on our day before dawn. We climbed like goats, the khan, who was wonderfully fit, setting the pace. Eventually we got to the required level and spread out up and down the mountain, with each of us walking along his own contour. The going was very rough, all large boulders and camel thorn, and very steep. There were masses of birds about, but we got very little shooting.

After about three hours the khan proposed that we should go to another place, and indicated another spur of mountain that looked a long way off, but not as far as it actually was. After almost another three hours' walking we reached it. I took the lower gun as there were no other bidders – the going was more severe than higher up, and I was probably as fit as the khan and far fitter than David who weighed fourteen stone. The result was that I got some first-class shooting at birds coming off the top and dropping on a dead wing like bullets.

The khan, who spoke very good Urdu and not the cross-bred Pushtu spoken by the villagers, was a delight and frightfully keen. The local people, too, were very pleasant and friendly and respectful, and out to help in every way. We got back to the village at about 4.30 p.m. having had quite enough. The khan promised to take me hawking which he considered more fun than shooting, and certainly he had some beautiful hawks.

Altogether we had a great leave. Plenty of sleep, plenty of exercise and, above all, plenty of cool fresh air without any dust. We broke all routine: went to bed when we felt tired, got up when we felt rested, ate when we felt hungry, and didn't bother about regular meals or anything else – no work and no worry.

The autumn and winter were the main training season when we left barracks and did manoeuvres of one kind and another, exercises which I very much enjoyed. We followed a regular and progressive course of training every year, starting with the individual soldier and progressing finally to the training of the full Regiment. Every individual soldier was trained and given an annual test to ensure his proficiency in all aspects of soldiering that he might be called upon to perform. That done, we went on to formation training.

First, the lowest formation, the section, six men or thereabouts, commanded by a lance dafadar (corporal) or acting lance dafadar (lance corporal), was again trained to full proficiency. Next came troop training – four troops to a squadron, commanded by a British officer. That, in effect, was the point at which I ceased to be the trainer, and became the trainee. Then the Regiment – four squadrons commanded by the Commandant. That gave him his chance to ensure that he and the whole Regiment were at the highest possible peak of readiness to deal with any duty the Regiment might at any moment be called upon to discharge. Usually we also managed brigade training. Higher training than that was more problematical.

It might seem that such training could be boring year after year, and indeed there could be an element of boredom, although much of it was very interesting and agreeable. I have a short account of a part of our Regimental training which was written by our Commandant, Jack Gannon, for the Annual Letter which he sent to pensioners and others.

> We first went to Sang Jani, north west of Rawalpindi, and then struck off in the Kohat direction and worked over the lowest range of the Kala Chitta hills into Fatehjung, then southwards in the direction of the Kaur oilfields. There is no proper road in this area, and it was a most delightful strip of country. The people were all delighted to see us, as troops never pass that way, and it is difficult to realise that we were only 25 miles from Rawalpindi with its political troubles and unrest. There were a good many old soldiers about, and one told us the story of how he was taken prisoner by the Turks at Kut but, later on, with a friend, contrived to escape. Politics seem to be unheard of in this happy valley where peasants, working in the fields, would leave their work and run to see us and salaam as we passed by. We covered 100 miles by the map in four days, though in actual work it must have been a good deal more.

In December David Gregson and I had one more period of ten days' leave in the hills. We left Rawalpindi in the borrowed luxury of a car, motored to Abbottabad some seventy miles away and, from there, took the west Kashmir road into the mountains to a place named Manshera, where we arrived at sundown. The keen air was very refreshing after the dust-laden plains.

One of our Indian officers had arranged with the Khan Sahib of Manshera, a friend of his, to allow us to shoot over his property. We were to camp at a village named Lhasan and do our shooting from there. However, we couldn't spend our whole time there as we had promised our colonel to arrange a couple of days' shooting for him near Manshera, as he badly wanted to get away from his office, and the dust, and what he called 'this herd of damned generals'.

We had a brigade commander in Rawalpindi, a major-general commanding Rawalpindi District, and a lieutenant-general commanding Northern Command. That winter, too, we received a visit from the Commander-in-Chief, Field-Marshal Lord Birdwood. He inspected our Regiment. I prepared myself with the answer to every possible question he might ask me. Eventually the crucial moment came: he arrived with his staff at the head of our squadron where I was standing. He may have been a fire-eating fighting soldier, but in his peacetime role he cultivated the character of a beneficent fatherly man. I was introduced to him, and he held onto my hand and looked in my eyes, and then asked me the last question in the world that I would have expected: 'How old are you?' I was momentarily flummoxed.

But back to our mountain leave. We stayed in the *dak* bungalow at Manshera. *Dak* means 'mail'. *Dak* bungalows were early staging posts all over India for the mail runners. They were quite substantial buildings, simply furnished with tables, chairs, beds and cheap crockery and cutlery, and had the usual primitive bathrooms with a zinc tub and 'thunder box' commode. There was a permanent staff, a caretaker who could do simple cooking, a sweeper, and possibly a *mali* (gardener). Anyone could put up for a night, or stay a few days, without notice, for the payment of a small fee.

We hadn't been long settled in when a young Indian walked in and introduced himself as the khan's eldest son. He gave us some information about the shooting and said that he intended to accompany us himself as he was keen on shooting and would like a few days' sport near Lhasan. He also said that his father wanted him to be with us to see that we were well looked after and made comfortable. He then took his leave, saying that all arrangements would be made for us to start our trek across the mountains at 9 a.m. next morning. There would be horses for us to ride, and donkeys and mules for our kit.

Next morning, more or less punctually, the horses and the young khan arrived, but we had to wait for the mules; so the convoy didn't leave the bungalow until 1 p.m. The horses were small hill ponies, but proved excellent for the job, climbing about most impossible places like mountain goats.

We trekked for about fifteen miles, arriving at Lhasan at about 4.30 p.m. We sat there to await our kit. It was a small village set in a pass in the mountains, over 4,000 feet up, and surrounded by crops and cultivation. For obvious reasons we didn't want to camp too close to the village, so we looked round for a suitable site, eventually finding an

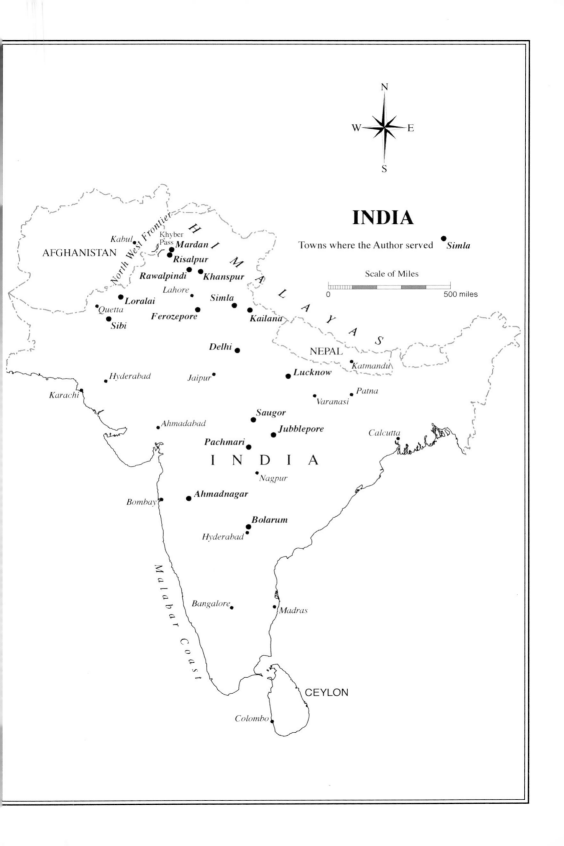

INDIA

Towns where the Author served   *Simla*

Scale of Miles

0   500 miles

N
W   E
S

AFGHANISTAN

Kabul
Khyber Pass
Mardan
Risalpur
Rawalpindi   *Khanspur*
Lahore
North West Frontier
Loralai
Quetta
Ferozepore
Simla
Kailana
Sibi

HIMALAYAS

NEPAL
Katmandu

Delhi
Lucknow
Hyderabad   *Jaipur*
Patna
Karachi
Varanasi
Saugor
Ahmadabad
Jubblepore
Calcutta
Pachmari

I N D I A

Nagpur

Ahmadnagar
Bombay
Bolarum
Hyderabad

Malabar Coast

Bangalore
Madras

CEYLON

Colombo

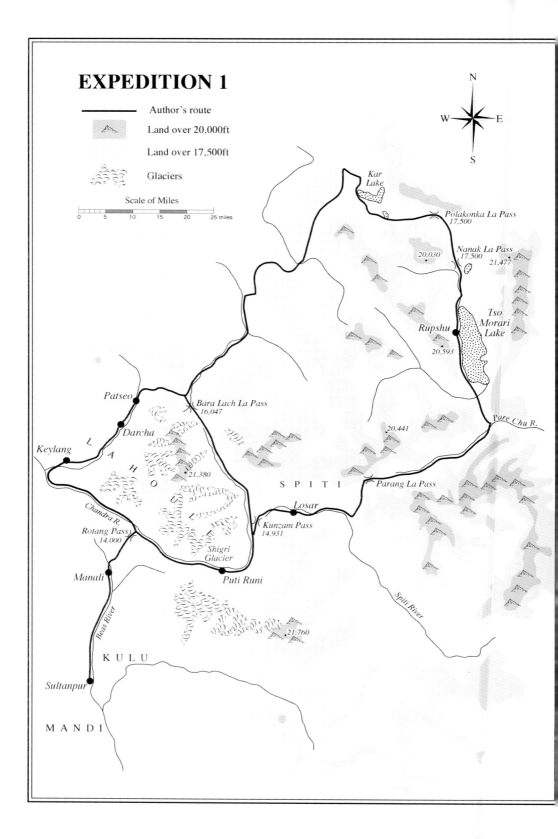

EXPEDITION 1

Author's route

Land over 20,000ft

Land over 17,500ft

Glaciers

Scale of Miles

0   5   10   15   20   25 miles

N
W — E
S

Kar Lake

Polakonka La Pass
17,500

Nanak La Pass
17,500
21,477

20,030

Tso Morari Lake

Rupshu
20,593

Patseo

Bara Lach La Pass
16,047

Darcha

L A H O U L E

Keylang

21,380

20,441

Pare Chu R.

Chandra R.

S P I T I   Parang La Pass

Losar

Rotang Pass
14,000

Kunzam Pass
14,931

Shigri Glacier

Manali

Puti Runi

21,760

Beas River

Spiti River

K U L U

Sultanpur

M A N D I

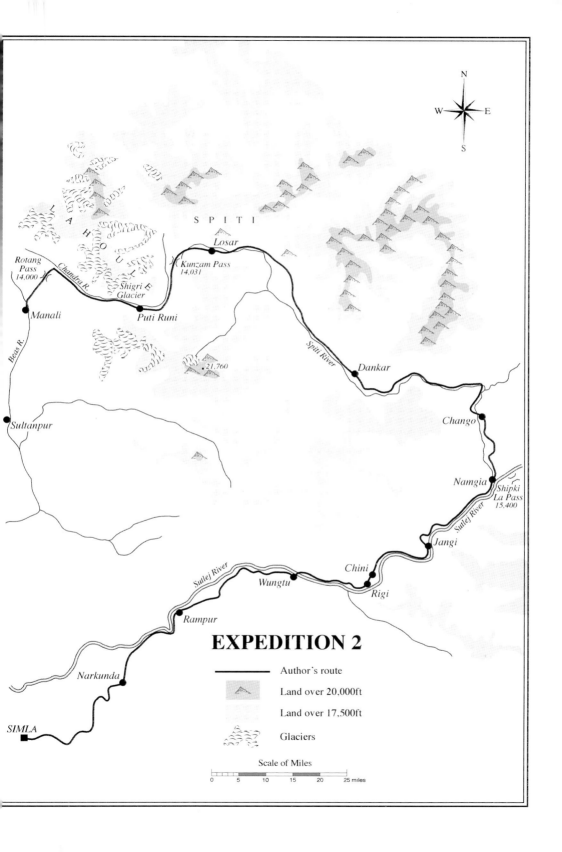

EXPEDITION 2

Author's route

Land over 20,000ft

Land over 17,500ft

Glaciers

Scale of Miles

0   5   10   15   20   25 miles

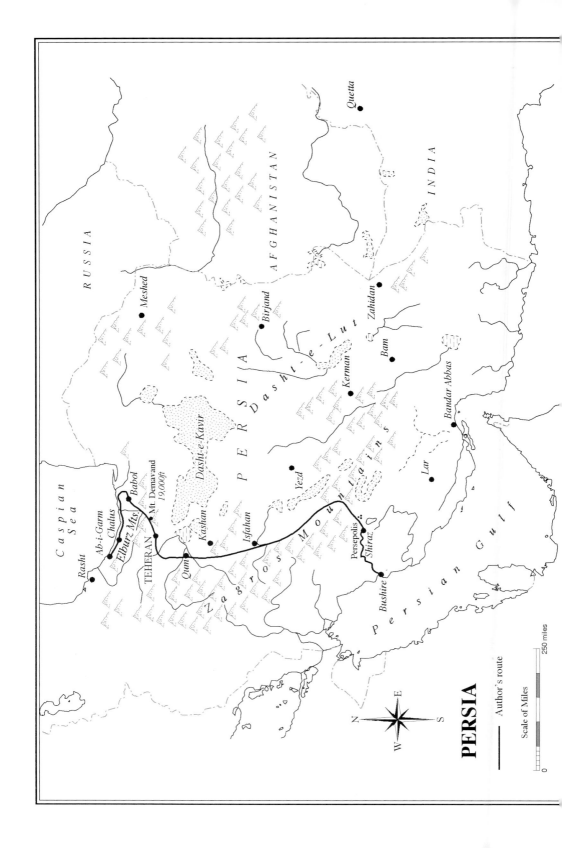

PERSIA

—— Author's route

Scale of Miles

0   250 miles

RUSSIA

AFGHANISTAN

INDIA

Quetta

Meshed

Birjand

Zahidan

Bam

Kerman

Bandar Abbas

P E R S I A

Dashi-e-Lut

Dasht-e-Kavir

Yezd

Lar

Caspian Sea

Rasht

Ab-i-Garm
Chalus
Babol
Elburz Mts.
Mt. Demavand
19,000ft
TEHERAN
Qum
Kashan
Isfahan

Z a g r o s   M o u n t a i n s

Persepolis
Shiraz

Bushire

P e r s i a n   G u l f

N
W   E
S

LEFT Risaldar Major Gurbakhsh Singh RIGHT Risaldar Hazura Singh

LEFT (back, left) Risaldar Muzzafar Khan RIGHT The Khan of Manshera

ABOVE Manali, near the head of the valley BELOW Yaks fording the Spiti river at Losar

ABOVE Tibetan and yak BELOW Tibetans in the High Himalayas

ABOVE *mani pani* wall with a *chorten* BELOW The Parang La Pass

excellent spot protected from the wind on two sides by enormous granite boulders, and on a third side by the mountains, leaving one side
open with a beautiful view away to the Kashmir snows. It was far
warmer at night than in Rawalpindi, though somewhat cooler in the
day.

Our baggage arrived at about 5.30 p.m., by which time David and I
had got our coats off and started pitching camp – it is black dark
twenty minutes after the sun goes down and we were working against
the fast reddening evening sky. The locals stood by amazed as bits of
wood and canvas and leather straps burgeoned into camp tables,
chairs, beds, etc.; and the young khan was somewhat shocked at David
and me indulging in manual labour. When I finally I took an axe and
started to chop some wood for a fire, it was too much for him. He
implored me to let a servant take over, as for him it seemed infra dig in
the extreme. We got our camp shipshape before dark, and settled in for
a comfortable night.

Next morning we were up with the sun and out on the mountain
after chukor, but birds were not as plentiful as at Ghari Habibullah.
The mountains were very steep but not difficult going as the rock was
all granite with no shale and with excellent footholds everywhere. The
cover consisted of thorn bushes, a type of heather, and a certain amount
of spear-grass, annoying stuff as it gets into all one's clothes and is the
devil to get rid of it. The bag was small but well mixed, and contained
chukor, black partridge, grey partridge, sisi (a very small partridge),
hares and snipe. A lot of the shooting was at driven birds coming hard
and fast. We were out on the mountains most days from dawn till dusk.

The weather was kind. One day it rained and continued blowing and
raining into the night, but the storm blew itself out before morning,
after which the sun shone from a cloudless sky for the remainder of our
leave. The young khan, too, was very good to us. Every day, when we
got back to camp, he would send us presents of fruit and vegetables and
honey – the honey was excellent and I consumed large quantities
hoping to make myself somewhat fatter. Then, when we packed up
camp at Lhasan, he insisted that we should go to his village, some two
miles from Manshera, and stay there as guests of his father.

We made the journey a shooting trip, and eventually arrived at the
khan's house about an hour before dark, having had a hard day over
very broken and difficult country. The village was on the top of a hill
with a winding path leading up to it that was worn deep into the rock
through generations of use.

Right at the top of the village, to our considerable surprise, was a very modern bungalow with a wooden roof and concrete verandah. This proved to be the guest house, set apart for us, and consisted of one large well-furnished and comfortable room containing two beds. The old khan sahib met us there and we had tea together. He proved to be a most interesting old man.

Next day we moved down from our 'castle' into Manshera and in the afternoon David and I climbed a neighbouring hill to inspect a huge boulder which must have been about forty feet high and was perched right on the summit of the hill. There are many legends about this stone. It is now worshipped by Hindus, but it is said to have been a holy place too for the Buddhists who once inhabited this part of India.

The land was fertile and, with a minimum of work, the villagers produced sufficient corn for themselves, without troubling to grow enough to sell. Vegetables grew well, and there was no difficulty about grazing cattle, from which they got milk and butter, and sheep and goats which provided them with meat to eat and skins and wool for clothes, footwear, etc. These illiterate people wanted no education. They were wonderfully cheerful and full of fun, and not a bit shy or afraid. Whenever we sat down anywhere near human habitation for a bit of lunch or a rest, someone came along with beds for us to lie on and with presents of eggs, fruit or vegetables, and asked for nothing in return. It was exhilarating to see a land so contented; even the dogs in the village seemed cared for and well fed.

It may seem that we took rather a lot of leave. The Indian Army did not go to the hills for half the hot weather, as the British Army in India did. Any time, therefore, we could get away from the summer heat was beneficial to our health. Ten days' leave started on Friday afternoon and included two weekends and a Thursday holiday, so it was only four working days' leave. There was no air-conditioning in those days, so we endured the full force of the heat day and night throughout the hot weather. Moreover there were very positive advantages for those of us in the Indian service to get out into the villages and to get to know the people better. And living out, and a bit rough, and having hard days' sport in the mountains certainly kept us fit.

The system allowed for every officer to take sixty days' leave annually – consecutive days, not working days. That was to enable people to get a good break from the hot weather. It was known as 'privilege leave', and it was made clear that it was a privilege and not a right – and indeed for reasons of duty, as with the Frontier troubles in 1930, we could not always take it; but a CO could give his officers ten days' leave as often as he could spare them and that was not deducted from privilege leave. We knew, of course, that we were liable to instant recall. Meanwhile our men also got very generous leave, including allowances to go home, for instance, to reap their harvest.

At the very end of 1930 a letter home said that I had gone to church on Christmas morning: 'I arrived late, but it was rather amusing, because the service started with "Hark the Herald Angels Sing" and, when I arrived, they had got to the second verse, and I wandered up the aisle to "Late in time behold him come".'

7
A Reunion and Other Diversions

Early in January I went up to Risalpur to stay for a few days with Robert Dorrien-Smith of the 15th/19th Hussars and to convalesce after a bad bout of fever. Two of their squadrons were out in camp combining training with 'showing the flag' to the local Pathans, and I called in on my own old 15th/19th squadron who were encamped at a place named Swabi. They had organised sports for the local inhabitants – tent-pegging, wrestling, races and a tug-of-war. All the local khans and dignitaries had been invited to tea and about a hundred came, together with a crowd of almost 5,000. The khans ate a tremendous tea and appeared delighted with everything. I talked at length to some of the old gentry, most of whom had served in the war or been in the Army – one in my Regiment.

It speaks volumes for the 15th/19th Hussars that one of their squadrons was able to mount such an occasion. They didn't have the facilities that we in the Indian Army had, with our contacts with the people through our own soldiers, and with our everyday use of the local languages. That it was good for local relations I have no doubt and there were occasional uneasy rumours to underline how important that was. At the time there was a Frontier report going around that local politicians were offering a reward of 8,000 rupees to any man who captured a white woman and brought her to the Tirah (the Afridi tribe's territory). When you consider that an Indian soldier's pay was 18 rupees per month, you get some idea of the value of 8,000 rupees locally. We imagined the ransom demand would be the return of the Kajuri Plain, an area of Afridi country across which we had just built a fortified military road to deprive them of a favourite jumping-off ground for their raids. In fact the rumour came to nothing, although there was an abduction some time later elsewhere on the Frontier.

One of the great pleasures of the Indian Army was the continuing association with old and retired soldiers and their villages. All our men were Punjabis and in Rawalpindi we were in the Punjab; so, although the

Punjab was an enormous province, we were not so far from our recruiting grounds that we couldn't keep in close touch with our pensioners.

However, in January 1931 we received a surprise. Sam Browne's Cavalry was due for a move, and we expected to be moved even nearer to the Frontier, perhaps to either the Risalpur or Sialkot cavalry brigades. I was looking forward to some involvement in Frontier operations which we seemed certain to have and the battle experience that that would entail. But instead we were informed that we were to move later in the year to the Deccan Cavalry Brigade in Bolarum/Secunderabad in Hyderabad State in southern India. A consolation, according to my letters, was that the Deccan Cavalry Brigade was what I termed 'a war brigade', with a good chance of participating in any operations there might be.

As I said in a letter home, we would be as far away from Rawalpindi as Vienna is from Dublin. Because, therefore, we would be out of easy reach of our pensioners for some years, Jack Gannon, our Commandant, decided that we should hold a reunion for our retired sirdars – our retired Indian officers. It was to last three days, the last day to coincide with the wedding of Betty Christie, daughter of one of our officers who had been killed on the Frontier, and who had been well known to many of the old sirdars. She was marrying Captain Freddie Walton of The Guides, and we had undertaken to give the reception in our mess – a duty that fell to me, as mess secretary, to arrange.

Apart from the pleasure of old friends and comrades, Indian and British, being able to get together for a few days, the reunion also had the advantage that the sirdars would go back to their villages full of regimental pride and enthusiasm. This should give them a renewed interest in persuading the best young boys to come and enlist in the Regiment.

A hundred and twenty pensioned Indian officers arrived, delighted to be 'back to the Army again'. The oldest was a venerable elder who would have been worth a fortune to Hollywood as an Old Testament prophet. He had gone on pension in 1894 with thirty years' service, so he would have been a boy of about ten at the time of the Mutiny.

The first event was a tea party under a large awning on the parade ground. Each British officer presided over a table at which about ten pensioner Indian officers were seated. During tea it was our job to make ourselves acquainted with the name of each pensioner, and something of his history. Then the colonel walked round, greeting them each in turn, and we introduced them and told him something about them. He then made a speech in Urdu which I suppose some clerk had written. It was short but faultless, and was answered by an excellent, and rather philosophical, oration by an ex-education jemadar who was obviously intent on making an impression on all present and talked slowly in very simple Urdu.

In a letter home I described some of the next day's events:

The recruits gave two first class displays, one in horse-back vaulting and trick riding; the other in physical training, showing the very high standard of gymnastics they must reach before being considered sufficiently supple and active to start riding. They were very good indeed, and it was an eye-opener to a lot of people to see what good training can do for these boys.

The real business started at four o'clock in the afternoon. The whole station had been invited and about 350 to 400 people turned up. It was my job as mess secretary to produce shade, seating and refreshment for the multitude. It was hard work and rather worrying as I did the whole lot myself. Apart from getting tables, chairs, cloths, crockery and a hundred and one other things, I made an extensive study of cookery books and food manuals in order to provide a wide variety of cakes, sandwiches and so on with the maximum of attraction and the minimum of cost. It all went off splendidly, and all the servants worked hard to make it a success.

The rest of the officers had worked like slaves at organising the sports and preparing the various displays. There were mounted jumping competitions for our own men and Indian officers, and for visiting officers from other units. There was a mounted tug-of-war and mounted wrestling, and a mounted sword, lance and pistol competition for Indian officers. There was also a tent-pegging competition for the pensioner sirdars, won by an ancient Indian officer who presented a fine figure as he galloped down the ground with his long white beard flowing in the wind. Other displays included a musical ride in all the different uniforms worn by the Regiment since we were raised in 1849.

Most regiments have a pet battle. Ours is the Battle of Ahmed Khel in the 2nd Afghan War, 1879. Although this was not strictly the anniversary, it was near enough for us to feel justified in calling it Ahmed Khel Day. As a grand finale, therefore, we fought the Battle of Ahmed Khel over again.

Firstly *sangers* (rock defences, as used by the tribesmen – *sang* means a rock) were erected on the parade ground, built of painted sandbags. Into these fortified posts crept the Pathans in their usual ragged kit, with rifles and bandoliers slung on their backs. They hid themselves and lay watching.

Soon, in the distance, appeared two scouts, dressed in the old red uniform of the time, trotting unsuspecting towards the enemy position. When they were about 100 yards away, two shots rang out. One of the scouts dropped from his horse and lay dead, while the other turned and galloped back to warn the Regiment.

A trumpet was heard to sound the 'gallop' and 'charge', and the Regiment (only about fifty men) appeared at full gallop. Ahead of the troops was the British officer, bearded, as were the officers of that day, waving his sword round his head and roaring encouragement to the men galloping behind. This was yours truly doing an unrehearsed turn. I had all the correct kit. The Pathans scattered wildly, and I jumped one of the *sangers*, decapitating a dummy enemy as I went, followed by the Regiment. Thus was the Battle of Ahmed Khel won.

The announcer then proclaimed that Ahmed Khel would be fought again, this time as it might be fought today.

My description of it records that we introduced Very lights, a smoke screen, motor cycles and armoured fighting vehicles kindly provided by a neighbouring unit of the Royal Tank Corps.

That night we had the traditional nautch – a dancing display by professional dancing girls. Our guests seemed overwhelmed by the beauty of the girls, and the British among us thought the funny man even more vulgar than usual. The performance was in the open air and, shortly after the start, there was a rough and tumble between our regimental guards and a lot of uninvited onlookers who had to be seen off. We learnt the following day that there was to have been a political demonstration in Rawalpindi city on the night of our nautch. The senior civil and police authorities were on hand to deal with it, only to find that it unaccountably fizzled out. The reason was that the toughs, usually hired at four annas a head by the politicals, had decided that the nautch would be more entertaining. However, as they got booted out of our lines, they neither saw the nautch nor got their four annas.

The next day we had the wedding. We dressed in our regimental full dress. I was an usher in the church, and also one of the four outriders which we provided to escort the bridal carriage on its drive to the mess. The bridal couple left the church under the crossed swords of Indian officers of The Guides and Sam Browne's. Then our Gunner friends produced a smart landau and team of six chestnut horses, handled by three of their officers, and we gave the bride and bridegroom a good liver shake as we took them full gallop from the church to the mess, about a mile and a quarter.

The old Indian officer pensioners came to the reception, and the reunion ended for them with an extra-special dinner, during which the Commandant and other officers went round to say goodbye. Then we packed the old gentlemen off home and I went to bed and didn't stir an eyelid till 8.30 next morning. When, being Sunday, I have no doubt that I got up and went for a ride and had mulligatawny soup for breakfast.

Six weeks after our regimental reunion some of us went for a polo tournament to Mardan, the actual and spiritual home of that famous regiment, the Queen's Own Corps of Guides. We stayed in their mess, a veritable museum of Graeco-Buddhist statuettes, relics of the invasion of Alexander the Great and other artefacts found locally, and of trophies of nearly a hundred years of Frontier warfare.

Mardan was in the North West Frontier Province, so we were back, for those few days, in the atmosphere of disturbance. This time it was the 'Redshirts', the militant wing of the Frontier section of the Congress Party. Although they engaged in dangerously provocative marches and demonstrations, and were not above attempting to promote the murder of British officials, they had recently been legalised.

On this occasion their leader, Abdul Gafour Khan, who had been released from jail, was due to attend a huge march culminating in a rally in Mardan bazaar. Steps were taken to keep them out of the cantonment, but they swarmed along the boundary, where the Indian police and Indian soldiers kept them at bay with creditable restraint and patience. Slogan shouting was a common feature of such demonstrations.

At about 9 a.m. large groups of marchers appeared, moving with some sort of military discipline towards the bazaar. They were dressed in their red shirts and were carrying banners, which they waved to shouts of 'Abdul Gafour' and 'Gandhi', and also a Persian word '*Anquilab*', meaning 'Revolution'. In due course Abdul Gafour arrived and addressed the enormous crowd, which was by now thousands strong. He commended them for their martial spirit and encouraged them to prepare for the great things to come – the outbreak against the British.

That evening a party of Redshirts went to the local police officer and protested. They were now a lawful body. Gandhi and the Congress leaders had been released from jail, and so had Abdul Gafour Khan, but what about this fellow Anquilab? They gathered he was still in prison. They seemed baffled when the police officer burst into fits of laughter.

A fortnight later we went to Abbottabad for the polo week. We were the guests of the 5th Gurkha Rifles and we won the tournament. There were also other pleasures. One day I went to Mashera and had a long talk with my friend the old khan; another day I went to Ghari Habibul-lah to see the sporting khan, and then went up the Khagan valley. The Khagan river was in high flood and full of cold snow water. I did a little climbing.

Later in the year Sam Browne's Cavalry won the Indian Cavalry Tent-Pegging Trophy, taking 23 out of 24 pegs and thus scoring 92 out of a possible 96 – a score that had been equalled three times before, in 1899, 1906 and 1914, but never beaten. The team, consisting of the risaldar major, Gurbakhsh Singh, the woordie major, Jemadar Muzaf-far Khan, and six other Indian officers and NCOs, took all eight pegs in their first run. That was a good start but not exceptional. However, in their second run, they repeated that score which put them in the lead, and the situation before their last run was that five pegs would give them victory.

The elderly Dafadar Gulamwaz Khan came first. He was rather deaf and quite imperturbable. He hit his peg but it failed to come out of the ground, but the next man took his peg clean, as did all the others. The last to go, Dafadar Ishar Singh, took his gallop down the ground to a crescendo of cheers from the crowd as he ripped the peg clear out of the ground on the point of his lance.

One of the team, Dafadar Munshi Khan, was of course, with that name, a Mohammedan, but as a boy he had been brought up in a Sikh village. The Sikhs in the Regiment recruited him and insisted on having him in the Sikh squadron instead of with the Punjab Mussulmans. I had him under my command at one time in the Headquarters Squadron. He was one of those characters who manage to get away with a good deal of eccentricity, and he was a volunteer for every difficult and dirty job.

My next interlude in the summer of 1931 was to go on the small arms course in Pachmari. I always enjoyed courses, because I met a lot of new people from many different regiments and arms of the service, and made some lasting friends among them. Besides, Pachmari was an agreeable place to be in the month of July, two or three thousand feet up in the rugged, jungle-covered hills of the Central Provinces and a great deal cooler than in the plains. I did some local climbing and explored the streams which ran down off the plateau.

The vicious forest wild bees were a real danger in Pachmari. They would attack and sting people to death. One day when I was jungle bashing on my own in the forest, I accidentally dislodged a stone. It crashed down the very steep hillside and hit a rotten fallen tree trunk out of which flew thousands of angry bees. I immediately lay flat and lay still. They were, I suppose, some twenty feet below me, and they ranged backwards and forwards along their own contour, and then settled down again without coming up to my level. So I survived the Pachmari jungles and returned safely, well stocked with up-to-date small arms lore, to my Regiment.

Walter Shoolbred, a Gunner, was on the Pachmari course with me and, like me, he was later to join Hodson's Horse. At the end of the course, as we were both going to the railhead at Itarsi in the plains and catching the same train, we travelled down the hill together. We had an hour or two to wait for the train. The sun had just gone down, and the light was quickly fading. We walked a little way along the line to get away from the heat of the railway station buildings and sat ourselves down on the warm rail to talk. It was wonderfully placid in the stillness of the hot weather dark, with a background of the jackals' whimpering chorus and muted wedding drum beats sounding from some distant village, and the air full of the smell of evening fires.

8

The High Himalayas

By July 1931 I had been in India for nearly three years and, although I had taken a number of short spells of leave, up to ten days at a time, I had taken none of the sixty-day spells of 'privilege leave' for which we could apply annually. This was partly because I had been too busy, and we had been too short of officers in the hot weather months, and partly because leave had been stopped because of the menacing Frontier situation. However, it meant now that I could apply for three, instead of two, months' leave and, as our officer situation made that possible, I did so.

Ever since I had topped the last rise on the hill road to Kailana with Ken Collen of the 60th Rifles and seen the Himalayas for the first time, I had been planning a trip into the interior of the High Himalayas. Now was the chance to realise it – on my own. The whole journey was some 450 miles at heights of between 10,000 and 17,000 feet. I went to places where no European had been before.

I chose the seldom-visited Spiti valley as my first target. It lies to the north of the first great Himalayan range. To the north again of the Spiti valley, the whole of which is above 10,000 feet, is another range with a contour of over 19,000 feet. To get at the Spiti valley from any direction involves days of difficult terrain. I decided to try to get in from the west.

On 8 July I left Rawalpindi by the Frontier Mail on my way to Kulu and thence to Spiti. I got to Lahore at 7.30 p.m. and had to wait there till 11.30 p.m. for the train to Pathankot. It was far too hot for my liking. Arriving at Pathankot at 4.30 a.m., I changed to the narrow gauge railway which runs up the Kangra valley to Joginder-Nagar. It was much cooler there than in Lahore. The narrow gauge railway is a work of art, winding its way up hill and down dale, and once past the town of Kangra – half way – never level. It was slow. It took ten hours to do 102 miles.

At about 7.30 a.m. we stopped at a wayside station where I was told that I might have breakfast. I was conducted to the waiting-room by a waiter who assured me that breakfast was prepared, and an excellent meal I should find it. This little refreshment room was run by Spencer's, big caterers all over India. They ran a wonderful show, and this place was no exception.

The sky was cloudy, so that it remained cool all day. It was altogether a very pleasant journey and we reached railhead, Joginder-Nagar, at about 3.15 p.m. I had intended to spend the night there, but some enterprising lorry firm called the Imperial Motor Company ran a service to Kulu, and their agent said he could get me to Mandi, the capital of Mandi state, by 6 p.m. I could spend the night in the *dak* bungalow there, which would be cooler and more comfortable than where I was. So I packed into the lorry and away we went.

At Joginder-Nagar, where we stopped, there was an influx of passengers, among them a woman covered in a powerful Indian scent who was proving a pervasive neighbour until an old man fortunately arrived with a bag of onions and agreed to sit between us. All the same I couldn't say much for the journey. The lorry was boiling most of the time, creaking along in low gear. There was an unpleasant hot blast of steam and a stench of burnt oil. But, for all that, we were making steady progress and I was reckoning we wouldn't be more than an hour late when, about ten miles from Mandi, we burst a tyre. The spare wheel belonged to another lorry and wouldn't fit. Luckily we had a spare inner tube, but it was carefully packed under all the luggage on the roof. I went for a walk. I thought it would be as well for me to clear out and leave them to their earthy jokes.

After about twenty minutes I returned to find the usual business going on with a broken pump: two men gripping a red-hot valve as though it were the Crown Jewels, another, sweating like a stoker in the Red Sea, working the handle, and the remainder standing round yelling advice. Eventually the tyre was pumped up and we all piled in and started off again. We then rattled along nicely until, about three miles from Mandi, there was an ear-splitting bang and another tyre burst. That was it: we had no spare tube and no means of mending the burst one, so the driver said he would walk into Mandi and get another lorry. An hour and a half later he returned. It was 10 p.m. when I reached the *dak* bungalow. Too weary to eat much supper, although I had had nothing since breakfast, I struggled with an egg, a biscuit and a cup of coffee, had a cold bath and turned in to sleep till six the next morning.

I left Mandi for Kulu (Sultanpur) at 7 a.m. and unloaded myself into the *dak* bungalow in Kulu village after an uneventful journey. I then went to buy stores in an excellent little shop called the London House run by a most obliging man who worked hard for the rest of the day to accommodate me. Then I caught a good trout for my supper in the Beas river, which runs alongside the village. It was the first trout I had eaten for three years.

On 11 July I started off at about 8 a.m. in a lorry for Manali, the last village of any substance near the head of the Kulu valley. It was a lovely day, with bright sunshine. The valley, with its green fields cut out of the hillsides contrasting with the dark pine woods, looked beautiful, with white foaming streams pitching down steep *nullahs* on either side to join the Beas river. Towards Lahoule, the mountains ruled the prospect to the north, the tops snow-clad and numerous glaciers running down the valleys. About 9.30 a.m. we reached Katrain, half way to Manali. I was told we couldn't move on to Manali till one o'clock because traffic was allowed only one way on account of the narrowness of the road. I lay down under an apricot tree and gazed up the valley to the snow mountains, but the warm sun soon sent me to sleep and I knew no more until the lorry driver woke me at one o'clock saying it was time to go.

We reached Manali safely, and I pitched my camp in a pine wood a few hundred yards from the village. The village *thekidar* said that it was not possible to cross the Hampta Pass into Lahoule as the path had been washed away, so I must go due north over the Rotang Pass – 14,000 feet. That would add a day to my trek. The *thekidar* said he would get me ponies for transport.

I had it in mind possibly to do some shooting, and I needed someone with knowledge of the hill languages, so I engaged a fine strong-looking man named Thakru who claimed to be only an inexpert *shikari*, but who said he was very willing to come with me wherever I might go.

The next day I did a bit of laundry work in the morning, and after lunch my pony drivers arrived, but without any ponies. They said they wouldn't fetch them until they had heard my plans, and then they would only come if my arrangements suited them. I thought some of this was probably bluff – they had after all thought it worthwhile coming to see me.

Their first point was that they wouldn't accompany me unless I undertook to employ them for at least a month. That I had no intention of doing because, as soon as I crossed the Spiti border, I intended to get yaks which would greatly reduce my expenses. However, I made an offer which, after much discussion, they accepted: I could pay them off whenever and wherever I liked, but would pay full hire for their journey back to Kulu. I thought that fair for they had no chance of getting employment for backloads from Spiti.

I reckoned seven ponies would be enough, but they said they wouldn't go with less than nine. They stood their ground, and I had to give in. Next, they asked for half the wages of a coolie. I gave them this. It didn't amount to very much, and I told them that if we didn't start off friends, we would certainly never get anywhere. Nevertheless, realising I suppose that they had done pretty well, they tried one more. We had to cross two passes. They said these were very difficult so I should give them a third over the rate for each pony for those days. Here I stuck out, and they gave way. We were now in agreement and they went off to get the transport.

We needed all these ponies because the country we were going into would often be uninhabited or, at most, very sparsely inhabited, and certainly very poor in resources, so we could not expect to be able to get any supplies except perhaps meat now and again if I could shoot it. We therefore had to take everything with us for nearly three months.

The next day, 13 July, didn't go according to plan owing to the pony drivers. They did not arrive till midday. They had three mules with them; the rest ponies. That annoyed me as they had promised ponies, and mules are apt to cause trouble. The drivers made no end of a song and dance of loading up, and we had not gone half a mile before one of the mules kicked off his load.

After that everything went well. The path was very good. I stopped at a little forest rest house a mile short of the village of Rhala, the last village in Kulu before the high mountains. This saved pitching tents, so that we could be off quicker in the morning, and there was good grazing for the ponies. We ended the day well up the Rotang *nullah* (valley) and about seven miles from the top of the pass.

The Solung *nullah*, west of where I spent the night, presented a wonderful view as we marched up from Manali with, at the top of the *nullah*, not more than ten or a dozen miles distant, a continuous ridge of snow mountains rising to 21,000 feet, streaked with glaciers which looked lovely shining in the afternoon sun.

A little boy came to me with a huge leaf full of wild strawberries. He was a nice little chap, and understood my Urdu. Before going off, he had another look at the strawberries and said, 'I don't think this is nearly enough for you, sahib, so I will get more', and he went scampering off up the mountain to collect another leaf full.

Not far from Manali was a boiling hot sulphur spring gushing out of the side of the mountain not a yard from a spring of ice-cold pure water. Below them a bath had been built. When local young women reached puberty they had to go there and bath themselves. The women there were a bit primitive in their toilet arrangements, and bathed quite openly by the side of streams with no arrangements for privacy.

During part of the disrupted bus journey up to Kulu, I had sat next to a young *sadhu* – novice, I suppose he could be called – from an Amritsar ashram. I asked him where he was going. He was on a pilgrimage to a well-known Himalayan shrine.

'You have got to go over the Rotang Pass', I said, 'to get there. I am going that way myself. I hope you have plenty of warm clothing. It will be bitterly cold up there.'

'I have this,' he said, showing me one of those very fine Kashmir shawls that can be pulled through a wedding ring.

'Useless,' I said. 'You'll die of cold with only that round you.'

'No, I won't,' he replied, 'I shall be perfectly all right.'

'What makes you think so?' I asked.

'I can control my body temperature. Animals and birds can do it, and so can I.'

Rubbish, I thought. We parted somewhere en route.

The day following my night-stop in the forest rest house, we were off in good time and reached the top of the Rotang Pass without difficulty. There was half a mile of snow on the top, which we crossed quite easily. But there, also crossing the snow, and wearing his thin Kashmir shawl, was the young *sadhu* I had met on the bus.

'Aren't you dying of cold?' I asked.

'No,' he replied slightly testily. 'I told you I can control my body temperature.'

As the Himalayas are very steep, it is difficult to find suitable camping sites, but we found a good enough spot a couple of thousand feet below the north side of the pass. We were then in Lahoule and, a thousand feet below us, rushing down from the Spiti border, was the Chandra river – a most turbulent torrent. We were in the midst of a sea of high snow peaks, and the evening grew cold. I donned my fur-lined Gilgit boots and fur-lined coat, and I needed mittens for writing.

At about 12,000 feet, we were now well above the tree line but, though no botanist, I was struck by the profusion and beauty of the wild flowers. In my ignorance I could recognise, and noted that I had seen, a beautiful small blue iris, forget-me-nots, small pink primulas, a variety of daisies and buttercups and – a surprising mixture – some heather.

Ahead of me, I had several days' march eastward up the south side of the very rough, uninhabited, and uninhabitable, valley of the Chandra river. I knew that the only way to tackle it was to keep as near to the dangerously torrential river as possible. Steep patches of hard-packed snow, rocks, and cascading streams to cross would be our problem – and one major obstacle, the Shigri Glacier.

On 15 July, chiefly through the excellent work of the transport men, we were once more safely encamped with all gear complete. It had been a very hard march. I enjoyed it, but it was very dangerous, not for myself, but for the ponies and the kit, and I thought we were lucky not to have lost anything.

We didn't move off early, for the men said it was no good going till the sun had melted the top of the snow slightly so that the ponies could get a foothold. The sides of the valley were so steep, running sheer up to 15,000 and 16,000 feet from 10,000 or 11,000, which it was in the river bed, that the sun had to be high before its rays could reach the bottom of the valley.

In the first mile we got into difficulties as we had to pass along a steep rocky shoulder with big boulders everywhere, and often it was difficult to get a loaded pony between the boulders. There were also some nasty stream beds to cross; not for any depth of water but because the descent into them and the ascent out the far side was very trying for the ponies, clever though they were at picking their way. There was a path of sorts but it was nothing more than a goat track and, if you did not keep your eyes glued on it, you would soon wander off and get stuck in some bad place.

After this we crossed some snow patches which the ponies seemed to find quite easy, though why they did not slip and go head over heels into the river I could not make out, for I had to go with the greatest care.

The men worked it so that they could go diagonally downhill on the snow, and the animals, using their forelegs in turn as brakes, could slide their hind feet, sometimes almost on their hocks.

We made our way more or less on the same contour for a considerable distance. The path was very narrow, and I expected at any moment to see a pony go tumbling down the hill. We came across some Spiti people in trouble at a stream where one of their ponies, a weak-looking ragged little mare, had fallen in. We got her on her feet again and they were able to move on. Soon afterwards we struck the river bed, all snow, but level, and we crunched along this for a mile or more.

When we left the river bed again, we had a steep climb up onto a little plateau of lovely thick grass on which hundreds of sheep were grazing. It was getting up this slope that we had our only accident. We were about half way up, and had just crossed a long snow bridge and were working over a bad bit of steep loose shale, when one of the ponies – perhaps his hoofs were clogged with ice – slipped and started sliding down the hill. The men tried to hold him up but it was no good and he slithered down onto a patch of snow, bringing an avalanche of stones with him. His load of course came off and clattered down with him. But he got up quite unhurt and we found no damage had been done to the baggage, which consisted of two tin boxes, one containing clothes and the other bags of flour and rice. The pony was soon loaded up again and we continued our march on very good going. I thought we had reached the end of our troubles as we went along over grassy downs.

We were climbing slowly all this time and must have been more than 500 feet above the river. Eventually the time came to drop into the valley again and this was the worst bit of all. We had to pick our way foot by foot down a precipice covered with loose broken rocks; it took three-quarters of an hour to go less than half a mile. We had to hold the ponies up by their tails to stop them falling, and often had to place their feet for them. Eventually we reached the river bed again. There was no snow or ice, so we wandered slowly over the rocks.

The transport men refused to go any further than that. I wanted to go on about another mile onto a little plateau which we could see ahead, but the men said that the ponies were too tired and wouldn't face the climb. They were probably right, and there was a steep bit of snow to cross which might have been difficult.

We had one casualty – a slightly sprained ankle, which happened to one of the drivers when the pony fell down the hill. I told him to stand it in a stream for as long as he could bear the ice cold water, after which I would tie it up for him.

The next day the men wanted to wait for the sun again before starting, but I was not satisfied with their talk about the snow being too hard for the ponies to cross, so I got up at five o'clock and went to a bit of snow beyond the camp to test it. It was perfectly safe, being quite soft on top, so we loaded up and moved off. The day was a repeat of the day before. At one point we had to cross a heavy stream which we managed safely, the little ponies up to their girths in the running water. We also came upon a very smelly Spiti family carving their mantra, *Om mani padme hum*, on a rock. One of them was spinning his prayer-wheel, which could contain hundreds of inscriptions of the mantra on thin paper so that every time he spun it one revolution clockwise, he believed himself to have said as many hundred prayers.

We camped at a spot well known to the shepherds. There was a huge boulder there split in two, and the shepherds called the place *Puti Runi*, the local onomatopoeic words for a broken rock. It was as well to camp where the shepherds camped because, as there was no firewood, the dung could be used for a camp fire to cook one's supper.

It rained throughout that second night in the Chandra valley and was still raining at five o'clock next morning. We had to cross the Shigri glacier that day, and I decided against tackling it unless the weather improved. But the clouds lifted soon after 7 a.m. and it looked finer, so we packed up and started marching. It came on to drizzle again and, by the time we reached the glacier, it was raining quite hard, but there was nothing for it but to go ahead. To return to Puti Runi would entail re-crossing a flooded stream in which two ponies had fallen and soaked their loads, and there was nowhere else we could pitch a tent.

I was somewhat shaken at the sight of the bottom end of the glacier. Since I came into the valley, I had admired, at a distance, the beautiful jade green of the upper parts of several glaciers, but this was quite different. The ice field we had to cross was somewhere between a mile and two miles across, and consisted of mountains of jet black ice, 300 to 400 feet high in places, and covered with stones and boulders varying in size from a football to a suburban villa, all loose – they were continually moving as the glacier moved – and falling about.

On the glacier there were precipices like polished glass, often fifty or more feet deep. They were extremely dangerous, for you suddenly came on them, and should you happen to do so at the same moment that a chunk of ice and a few boulders dropped down to the bottom, you might have gone with them. From time to time shepherds had put up little pillars of stone to mark the best way across, but there were so many of these that they were misleading. The going was terribly slow owing to the frightful surface and the looseness of the stones. We got about half way across in a couple of hours, but the weather started to get worse, so Thakru and I and my bearer decided to push on and look for somewhere to camp.

We finally reached the far side of the glacier and dropped into a trough from which the mountainside reared up in a steep incline of loose slate shale. Here we found quite a good path which we thought the ponies ought to be able to manage, and we ourselves climbed up a bit and sat down to wait for the transport which we could see wending its way slowly towards us. Every now and then the animals would stop and we could see a man go forward to find a way by which they could get on a little further. It was still raining but there was not much wind. We were very wet but that didn't much concern us: the baggage was so packed as to keep out most of the damp, and we knew that once we pitched camp we could make ourselves fairly comfortable.

However, we had angered the gods. Almost from nowhere a thick cloud came down and shut off everything from view, a strong wind got up and in a minute we were in a dark fog of driving mist and rain. Thakru said we ought to make straight up the path as it was dangerous to sit where we were: the wind and rain would bring down stones from above. We fought our way up through the storm and reached a level grassy ridge, or so it seemed for we couldn't see far. It was no good staying there as there was no shelter, so I said we should try to hit the river valley and make for the camping ground a few miles up the river which was our aim. The transport would follow in due course. We stuck to our path, waded a dangerous-looking torrent, and shortly came down onto the bed of the river, a wide stretch of sand and gravel. Then we kept going. We were particularly concerned to find some grazing for the ponies. Eventually we were stopped by a stream in high flood that we could not ford, but it was a good enough place to camp and there was some grass on the mountainside for the wretched ponies.

We sat down and waited. By 4.30 p.m. there was no sign of the ponies, so we decided to go back and look for them. There was now a strong wind, and it was very cold. As we went, I noticed some smoke coming out of a little heap of rocks. It proved to be a Kulu shepherd crouching over a smoking heap of wet sheep's dung. I asked him where his flock was. His partner had them on the hill, he said, and would be back soon. Meanwhile he would prepare the evening meal when the fire got a bit warmer. I told him I might be back myself before long to share the warmth of his fire.

We pushed on back toward the glacier, but without finding the ponies. Thakru suggested that the bearer and I should stay with the shepherd where he could find us, while he went further back to look for the ponies.

It was nearly dark when Thakru reached them. They had had a terrible time in cloud over the last bit of the glacier and, when they reached the edge, could go no further, and sat in the hopes that we would come back to them. Thakru told them it would be impossible for us to get back to join them, so he took my overcoat and started back to where we were waiting. However, owing to the mist and darkness, he was unable to cross a heavy stream and was forced to take shelter under a rock for the night. The transport men, meanwhile, fared better for they had the kit, but the poor wretched ponies had to lie on the rocks and shiver for there was nothing for them to eat.

The bearer and I, in inadequate and very wet clothes, spent the night in the open with the shepherds at 12,000 feet, not far from millions of tons of ice, and felt the cold acutely – particularly as, ten days earlier, we had been living in a mean temperature of over 100°F.

The Kulu shepherds, who take their flocks into those high regions in the summer, are wonderfully hardy. They do not have tents. They live in the open, no matter what the weather. But their clothes, of homespun, thick sheep's wool with the natural grease in it, are very warm and adequately waterproof. In addition to several layers of clothing, the shepherds have a similar heavy blanket each. Our two that night had a little walled enclosure about eighteen inches high, the crevices stuffed with sheep's dung to keep out the wind. They had no head covering but, after their simple meal of chapatis, cooked on the very inadequate smouldering and reeking sheep's dung fire, they wrapped themselves in their blankets and slept soundly all night, even when restless sheep and goats walked all over them. My bearer and I – so-called civilised folk – were a sorry contrast, cold, wet, miserable and short of sleep.

As soon as it was light, he and I walked about to get the stiffness out of ourselves while the shepherds slept on. It was a fine morning and we soon made contact with Thakru and the transport men. It turned out a beautiful day. We finished the march of the day before by noon, pitched camp, and got all our wet stuff out to dry in the sunshine. We also had something to eat for the first time for twenty-four hours. Thakru and I had a self-denying ordinance that day against fording rivers. We had had enough wetting for the time being, so we went well out of our way to find snow bridges on the line of march.

The next day I reached Spiti and camped near the village of Losar (13,500 feet). We had a delightful march and, though the longest we had had, it was the easiest, with only two streams to ford, neither of them difficult. It was a long ascent up to the Kunzam Pass (14,931 feet), but again quite easy.

The Kunzam ridge is the watershed between two of the great Punjab rivers. The Spiti river rises near the pass and flows eastward into the Sutlej. The Chandra river, up which we had come, flows west into the Chenab. Eventually both the Sutlej and the Chenab flow into the Indus. The water that was then on our boots from these two different sources, separated by the Kunzam Pass in the High Himalayas, was therefore destined to meet again in the scorching plains of India 500 miles away as the crow flies – 1,000 or more, no doubt, as the rivers wind. As it turned out, the two easiest days up the Chandra valley were the days we crossed the passes – the Rotang and the Kunzam.

Looking back into Lahoule from the top of the pass there were three high gaunt snow peaks, and two glaciers. Looking east into Spiti was a very different view. In the distance was a huge line of purple snow-capped mountains, and nearer were precipitous cliffs of brown shale, which appeared to be bare of vegetation. From the pass itself, on the Spiti side, beautiful grassy downs sloped up to the snow-line.

In Lahoule, the snow-line seemed to be about 15,000 feet, and there was a lot of snow much lower than that, but in Spiti it was more like 18–19,000 feet. I have no idea what causes the difference. The mountains, too, are of different substance. In Spiti it is all slate and shale. In Lahoule it seemed to be mostly granite.

I had learnt that two Sapper officers had gone up the Chandra valley a couple of days ahead of me, and indeed I had found a trace of one of their camps. On arriving at Losar in Spiti, I met them, and they were more than surprised to see me, as they had no idea that anyone was following them. They had very bad transport men and took a day longer over their journey than I did. Exactly the same thing happened to them on the Shigri as happened to me, and they also spent a wet night out with a shepherd; he however was able to lend them each a blanket, and gave them rice to eat. But I was more fortunate than they, for one of them fell into the ice-cold Shigri river and was washed about a quarter of a mile downstream and nearly drowned.

Was it just coincidence that they were both Irishmen from exactly the same background as myself, Michael Perceval-Price of Saintfield, Co. Down, and Eyre Ievers of Mount Ievers, Co. Clare (the one who nearly drowned), or was it that our blood, or more likely our upbringing in the wild bogs of Ireland, left us with a strong call of the wild? Or was it, as Kipling says in *Kim*: 'From time to time God causes men to be born … who have a lust to go abroad at the risk of their lives and discover news – today it may be of a far off thing, tomorrow of some far off mountains.'?

They pointed me out a good place for a camp and asked me to have supper with them. I pitched my tent a few hundred yards from their camp on a little stream and had a clean-up and got changed into warmer clothes.

I then paid off my pony men and, at about half past six, went back to the Sappers. They gave me an excellent supper of curry and stewed apple, after which we got out maps and discussed plans. They were mainly on a shooting trip, and were going on eastwards the best part of another 100 miles to shoot along the Western Tibet border. I was mainly following my nose exploring the country, with possibly some incidental shooting thrown in. The shooting is exceptionally difficult stalking, in precipitous mountains, for wild mountain species of goat and sheep – ibex, mahkoor, buhrel and ovis Ammon.

I was not going as far down the Spiti valley as they were. There is a range of mountains 100 miles long along the north side of Spiti with a contour of over 19,000 feet. I was intending to look for some shooting in Spiti, and then to try to find a pass northwards over the mountains into Rupshu and Ladakh.

The Sappers moved off the next day. Although both served their full time in the Army and became colonels, I never met either of them again. More than fifty years later, however, I received a letter from Colonel Perceval-Price telling me that he had read my book, *Umma More*. His son, who is a writer, was one of those who reviewed it.

I decided on a day's rest, and I saw the *lambadar* of Losar village and arranged for him to supply me with yaks for the next stage – which he did, although they were very slow in arriving the following day and the men took some time to load them. When we eventually set off our first challenge was to ford the Spiti river. The *lambadar* brought his own pet yak for me to ride through the water. I think I got almost as wet as I should have done walking: my legs were already trailing in the quite deep current and the old yak lashed more water over me with its tail.

We were now in Tibetan country. The people were Mongoloid and the language was a dialect of Tibetan, of which we picked up a smattering as we went along; not least the words *kishi mishi* which mean 'early morning', for we were always keen to begin marches and hunting operations around dawn, if not earlier. For the first time, too, we encountered *mani-panis* – the long walls, several feet deep and up to perhaps four feet high, made entirely of loose stones each with a device carved on it; many simply with the words *Om mani padme hum*, and others with the figure of Buddha, some of them very well carved. This was recreational and devotional work, done on the long cold winter evenings.

A couple of days' rough march took us some twenty miles down the Spiti valley to an area where some Kangra shepherds told us they had seen a flock of burhal (mountain sheep) grazing on the mountain slopes to the north. We decided to make camp on a nice piece of ground beside a stream, far enough from any village not to be worried by children or dogs, and to do some hunting. The shepherds said they would supply us with sheep and goat's milk.

After four days in that camp while we reconnoitred for ibex, we located some near a high rugged cliff and decided to move camp to that immediate area. Here I was pleased and surprised to find quantities of wild rhubarb growing on the hills; the stems were only about three inches long, but I made an excellent rhubarb pie for supper, which I had with cream scraped off the top of the milk. The rhubarb was particularly welcome because we could get no fresh fruit or vegetables, although I had brought a sack of onions and a sack of dried apple rings with me. Indeed these, together with sacks of wholemeal flour, were our main diet, along with some salted meat and such fresh meat and milk as we could get. We also had some potatoes and rice, and a few delicacies to add some variety: raisins, golden syrup, macaroni, a few pounds of chocolate, a few pounds of dried ginger, a small bottle of orange essence, and another of peppermint; and we could ring the changes for drink on tea, coffee, cocoa and Bovril. I was never able to get a taste for the tea which the Tibetans brew in copper urns and drink all day long – green tea, which comes overland from China, and which the Tibetans mix with salt and rancid butter. But there was one error in our commissariat. I brought a quantity of dahl, a very sustaining small Indian lentil, but it wouldn't cook at high altitudes where the water boils at a lower temperature.

In hunting the ibex, we were not only trophy hunting; we were pitting our wits and skills in very difficult terrain, and needing considerable hardihood, against much more agile creatures than ourselves, with an enormously highly developed sense of their own security. Also, we did need the meat. Moreover, in such shooting as a very few of us did in the high and far Himalayan uplands and valleys, we were shooting only the older male animals, and very few of them, so we were hardly doing more than assist the wolves and snow leopards in the natural cycle of culling. If that seems like a salving of conscience, so in some measure it is, for although I was not then troubled by what I was doing, the time was to come when I no longer felt able to shoot wild creatures and birds.

Certainly that sort of shooting, mainly for trophies and sport, is less acceptable today. In those days it was customary. And there's no denying that a large number of people, some at great expense to themselves, still enjoy the hardship, the skill and the excitement of deer-stalking in Scotland.

On the day we spent hunting the ibex there was a very good moon in the early morning, so we were able to get away before there was any glimmer of daylight. I wanted to work as far down the ibex cliff as possible.

The slope of the hill looked very steep and bare, so we thought it best to keep along the edge of the cliff. This enabled us to keep a good view of the country ahead. At every ridge we came to, I crawled to the top and searched the country with field-glasses. For some time we saw nothing, though we found a quantity of fresh markings.

The whole of the hill was very difficult to move over; it consisted of sharp ridges of rock between which were wide stretches of steep polished stone which had obviously at some time been the beds of glaciers. On the top of this was a thin sprinkling of gravel and small loose stones, which through heat and cold, wind and rain, had been chipped from the rock face. These little bits of stone, almost like ball bearings, made effective and unwelcome casters between one's feet and the surface of the hill, and every now and again I managed to take a sudden plunge for twenty or thirty feet down the mountain till stopped by some crack in the rock. The result of these little expeditions was that I was cut to ribbons and covered with bruises. Still, the alternative to an occasional slide down the rock would have been a header over the cliff, here almost sheer, into the Spiti river some thousands of feet below.

Then, on looking over one of the rock ridges, I saw some 300–400 yards ahead a huge ibex; he looked more like a horse. I couldn't see much of his head as he was standing with his back to me, but his horns were a very wide spread. As I watched him, he walked slowly away from me and disappeared into a hollow. A few minutes later he reappeared accompanied by two more ibex but not as large as himself. They were all walking slowly away from where I was watching. They dipped into another hollow and came out on the far side onto a little patch of grass, where they stood and grazed for a few minutes and then lay down. Two of them, including the big one, lay with their heads towards me, the other, on lying down, became invisible.

For about fifteen minutes I watched them, but they didn't move, so I reckoned they would probably stay there for the day. They were about half a mile away and not more than a hundred yards from the top of the cliff and the job now was to stalk them. There was no chance of getting along the back of the cliff, without wings. Going straight ahead was not really an option: there was a steady, though very mild, breeze blowing from our direction, and, besides, there was no cover and we should have been in full view nearly all the way. There was only one plan, to go down the mountain under cover of our ridge, get below the ibex, climb the mountain again behind them, and then do a stalk making use of a ridge a short distance to their rear.

That it was a difficult operation is evident from the time it took. It was 6.30 a.m. when we started our descent, and at 11.30 a.m. I reached the top of the ridge behind the ibex. Except that there were no ibex; they had gone. We went and examined the spoor. There was nothing to show which direction they had taken, for the little grass patch was covered with footmarks and all around it was bare rock. I decided to make for the top of the cliff, where the going was easiest, and work our way home.

We had not gone far when we saw the ibex again. This time there were five of them. The big one was there and three of the others were shootable, the fifth was on the small side. They were not more than 300 yards away and, had I had a good reliable weapon, I should have fired at the big one who was standing broadside to me facing down the hill.

We watched them for a bit, and then they started to move off. Something must have frightened them; perhaps they got a scent of us, for the breeze could play queer tricks round those broken hills during the day. They broke into a trot and then galloped away; looking magnificent as they bounded across that treacherous rock with the utmost ease, leaving a trail of rattling gravel sliding down the hill behind them. On the next ridge they stopped for a moment, silhouetted against the sky, and looked back towards us; then they turned and dropped over the ridge, disappearing from view. I almost felt glad that they had been too clever for us, but for all that there is a wonderful fascination in hunting them.

I thought it was time for a rest, so we sat down for a couple of hours and ate our lunch. After this we worked slowly homewards, keeping a close eye open for the ibex which we knew must be lying up somewhere ahead. Late in the afternoon we stopped in a good concealed position to see all the country ahead as far as the camp *nullah*; there was a good chance of the ibex coming out of their hiding for their evening graze and working back towards us, especially as the wind was now in our faces. Eventually I spotted them a long way ahead, but it was a tedious job getting to the place, and they were out of sight before I reached it. I followed their tracks for some time, but darkness came on and I was forced to give up the chase and return to camp. It had been a pretty hard day, and I was tired and somewhat cut about and bruised.

The next morning Thakru and I went after the ibex again. By about two o'clock in the afternoon I had had quite sufficient scrambling over rocks, so we took our hats off to our quarry and, giving them a graceful bow for their skill in evading us, we turned our backs on the hill and made for camp.

On the following day we moved camp to within a couple of miles of the Parang La Pass. So far as I could discover, it was the only way out of Spiti over its high northern mountain barrier. There had been another and lower pass, but it had become blocked by a rock-fall. The Parang La is open only for a few weeks in the late summer. I think that none of the passes I crossed are open for more than about three or four months in the year, and they can be very dangerous. Over 100 men were lost one day in a storm on the Rotang Pass.

Before crossing the pass, Thakru and I had another day and a half stalking and I got a very fine burhal head. Unfortunately I didn't kill the old ram clean, and he staggered along a cliff and then fell into a ravine. We had an adventurous job getting to his carcass, butchering it, and bringing back the meat. We were very glad to have the fresh mutton.

We were now about to leave Spiti. It is a very sparsely inhabited valley with a few very small villages. A little stunted barley and a sort of pea grew in small patches. Grain was brought into the valley by the Kangra shepherds, each of the goats in their flock carrying two saddle-bags of grain, about 20 lb per animal. They also took a backload of salt down to India. The Spiti people have a fine breed of beautiful ponies, as well as yaks and donkeys – and I discovered, in that context, that there are wild asses, the kiang, the Tibetan wild ass, living permanently above 15,000 feet in Ladakh, indigenous to that altitude and climate.

The houses in Spiti were good square stone blocks thatched with some sort of heather or brushwood. But some of the architecture was fantastic, with buildings perched on precipitous cliffs. For the inhabitants, it could hardly have been more than a subsistence existence, but they looked healthy, cheerful and well fed. They were well clothed, too, in their own very warm, and in some cases colourful, homespun clothes with good, fur-lined, leather boots, and also thick felt boots up to their knees. I never saw anyone washing or bathing in the streams. They were very smelly. I suppose they washed very little, and bathed even less, if ever. Perhaps it preserved the natural oil in their skins and kept them warm. Personally, I only bathed in the warm part of the day on rest days in my small canvas bath. Otherwise, morning or evening, it was too cold. Even then I could only do so where we could get enough fuel to heat up the water.

I visited a little Spiti village called Chikim. It was a filthy place built into the mountainside; picturesque from a distance but too highly scented with the dirt of ages to be attractive. There were two temples, so called, which I was allowed to look into, though I was told I must remove my boots if I wanted to go inside. I preferred to stay out. In one was a large figure of Buddha and, on a little altar before him, some small brass bowls and lamps. The rest of the room, which was very small, was hung about with draperies and flags inscribed with characters and painted in various colours. I didn't stay long because I couldn't stand the smell, nor did I like the look of a very ancient lama who sat on the floor, dressed in rags, spinning a copper prayer-wheel.

The second temple was smaller still, but seemed to be more important. It was the shape of a dome painted white outside with figures of animals which might have been horses or dragons (very fierce whatever they were meant to represent) painted in colour over the whitewash. The interior of the building was a mass of painted flags and screens. I could see no Buddha, but there was a small altar and more brass lamps. In front of the temple was a little mud terrace with a stone wall in which were planted poles, some with flags, others with yaks' tails suspended from them, and in one corner of the terrace was a pillar on which were fixed the horns of a very fine ibex and also some burhal.

On the terrace were three lamas, one beating a drum, a second playing a kind of large flute, and the other yelling with the full force of his lungs. All three were very drunk.

The village *lambadar* came to me with some drink in a silver bowl. This I declined to accept though I gave him some money as a mark of gratitude for his hospitality. The people of this country were very fond of liquor and frequently fell foul of excesses of their home-brewed whisky, *chang*, a colourless liquid distilled from barley.

While I was there a ceremony took place. The first item was a procession on horseback to a sacred rock somewhere up the mountain. On returning from this pilgrimage everyone would dance in front of the temple, refreshing themselves frequently with *chang*. The dance, I gathered, would increase in fury till everyone became so drunk that they could dance no more.

Having spent a fortnight in Spiti, I set off on 4 August 1931 to cross the Parang La Pass that day if possible. We dropped down into the Kibar *nullah*, up which we had to climb, by a very steep and twisty path, till we reached the bed of the stream from where it was about 3,000 feet to the top of the pass. We forded the stream which, though very rapid, was only knee deep, and followed a path up. The gorge was never more than thirty yards wide with mountains going straight up in sheer cliffs on each side for thousands of feet.

When we were near the top, we became enveloped in cloud and freezing rain. I had been told that on the top of the pass there were two or three miles of snow and ice to cross, so, with the Shigri glacier still fresh in my mind, I decided against going further that day and we pitched a cold camp for the night at about 18,000 feet. Although we had some rain and snow during the night, the next day turned out fine. We had a steep climb and then when we got to the top, instead of the black, rough rock hillside, a huge snowfield lay before us glittering and sparkling in the bright morning sun. All the ice on the glacier was covered in fresh snow which lay in a smooth sheet reaching to the top of the peaks on either side of the valley.

We had a short rest on the top, and then began our journey of some two miles across the glacier to the valley which runs down into the bed of the Pare Chu river. I had a mixed bag of transport – some yaks, some donkeys, and some load-carrying coolies. We had agreed not to take the yaks beyond the top of the pass because of stories of some rampant yak disease in Rupshu and Ladakh, and so the yaks were sent back from the top of the pass and the coolies replaced them. We had a few little donkeys which were very strong and could carry heavy loads, but were not able to carry much up the steep route to the top of the pass. They were therefore loaded with fodder for themselves and the yaks, while the latter did the real hard work.

I had gone on ahead to take a look at the glacier to enable me to judge what faced us. Having done that, I sat down in a little sheltered saucer at the top of the pass to await the transport. I found that I was sitting in a nest of fossils. I put a few in my pocket. Years later, I happened to put up a man who was in need of a bed for a night, and who turned out to be a geologist. I showed him the fossils. 'Oh, nothing unusual,' he said, 'very common marine fossils.' I had been sitting on the one-time ancient bed of the ocean at 18,000 feet above sea level. I later learnt from the British Museum that the fossils were 140 million years old.

For the next three days we marched northwards up the uninhabited and desolate Pare Chu valley. It was almost bare of vegetation, and there were very few signs of life at all; not even flies. There were some stunted gorse bushes, and another bush with a dry root that made excellent firewood. None of the bushes at that altitude, about 16,000 feet, was more than a foot high. One day I saw a few birds: a hoopoe, a green sandpiper which I could not identify, and half a dozen pretty little birds which, for want of a name, I called stone larks. They were very tame, and one of them shared my lunch.

A local Spiti man named Tashi Dundu had attached himself to us as a sort of guide and know-all for this part of the journey and, on the third day in the Pare Chu valley, he told Thakru what our road would be and went off to look for game. He later reappeared and said he had spotted a flock of burhal. I followed him to where he said I would be able to see them. I took out my glasses and crawled up the hill and looked over the top of the ridge. The view was so superb that the burhal went momentarily out of my mind. Some miles away, in its basin of undulating purple hills, a vast expanse of water, the Tso Morari Lake, lay glittering in the early morning sunlight, the deep blue colour of a Riviera sky.

I turned my attention back to the burhal. There were fifteen or twenty of them grazing about 200 yards from me; but they were all ewes and lambs, and no ram with them. I watched them for about half an hour, after which they moved into a valley out of sight. One old lady obviously suspected my presence as she was very restless and kept stamping on the ground and climbing rocks to have a look in my direction. As soon as they were out of sight, I moved cautiously after them. When I reached a position from which I could see down into the valley, I found that there was still no good head to be seen, so I stood up and walked towards the little flock. They turned and watched me, and I was within 100 yards of them before they moved off. They then trotted away a short distance and allowed me to approach them again. All this time they were making harsh twittering noises which I supposed was their warning sign. But it was extraordinary how tame they were.

On that day's march we left the Pare Chu river, which swings east-wards into Western Tibet, and continued north west over a low (comparatively!) pass (15,500 feet) and down a gentle slope into the amazing basin of the Tso Morari Lake. We made camp at the water's edge at the lake's south-west corner.

The lake is truly a basin. It is some fifteen miles long, and five miles across at its widest, and is almost 15,000 feet above sea level. A number of quite significant streams run into it, but all the surrounding country is above the lake level, so there is no outlet. Two of the streams are sufficiently substantial to be building up deltas at the north and south ends of the lake. There are some salt deposits, and the water is said to be brackish. It may be technically so, but it tasted sweet. Looking into even deep water from any high ground, the individual pebbles on the bottom are crystal clear. There is no weed in the water, and there are said to be no fish. Even when you were standing on the shore, the lake appeared to retain its amazing sapphire blue colour.

The mountains immediately surrounding the lake did not look high, partly because they were rounded and not precipitous. They rose to just under 22,000 feet. At that time of year there was little snow on their summits and it was possible to walk to that height, as on a Scottish moor, without any technical climbing. Geologically it was granite country, much easier to walk on than the slate and shale of Spiti. But the hills were very bare, with very sparse vegetation. One evening we had a glorious sunset, and the precipitous snow-clad 23,000-foot Mount Shillar, thirty miles to the south of the lake, continued to shine and reflect the sun, long after the light had gone from the lower hills.

On the lake shore there were plenty of kiang – the wild Tibetan ass – which were not very nervous. They let me get within 250 yards of them to photograph them. There were also large marmots. I could get within twenty yards of them before they bolted down their holes

Some days later, four marches beyond the Tso Morari Lake, I came to the smaller Kar Lake. There I saw geese, a large number of ruddy shelduck, some with young birds, and teal. There were also redshanks and other waders, and – to me most interesting – a large number of gulls. There were terns on the rivers and marshes in India, but I didn't remember ever having seen gulls. These were about the size of a black-headed gull and they looked like them in flight. On alighting, they folded their wings with the same characteristic care.

In the Tso Morari basin, despite the altitude, and perhaps because of the sunlight reflected off the water, it was very hot in the day. The temperature in my tent got up to 108°F, whereas at night the canvas bucket of water standing outside my tent froze quite hard – a change of temperature in the day's cycle of some 80°F. Most of that temperature change took place during the hour either side of sunset. It was therefore imperative not to get caught out during that period with inadequate clothing. We had to pile on jerseys and whatever else we had, and we had to rely on our own body heat for warmth because we were seldom able to make good enough fires for anything beyond our simple cooking.

The ultra-violet rays at that altitude were very hard on the skin. From my first march out of Kulu I grew a beard to protect some of my face. We did not have the sun creams available today, and so, although I did have some skin lotion, and despite being accustomed to the Indian sun and being already sunburnt, my arms, the backs of my hands, the bridge of my nose and my cheekbones did suffer.

We spent three days in the Tso Morari basin. On the second day we moved half way up the lake to the tiny village of Rupshu. At 15,500 feet it must have been one the highest villages in the world. It was a filthy place consisting of two small blocks of dwellings, a long *mani pani* wall and six big *chortans* – cenotaphs beneath which are buried the relics of holy lamas. I pitched my camp half a mile away from the village on the shore of the lake.

The *Nono* – king – of Spiti was at Rupshu, a youth of eighteen who had come north to get married. He seemed quite pleased to see me. The local people told me that I was the first European they had seen for seven years. I saw only one woman in the village. She allowed me to take photographs of her as she was wearing an extraordinary headdress of iron and leather covered with a large amount of turquoise.

In those mountains women are scarce, and polyandry is the custom. Marriage was not a religious ceremony but, when a woman marries a man, she also becomes the wife of all his brothers, provided there are not more than three. Her children, if any, are said to be those of the eldest brother.

A couple of miles from Rupshu village was a large shepherds' camp. As our Spiti coolies and their donkeys would come no further and wanted to get back home, we needed transport, so Thakru went to see the shepherds. He had met some of them before in Lahoule. Not only did they agree to provide us with yaks, although they had lost many from disease, but they also sent us a present of lots of firewood and milk.

The following day Thakru went off to the shepherds' camp and spent most of the day there. He got a quantity of freshly shorn black sheep's wool which he began ingeniously spinning into yarn with hand bobbins from which he proposed to make himself some socks. The shepherds had found yaks for us and said they would bring them along in the morning, to enable us to get away soon after sunrise.

I learnt a fire-lighting trick from the shepherds. They didn't carry matches, but had little home-made leather purses with a short, smooth steel bar outside at the bottom. In the purse they kept some flint and some very greasy sheep's wool. With a deft spark from the flint and steel they set the sheep's wool smouldering and then blew it into a flame. Thakru and the coolie, being hill men, knew the trick and so I learnt to light our fires shepherd fashion. If, with that primitive equipment, I could coax some lumps of wet yak's dung into an adequate fire to cook even a rather inadequate supper, in a wet cloud, at 15,000 feet, I thought I had earned another Boy Scout's badge.

I now had a problem. When I decided to go north west from the Tso Morari Lake, I was going into country that I hadn't intended to visit. I had supposed that I would return to Kulu by the way I had come, but I decided that it would be preferable to see new and different country. My problem was that I ran off my map at the north end of the Tso Morari Lake, and would now have to get along as best I could without maps.

The yaks meanwhile were in wayward mood and we had great trouble loading them up. They butted each other and bucked off their loads, but luckily did no damage. Then, soon after we started, a Himalayan snow-cock – a large affair weighing several pounds – flew down to the lakeside and alighted with an extravagant flutter just in front of the leading yak, which promptly bolted and flung off its load. Thakru, who had already had quite enough of the yaks, said, 'I'll kill that wretched bird' and ran at it with his *khud-stick* (alpenstock). The bird flew up the hill and disappeared over a crest, but Thakru pursued it and about a quarter of an hour later returned triumphant with the dead snow-cock, which he had killed with his stick.

Snow-cocks are francolin, a species of partridge. There are two varieties in India, the Himalayan snow-cock and the Tibetan snow-cock which is somewhat smaller, and which is the bird we saw. Its habitat is between 15,000 and 19,000 feet.

That afternoon, after we had pitched camp, I went out on the hill and shot a couple of hares for the men to eat. We saw plenty of hares, too, the following day in the rugged mountain country after we'd crossed the Nanak La Pass (17,500 feet), but it was unwelcoming terrain – we could hardly find a suitable place to pitch a tent and there was scarcely adequate grazing even for the yaks. But now we were in ovis Ammon country.

The ovis Ammon is a large sheep that lives only at very high altitudes. The fully grown rams have enormous curly horns. To secure one in those days was to obtain a coveted trophy. We were told that there were very few in the area that year because of the scarcity of grazing after the late winter. However some, though not all, of the shepherds were reluctant to give us any precise information about the whereabouts of game. They were Buddhists of a sort, but in that vast area where small monasteries and small communities were very isolated, and altogether cut off from each other for months every year, no doubt many aberrant local forms of Buddhism had evolved. The various forms of Tibetan Buddhism fall under the generic name of Lamaism. Buddhism involves transmigration as an element in the maturing of the soul. We discovered that the shepherds believed that a lama's soul returned to a lama. The souls of ordinary people, however, might return either to other people or to wild animals. So the shepherds weren't prepared to have it on their conscience that, in giving us information, they might indirectly be instrumental in causing the death of some creature housing the soul of a former human being.

Nevertheless, three marches beyond the Tso Morari Lake, when we had crossed another pass, the Polakonka La (17,500 feet), and made camp in the early afternoon where there was a good patch of grass and a clear stream, one of the yak men did say that he would take Thakru and me up a *nullah* to a likely place. I wasn't that confident, so I sent Thakru off with the man to prospect and look at least for spoor and marks. They must have had a long walk as they said they'd been up to the snow (which would have been about 20,000 feet). They returned as it was getting dark, bringing with them the skull and horns of an ovis Ammon; not a very big one. I measured the horns to be 32 inches (each horn). The animal must have died within the past few months for there was still hair and skin on the back of the skull. The wretched creature must have had days of agony before it expired. It had evidently gone to the stream to drink and caught a foreleg in a crack in a rock. It had been stuck in this trap, unable to free itself, until it eventually died. Thakru and the yak man found the skeleton's foot still wedged in the cleft in the rock.

My aim, after leaving the Tso Morari Lake, was to work my way to the Bara Lacha La Pass into north-east Lahoule. From there we would get a path for the next two marches into the inhabited part of Lahoule.

To get to the Bara Lacha, we were marching over mostly very high undulating country at between 15,000 and 17,000 feet, with several relatively low passes under 18,000 feet. Some of the marching was very tedious over loose sand. At times, too, the weather was bad – wet, with very high winds and very cold.

For twenty-eight days, on most of which we marched, we were always at altitudes between 15,000 and 17,000 feet. We had relatively poor, relatively little, and very monotonous food. But we kept very healthy. I think none of us ever went above 21,000 feet; at the same time, none of us was adversely affected by the altitude, except that I came to realise that the pace at which we covered the ground was deceptive. We were so strong and fit that we strode out at a seemingly good four and a half miles per hour, but in fact we only covered the ground at about two miles per hour. The yaks did one and a half miles an hour. They clearly understood their own habitat, and knew what they were doing.

On two separate occasions we met Indian hill traders going with their mules laden with tea for Leh in Ladakh, and beyond. One party said they would have a backload of wool and carpets. We were puzzled by the backload of the others. It seemed as though it was a drug, possibly opium, but clearly not contraband or they wouldn't have told us about it. They made these journeys annually during the few months that the high passes were open.

Meeting these people brought home to me something which is important for the understanding of early history. That is that even in very early times ideas came to be shared by people very distant from each other because they were carried by small handfuls of enterprising traders and, for that matter, by ships' crews. Out of the whole teeming population of millions of Indians, probably not more than two or three dozen carried on this trade.

But what was particularly interesting was that here were just a few people doing this merchandising with nothing that much earlier people worldwide did not have many thousands of years ago. They were hill men, wearing homespun and home-woven hill clothes. Their saddle-bags were homespun, as were the ropes that secured them to the animals. They had pack animals only, and they themselves walked. They were traversing, in a few weeks, hundreds of miles of almost the hardest and most inhospitable terrain in the world. To encounter that sort of primitive trading going on in our own time suggests that it was almost certainly the case that in earliest times too small parties of people did move about the world, over great distances, for a variety of reasons, carrying ideas with them.

To give examples from many that could be given. Prehistoric jewellery found in Ireland was the same pattern as jewellery known in Ancient Egypt. But the design was not Egyptian. It was Indian. Carbon dating and other evidence suggests strongly that the pyramids of Egypt were the prototypes for man-made mounds in our islands. It is highly probable that 'engineers' in prehistoric Britain knew what was going on in Egypt. And in prehistoric times fairs were held in Armagh in Ireland. The skull of a Barbary ape has been found there carbon dated to 700 BC. Perhaps it was the stock in trade of some itinerant North African entertainer.

Marching was not all that we did. During all the most active part of my life, my rule was 'to have the road behind me, and the day ahead of me'. We marched as soon after sun-up as we could get away and, if we could, made camp at 2 or 3 p.m. That had two advantages. It gave us time to collect up any sort of fuel we could find for our evening fires. It also tended to ensure a safe and reasonably long march. There are numerous rivers in the High Himalayas, but no bridges. All rivers had to be forded. In the early part of the day we could usually find a safe crossing, and not so deep as to wet the baggage. After midday they become swollen with melting snow water. One of them may then cause a halt to be called to the day's march, or present a dangerous alternative. So I believe the worst danger for the unwary traveller in the High Himalayas is, curiously perhaps, drowning. There is a substantial risk of a bad sprain, or even a broken limb, but one could get out on a yak. The only other irremediable danger would be a burst appendix or some other serious illness needing medical assistance. But that is a reasonable risk.

The fact that we usually managed to make camp with four or five hours of daylight still left meant that we had a large part of the afternoons to explore the *nullahs*, look for game, admire the scenery and, in my own personal case, make notes which I had undertaken to do for the survey of India.

Five marches after leaving the Tso Morari Lake, we were in Mangrik, where we camped by a mountain river. We were surrounded by high granite mountains covered in snow, a welcome contrast to the previous few days of hills and sand. Two men soon appeared from the village immediately to our north and Thakru went off with them to talk to their *lambadar*.

The fact was that the Tso Morari yak men did not want to come any further, so we needed fresh transport. The next day Thakru returned to camp about midnight, wet to his neck, having nearly drowned himself trying to ford a river in the dark. The village had been further away than he had been led to believe, but he had made arrangements for yaks for our journey.

It was at the end of the next day's march that I came upon a habitation – more of a camp than a village – which those living there called Karnak.

The dwellings had walls of loose stones, built one upon the other without any form of cement, and were roofed with stout sacking of closely woven wool, here and there supplemented by the skins of animals. Most of the dwellings were ornamented with poles hung with yaks' tails and religious flags.

Every man, woman and child throughout these parts seemed to carry a bundle of wool and a bobbin by means of which they spun the wool into yarn. They were very clever at this, and must have spun yards and yards in the day. The shepherds all did it as they wandered along with their flocks of sheep and goats. They could also knit and, I dare say, weave as well. All their soft goods, all clothes and blankets, saddlebags and ropes were made of home-spun yarn from their own animals.

I shouldn't like to estimate the number of sheep and goats owned by that village. It was interesting to watch them coming down the valleys at sunset to the village where they were kept penned in stone kraals. There were also a large number of yaks, from which milk was obtained and turned into butter, made so as to keep for long periods. The yaks objected to being milked and every now and again a few broke loose and tore round the village kicking up the dust and scattering everything before them; they are powerful beasts and were not to be trifled with when in recalcitrant mood. But the villagers knew their tricks and made short work of cornering them and tying them down. The best way to anchor a yak, or several yaks, is to tie them together by the horns, for then when anything excites them, rather than go forward and receive a good butt on the head, they back away from each and so tighten the ropes, with the result that they merely become more securely fixed.

During our march we were greatly worried by dust devils. Never before had I seen them so violent or in such quantity. At a distance they were a magnificent sight, whipping up the sand and grass and dust in spirals hundreds of feet high, but when they came near one had to sit down and hold on tight to one's hat.

I continued to suffer considerably from sunburn. A lot of skin peeled off my face and arms, and my right hand had to be in a bandage for ten days, owing to the back of it becoming septic from the sunburn. I also had to deal with some sick and suffering people. Sores and cuts were easy to doctor, but I was asked to effect the cure of one unfortunate girl who had an ossification of the knee joint, which I supposed was arthritis. Of course I could do nothing for her and told her relations so, at the same time advising them to send her to Lahoule where, at the capital, Keylang, there was a mission post with a doctor. However, I thought I must do something for her, and there can never be much damage done by the administration of a small dose of Epsom salts, especially to people who eat nothing but grain and a little meat, having no fruit or vegetables.

I decided to spend two or three days near the Karnak encampment. I went to the top of the valley where a path crosses a pass on the summit of which is a large *mani pani* containing some very well carved stones. On one, three *chortens* were carved in detail. The *chorten* is a type of cenotaph which either contains the relics of some saint or holy man, or else is erected in his memory. The various parts of a *chorten* have significance. The base is a solid plinth which represents the earth; resting on this is a hemisphere which represents water; from the top of the hemisphere rises a cylinder, or cone, which symbolises fire, resting on top of which there is a crescent for air, and in the centre of this is placed a three-pronged fork – sometimes replaced by a bush of twigs; this is the ether. These *chortens*, some well built, some rough and crude, are to be found everywhere, and a carving of one will be seen on most mani panis, somewhere among the multitude of stones bearing the ubiquitous mantra, *Om mani padme hum.*

When we moved on from the Karnak camp, the *lambadar* kindly said he would send a small flock of goats with us to keep us in milk until we got to Lahoule. We all found milk a useful comfort. Although our eight goats only supplied one and a half pints a day between them, it was as much as we needed. But we had to take care of the animals at night because of the danger of wolves and, possibly, snow leopards.

The weather was variable. Clearly we were getting the tail end of the monsoon which had not wholly expended itself on the ranges to the south of us. We didn't much object to the rain because it meant cool marches, but clouds hid the scenery and there was always the threat of sickness in the camp through sleeping and living in wet clothes. Towards sundown, however, the clouds rolled up to the higher mountains and the rain ceased. The view and the colours were superb. The higher ground was sprinkled with a fresh fall of powdery snow, and in the valleys there hung wisps of grey cloud like smoke on a still summer's evening.

After one of our marches we dropped down many hundreds of feet into the bed of a river which the yak drivers called the Parama Numa, and we encamped there. About half a mile up the river was a little tent containing a woman and two children. They were starving but, as we were unable to converse with them, it wasn't possible to discover the cause of their miserable condition. The woman, though dressed like the other people of the area, was obviously of Indian blood as her features were not those of the local hill folk. We gave her some food, and money for purchasing more food from Indian travellers, as she was living by a well-worn track to Ladakh.

But how on earth had she got there, at 16,000 feet, beyond the main Himalayan ranges, and seventy-five miles on foot over awful country from the nearest sheltered habitation? She would not have gone up so far into the wilderness of the high Himalayas by herself. She must, too, have had some transport. Whoever was with her may have been drowned. More likely she had been abandoned, not necessarily maliciously. Her man – there must have been one – may have gone off with whatever transport there was, to get supplies or something. Or was she, for some reason, a modern-day Hagar, an outcast?

One day we crossed a pass and descended onto a sandy plain. Coming down onto the plain we saw a number of little creatures called mouse hares. They live in holes and, as you approach, scuttle into them for safety. I managed to catch one. He thought to hide himself under a flat stone, but I seized him by the hind leg and pulled him out. The coolie told me to be careful in case he bit me but, after a preliminary squeal of fright, he kept completely quiet and showed no pugnacious tendencies. In fact he sat on my knee while I stroked his back. They are well named, for they are no bigger than a large rat and have the head and ears of a mouse, while their coat is that of a hare or rabbit, and they have a short tail. When I liberated him, he ran away a few yards then sat and looked at me, making no effort to seek the shelter of a nearby hole.

A fortnight after leaving the Tso Morari Lake, I was on the map again and could give up my North Star reckonings. My maps dated from 1863. They showed that we were two marches from the Bara Lacha La Pass into Lahoule, and I decided to stay in the area for a few days and do some hunting. We were short of food, and wanted some meat.

Thakru and I went up one of the *nullahs* to look for game, and spotted what we took to be a European and his party erecting tents about three miles from our camp and a couple of thousand feet below where we had climbed. It was dark when we got back to our camp, but next day I went to look for the other party. They had already started their march, but I caught them up. I found myself confronted by Colonel C. H. Stockley and a Gunner officer whose name I did not record. Stockley was one of the best-known explorers and big-game hunters in India at that time, and I knew his books on those subjects. He told me that he had intended to spend a week in our present area, as it was very good for game, and he thought we ought to find ovis Ammon. (Indeed Thakru and I had seen both ibex and burhal the previous afternoon.) However, as I was already installed, he would move on. He was going to follow my route back to the Tso Morari Lake. He said that only two people had done it in the past sixty years or so. He also said his party had had an awful time crossing the Bara Lacha La Pass as it snowed and rained and blew a gale for three days. The Bara Lacha has a very bad reputation.

I moved my camp a few miles that day in order to be nearer the area that we wanted to prospect for game. We maintained that camp for four days, which we devoted to hunting. The second day, in very difficult country, we came on a small flock of burhal ewes and lambs with one young ram. Taking care not to frighten them, we pressed on upwards towards the snow at about 20,000 feet. Eventually I spotted another small flock of animals lying down a long way off. It was not until after a long and difficult stalk that I got within shot of them at about 6 p.m. There were ten burhal rams, five of them shootable heads. We needed the meat and I shot three of them. I also thought that there was no harm culling them because there must have been many more than were needed to serve the local ewe population. We took some of the meat back with us but it was almost dark when we started out for our camp. We had many miles to go, but there was a good moon, about full, without which we might have had to spend the night on the mountain.

The next day we toiled up the mountain again to get the meat. It took us four hours to get there. Thakru and some of the yak men dealt with two of the burhal while I went down a steep *nullah* to look for the third which had dropped down there. It was an awful place with a most uninviting dark ice tunnel in it. I was joined there by one of the yak men whom I had christened 'Mani-Pani' because he was for ever spinning a prayer wheel.

We found the burhal and cut it up, and wrapped the meat and the head in the skin. Then 'Mani' slung the whole load on his back and we were ready to move. I had difficulty in conveying to 'Mani' my pleasure at the work he had done. I told him in five languages that he was a good fellow, yet I could not say it in Tibetan. However, I had some money in my pocket and I gave it to him.

Rather than climb back up the mountain again with the load, we decided to go on down the very difficult valley that we were in. It was a deep ravine, very narrow, with steep bare rock cliffs on each side, so high that we had only a diffused light. We could only see a short way down the ravine on account of the twists and rock promontories, but it appeared below to get even narrower. There was nothing for it but to tackle it. For some time we progressed with the greatest difficulty, as the whole water course was choked with huge blocks of ice and boulders. The ice was the worst, for it was hard and smooth and it often seemed that it would be impossible to climb over the big pieces. Even my iron-shod staff made very little impression on them.

After half an hour or so we reached more open ground and had good going over the pebbly stream bed. I strode on thinking that the rest of the way would be easy. I passed a valley leading up to the central mountain ridge, but decided not to climb it. (As it happened, 'Mani', when he arrived at this place, took that route and had a much better march than I had.) So I continued for a short way along the stream bed and then the valley shut in again. Few people can have travelled by a stranger path than that by which I was forced to go for nearly two hours. The water here had cut its way through the solid rock and was flowing through a deep narrow chasm. There was very little light, and I was wading all the time. Sometimes the water was only ankle deep, other times it was up to my waist and in one place only my hat was saved a wetting. It was so narrow in places that I don't believe a fat man would have got through. As I went along I had two hopes: one that when I rounded the next bend I should find a more open valley, the other that I shouldn't come to a waterfall or impassable precipice. I was worried, too, over 'Mani' and his load, but I couldn't wait for him owing to the intense cold.

After an hour I was so numb that it was only with the utmost diffi-culty that I managed to struggle along at all, floundering through the water like a cow in a brook. I kept thinking I must be nearing the end of this frightful passage and anyway it was too late to think of turning back; so there was no alternative to going on downstream. And so eventually I came out into the open. There was a strong wind blowing, which in this temperature, and in my condition, frozen from the icy water, only tended to increase the discomfort. On reaching camp, however, and getting into dry clothes and after a warm by the fire, I felt normal again. 'Mani' made a slow journey, and came in very late by moonlight.

We spent one more day in that camp. The next day we marched south. With no bridges in that high barren country we seemed to spend our time fording streams and rivers. On that day's march the yak men wanted to get on and camp early. I told them they were on no account to attempt to ford the river at the end of the day's march. They disobeyed my orders. The river was deep and all our kit, food, bedding, etc. was saturated. The next day we stayed where we were but we were in a cold wet mist after a night of wind, snow, hail, sleet and rain, and we couldn't get things dried out.

We were lucky to have fine frosty weather to cross the Bara Lacha La Pass (16,047 feet) into Lahoule, bringing us back into directly administered British Indian territory. At one point we had to cross the Bhaga river, where some men were building a bridge. They were Lahoulis, but the foreman spoke Urdu and he told me that about three weeks before two men were crossing a little temporary footbridge of planks when they overbalanced, fell into the water and were never seen again. The river was quite small, but the water was rushing down with alarming force. Our yaks managed to cross about a mile upstream at a shallow place, so that none of our kit was damaged. Even the goats crossed with no trouble. Then we had a long downhill march through to Patseo camping ground, where we were below 15,000 feet for the first time for a month. Here there was another hut and a few more Government coolies with a foreman whose job it was to keep the path in repair.

On 2 September I wanted to get to a place called Jispa but, on reaching the Kado Tokpo river, we found it to be a huge torrent and unfordable. There was a bridge but the yaks had never seen a bridge before and wouldn't cross it; even the yak drivers were afraid of it. One of them crawled to the middle of it on his hands and knees and then came back with his nerve quite shaken. I decided to pay off the yaks, and if I couldn't get ponies from the village I would send to Keylang, the capital of Lahoule, for transport.

Darcha, the most northerly village in Lahoule, is just under 11,000 feet up and some sixty miles north of the Rotang Pass over the main Himalayan range into Kulu. There, save for the tiny village of Rupshu on the Tso Morari Lake, we came upon the first houses we had seen since leaving Spiti exactly a month earlier. I felt we were out of the wilderness. There were plants and shrubs everywhere and quite a number of small coniferous trees. We were using for firewood a bush with a grey leaf from which Thakru said oil was extracted. I enjoy the smell of a good log fire, and this bush gave off a particularly pleasing scent as it burned. It was all I could do to keep myself from sitting on the smoky side of the fire.

There were many old friends among the birds again, including the whistling thrush and my favourite of all the birds of India, the white-capped redstart. He is seldom found except flitting from stone to stone in some mountain torrent. His song is cheerful, the top of his head has a snow white cap, his wings and body are jet black, while his rump and tail, which is never still, are a brilliant red.

Having had to get rid of the yaks – and the goats – we had to arrange more transport. There was none to be had in Darcha but Thakru met an acquaintance who said he would go to Keylang to fetch ponies and promised to be back in the early morning. We expected he would arrive at about midday but, true to his word, he arrived at dawn, thus enabling us to make an early start and complete the journey to Keylang, a distance of more than eighteen miles, in quick time. There were villages scattered all along the valley and every patch of ground which was not a wall of rock was cultivated and grew either barley or potatoes. Were it not for an elaborate irrigation system this cultivation would not have been possible; hence all the mountain streams were cut and diverted in channels so that they not only watered the ground but also flowed through the mills which were used for grinding the corn.

About three miles out of Keylang I met an Indian on a pony who said he was the local schoolmaster and a servant of the Moravian mission. He invited me to go down and stay in the mission quarters. This seemed very suitable so I accepted his invitation. The mission was run by a very nice man called Asboe who had been there for ten years. He was married to an Irish woman, also very charming. I called in at their house and had some tea with them. They told me that there was another man staying in the guest house, a little further down the mountain, and that they would send down for him and get him to come up for tea. He turned out to be an officer in the 2nd Lancers named McCoy who had the next room to me at Pachmari. He had been in Lahoule for six weeks looking for ibex, but hadn't seen a single one.

There was only one room in the guest house, so I pitched my tent in the little orchard and McCoy and I arranged to feed together in his room as long as I stayed there (he had soon to go back to Kulu). His bearer was an excellent cook, so I got a much-needed rest from my rice, dried apple rings, and unleavened pancakes, chapatis, which had rather lost their allure.

The Moravian mission in Lahoule – which was over 10,00 feet up – had been there for seventy years at that time, and there were forty converted Christian Tibetans. Mr Asboe spoke fluent Tibetan, but no Urdu. I suspect that he also had some medical training, which would explain the information I had been given that medical help could be obtained at the Lahoule mission. It was snowed in for months during the winter and, apart from the occasional summer visitor like myself and Sam McCoy and Colonel Stockley, the Asboes had no European company. They had a good garden and the orchard seemed to respond well to the care and attention they devoted to it, with trees well laden with apples, pears and apricots. They plied me with cabbages, beans, fruit and fresh butter, all great luxuries. I was also able to borrow books from Mr Asboe; he was, as one might expect, widely read.

Sam McCoy and I stayed four days at Keylang and, as recompense for their kindness (they would take nothing else), he and I decided to give the Asboes a hand with this and that. We picked Mr Asboe's apple crop for him and, one wet morning, joined in the niceties of a jam and butter making day. We were entrusted with cracking the stones of apricots to extract the kernels, and of churning the week's saving of cream into butter. Then we rolled up our sleeves and made a quantity of bread and scones.

After lunch the sun came out, so McCoy and I climbed the hill above Keylang village to look at the biggest and best of the numerous monasteries in the area. But we found when we got there that all the lamas were away at a funeral and we couldn't go in. So we dropped down into the Shakas Lungpa valley where we decided to visit some Russians, the Roerich family. Russians encamped so near the frontiers of India were inevitably objects of interest, if not of suspicion.

The head of the family was Professor Roerich, a venerable figure with a white beard. He was an artist and showed us some of his attractive pictures of the Himalayas. He also collected curios and art treasures from Tibet and the neighbouring countries. He had a wife living with him, who didn't make an appearance but was said to be a princess of royal Russian blood. She was also said to suffer from a weak heart and high blood pressure. It therefore seemed curious that she managed a sixty-mile pony ride from Kulu every year, negotiating a 14,000-foot pass, in order to spend the summer months in Lahoule at 10,000 feet, a fortnight's journey from any sort of expert medical assistance.

There were two fair-haired Slav servants and a fair-haired woman secretary, an alert creature of about thirty, dressed like a cowboy, who bubbled with interrogatory conversation. Equally interrogatory was George, the professor's clever son, whom I liked. As well as English, he said he spoke Russian, Urdu, Tibetan, Persian and Turkish. We had tea and afterwards he showed me his tent. There, on the camp table, I saw a French novel and a magazine with a cover in Chinese or Japanese characters. So he seemed to be familiar with at least eight or nine languages. Interestingly, the Asboes told us later, when we got back to our base in the mission orchard, that the Russians had been a considerable nuisance to them and had tried to get the mission turned out of Lahoule.

The following Sunday Mr Asboe held a church service. It was the oddest service I had ever attended. The proceedings were conducted in Tibetan, with the Tibetans squatting on the floor. Mr Asboe accompanied the hymns on a little portable harmonium. McCoy and I sang the hymns in English which didn't quite fit in with the Tibetan version, but there was anyway such a braying and confusion of noise that it didn't much matter what words or tune we uttered. Because of the altitude it was impossible to find sufficient breath to sing standing, so we sat for the hymns and, as compensation, stood for the prayers.

After church we lunched with the Asboes at the mission bungalow. They seemed capable of total generosity, the true charity of the widow's mite, for they could scarcely afford to clothe themselves. Then, after lunch, McCoy and I climbed up to the big monastery again – it was a lovely day and I wanted photographs. We found the monks at home and they showed us the interior of the building. It consisted of several storeys, on each of them at least one chapel. In the passages leading to these were rows of prayer-wheels which one spun while walking past, thus saying many thousands of prayers and making easy the road to heaven. In the chapels themselves there were busts and carvings of the various gods and saints who are worshipped, and also bowls of holy water and burning oil lamps. The walls were hung with some fine oil paintings of gods and demons, some of them very obscene.

We were also shown the long trumpets and drums which play such an important part in the religious festivals, and also the masks used in the devil dances. One trumpet was made from a human thigh bone; but human bone was commonly used in these parts for beads and rosaries, a not so very distant legacy of human sacrifice – practised even as near India as this.

One room in the monastery was a library, with a quantity of parchment manuscript bound in bundles of cloth and kept in place with stout wooden boards. Once a month the monks met here and studied these 'books' containing the laws of their faith. Their religion, Lamaism, was a corruption of Buddhism, but infused with many of the ceremonies of the Roman Catholic faith, which was introduced by a missionary many centuries ago and made use of effigies, rosaries, holy water, incense and so forth.

Having seen all there was in the monastery, we returned through a village in which we saw a prayer-wheel which was turned constantly by the water of a stream – so enhancing the spiritual welfare of the inhabitants. And we ended the day with another couple of hours' talk with the Asboes. I think they were rather sorry to lose us as they welcomed a little companionship from civilisation.

The next day we were off at crack of dawn. Three long marches round the western end of the snow-clad peaks and glaciers of the Lahoule central massif took us back over the Rotang Pass into Kulu on a beautiful day, and down to Manali where I set up my camp again in the pine forest. There I dug a hole in the ground six foot six inches long, eighteen inches wide and a foot deep. I spread a tarpaulin in it. There was all the firewood we wanted in the forest. I boiled a mass of water, poured it into the tarpaulin-lined hole, and had the first real bath I had had for two months.

I had been just under two months in the territory I had always promised myself – beyond the snows. We had had thirty-six days' marching, averaging, I suppose, about twelve to fourteen miles a day – somewhere about 450 miles, plus many additional miles of mountain climbing and stalking.

Sam McCoy had two days' leave left. There were trout in the Beas river in Kulu and I decided to teach him to fish. With the last cast on the last day of his leave, he hooked a two and a half pound trout in that exceedingly turbulent water and, in great excitement, brought it in.

The fact that Colonel Stockley, the two Sappers, Michael Perceval-Price and Eyre Ievers, and I were the only British, out of all the thousands in India, to venture that year into those high and remote Himalayan regions indicates how few people fell for what was to us an irresistible temptation to push a little further beyond the familiar frontiers of our lives. I once met a naval officer wearing the polar medal ribbon. He had been on several expeditions. I asked him if he would go again. 'Of course,' he replied., 'it's a disease.' The High Himalayas are a disease too, against which I had no immunity. I couldn't wait to get back there again, and had already planned my next trip, but it would have to wait at least four or five years before I could expect to get three months' leave again at a stretch. I remained in Kulu for some days fishing and exploring the valley. Then, instead of going by lorry to railhead at Jogindar-Nagar, I took to my feet again and did the journey in five marches.

And so, back to my Regiment, and to a paradox. Civilisation has been a liberating force, but somehow, coming down from the mountains and the great wide spaces of the High Himalayas to the dinner jacket world I found not so much liberating as restricting. And I had another sensation. I felt I was walking taller than those who had stayed below and hadn't shared my experiences. Achievement gives at least a temporary boost to our morale.

My motives for going were threefold. First, curiosity: a strong urge to see for myself what lay beyond the Himalayan snow ranges that we could see from India, and to have the experience of breaking through those ranges to get to the other side. Second, a desire to face, overcome and even enjoy whatever difficulties and hardships might be encountered in those vast and inhospitable regions. Third, to have a good holiday, stretching myself to the limit.

For many men a degree of hardship can be an attraction. Perhaps it is a genetic impulse deriving from the long ages of primeval existence when the man's lot centred on the difficulties and privations of being out in the wild hunting for food.

9
Bolarum

While I was on leave in the Himalayas, my Regiment carried out its move – by train, without its horses – from Rawalpindi in the north-west Punjab to Bolarum in Hyderabad State in the Deccan, a distance of 1,600 miles.

The Deccan is the southern peninsula of India which juts southwards into the ocean – very roughly that part of the old India lying south of a line drawn from Karachi to Calcutta. We were in the tropics – latitude 30 degrees north – on a 2,000-foot plateau and the weather was warm the whole year round, but never very hot. Throughout the winter months, October to March, there was a hot but not too unpleasant sun by day, and nights when at most a thin blanket might be needed.

Hyderabad State was a huge area roughly in the middle of the Deccan and ruled over by the Nizam, who was in treaty relationship with the British. Under the treaty, the British kept substantial forces in his state – a cavalry brigade, an infantry brigade, a battery of horse artillery, and two batteries of field artillery. These forces were part of a division (under a major-general) known as Deccan District, which had its headquarters in Bolarum and had also under its command two more infantry brigades stationed elsewhere in southern India.

We replaced the 8th Cavalry and took over their horses, a splendid lot of Walers – Australian horses so called because they came from New South Wales. The 8th Cavalry took over our horses in Rawalpindi. Because we were a sabre regiment and they were a lancer regiment, the first time they mounted our horses with an unaccustomed flurry of lance pennants, the horses bolted.

We were brigaded with a British cavalry regiment, The Royals, an Indian cavalry regiment, the 16th Light Cavalry, and 'G' Battery, Royal Horse Artillery. The Royals soon left us and were relieved by another British regiment, the 17th/21st Lancers. The 16th Light Cavalry, too, were soon relieved by the Scinde Horse, with whom we remained brigaded for the next four years.

There was a sense of history in our surroundings in Bolarum: the British had been in that part of India for much longer than they had been in the Punjab, and that sense of history was underlined that year by the loss of our Colonel-in-Chief, General R. Clifford, aged ninety-one, whose first active service had been in the Indian Mutiny. Equally set in the past were the old-fashioned time signals, a six o'clock morning gun that reverberated through the whole cantonment and set all the pi-dogs howling, which was repeated at noon. No one took any notice. It was just a 150-year-old habit.

In earlier times the force that had been stationed there was called the Hyderabad Contingent, and we were fortunate enough to take over its fine old mess building, complete with ballroom, billiard room and squash court. Indeed there was much about Bolarum that had not changed since the early nineteenth century, including curious financial accounts which had been inherited from Victorian times.

The British and Indian forces were strung out in a number of cantonments running north and south. South of that complex was Hyderabad city where the famous Golconda Palace is situated. The Nizam lived there, as did the feudal barons – the nawabs – who surrounded him, and the Nizam's own army, known as State Forces, about comparable in size to the British contingent, was also there. We played polo with their officers and got to know them well. Some were Arabs, some French, the rest from local Hyderabad families. The two royal princes, the Nizam's sons, also played polo. They were married to two beautiful girls, daughters of the ex-Sultan of Turkey, who used to come and watch the polo in their rich saris.

The first cantonment to the north of Hyderabad city and its great artificial lake, the Hassan-Sagar, was Secunderabad, the infantry brigade station; and north of Secunderabad was Trimulgherry, where the British cavalry and artillery were stationed. *Secunder* is the Hindustani for Alexander, and derives from Alexander the Great's invasion of India. *Secunder abad* means 'the abode of Alexander'. 'Secunder Sahib' was still talked of in some parts of India as though he had been there only very recently rather than more than 2,000 years ago.

It was some twenty miles by road from Bolarum to the centre of Hyderabad. India was a hospitable place and lunch and dinner parties were frequent, particularly at weekends. Before motor cars were common, the problem of going out to dinner twenty miles away in Hyderabad had been ingeniously solved. You rode out to dinner on your horse, taking your orderly or a syce with you on a spare horse to take your horse home. Your bullock cart, drawn by two bullocks, had meanwhile set out for your host's house. In it was your bed, already made up

by your bearer. After dinner, having bidden farewell to your host and
hostess, you got into your bullock cart, took off your clothes and went
to bed, trundling back through the night in time to be home for the
usual pre-breakfast ride, or early parade if need be, next morning.

Before The Royals left Bolarum, they had their annual boxing competition, where I witnessed the best fight I have ever seen in Army
boxing. It was not part of the regimental competition, it was a special
match. A trooper in The Royals, who was a very good boxer, got
himself into trouble and found himself incarcerated for a period in the
glasshouse – the military prison. While there he fell foul of a sergeant
on the supervisory staff, and said to him, 'Wait till I get out of this, and
I'll knock your block off.' The sergeant replied, 'You try.' And when the
man did get out, he challenged the sergeant to a boxing match, which
the Regiment undertook to include in their annual programme.

They were both lean, wiry, lynx-like men, and the atmosphere was
tense as they entered the ring, both clearly grimly determined. The fight
was three rounds of three minutes each. They were both good boxers
and they went for each other pitilessly – each with a point to prove. It
was an exceptionally even fight but I was happy that, in the outcome,
Authority got the verdict. The Detention Corps sergeant was judged the
winner, I imagine by a very narrow margin.

The Royals, among the elite of British cavalry, were a wonderful regiment. They set themselves the highest possible standards in everything
they did. During our time with them in Bolarum, the General Officer
Commanding Deccan District carried out his annual inspection. One of
the officers on the general's staff was Major Roy Bucher of the 13th
Lancers (Indian Cavalry). To be controversial was part of Roy Bucher's
stock in trade, and that day he made a point of making it plain that he
thought The Royals had overdone the touching up. Some wooden rail-
ings outside a cookhouse had been lavishly coated with red raddle. Roy
Bucher ran his finger along the top of it and then held it up conspicuously to show the red that had come off on it. The Royals Quartermas-
ter, one of those sterling old soldiers who had risen from the ranks, had
been following Roy with increasing exasperation. At this he snapped.
'That's right!' he said. 'Now rub it on your nose, and it will be the same
colour as your arse, and you'll look like a ——ing orang-utang.'

The poor man was afterwards so ashamed of himself that he went to
his Commanding Officer that evening and offered to resign his commission – which was of course refused. There were fitting apologies and
that was all. Roy Bucher was much too big a man to take any offence.

During the war, when he had very heavy responsibilities, he used to confide his problems in me, and he told me that he was fully aware that he had a well-deserved reputation for not being over-tactful. He ended his career as a full general and the last British Commander-in-Chief in India: a quite unforgettably unusual character. His charming first wife, Edith, I also knew. Sadly she died in India too young.

In Bolarum we not only had the sumptuous mess which, as mess secretary, I worked hard to decorate, but we also had enviable quarters. I had two large rooms in a well-built stone bungalow with stone-flagged floors, and the bungalow had a compound of several acres. Outside my bedroom was a large tree which was almost inexplicably popular with the local birdlife. My count got up to fifty-seven different species.

The horse lines were a mile from the mess and from our bungalows, but I never found that any inconvenience. It took only minutes to get there on a horse or on a bicycle. I particularly enjoyed bicycling down to the horse lines on a warm moonlit night to see that all was well and have a word with the sentries. We had two lines of mangers, one under cover, the other in the open. When the 600 horses were under cover at night, after going my rounds and talking to the sentries I would often sit in the moonlight on one of the dried mud and straw outside mangers, which were still warm from the day's hot sunlight, and enjoy the peace of it all to the low-key background of the horses' stirrings.

One night when I visited the horse lines as orderly officer, wearing my blue patrol uniform, I found a kitten playing with a snake. She was catching it by the tail and throwing it over her head. It seemed an unhealthy occupation for the kitten, and in any case snakes in the lines were to be discouraged, so I drew my sword and killed it. It's a very odd credential, but there can't be many people around who have killed a snake with a sword.

Snakes were abundant in southern India. We once found seventeen in a bush fence we were dismantling on our parade ground. I developed an instinctive awareness of them but we were of course very snake-, scorpion- and tarantula-conscious as, except in the monsoon season, we all slept outside. You shook out your slippers before you put your feet in them. One night the head clerk's orderly got out of bed for some purpose. When he returned to bed, he pinned a note to his pillow which said, 'If I'm dead in the morning, it will be because I have been bitten by a snake.' Poor boy; he was dead.

I loved the country in that part of the Deccan. It was natural, undulating grassland of tall dry grass, with dramatic outcrops of extraordinary rock formations. The most extraordinary was an enormous bubble of smooth rounded rock, a sacred place named Maula Ali – supposed to contain a footprint of the Imam Ali, the Prophet's son-in-law. *Maula Ali* is Arabic for 'The Lord Ali'.

The countryside was full of little lakes which irrigated cultivation locally. There were also toddy-palm groves – real picture-book India. The toddy-palm has a tall, slender stem with an umbrella of long fronds at the top and, just under the fronds, there would be a cluster of brass pots to catch the toddy, which was collected by the tree-climbing 'toddy-wallas' and made into an intoxicating drink (rather like gin). Each tree paid one rupee per annum tax into the Nizam's coffers, which was an easy way of collecting excise duty.

'Snaffles' (C. J. Payne), whom I knew, and who so accurately captured life in India with his pencil and his brush, particularly the life of us cavaliers, wrote this description of the toddy-wallas and their craft on an occasion when he was staying in Bolarum. He also drew a picture of them.

> The toddy-wallas seem a race apart from any other trade caste in India. They posses more muscle than the average native, and an odd thing about them is that they never seem to be either very young or very old. Probably the older ones fall out of their loops; or perhaps the toddy (so easy to come by) affects their nerves, and they retire with discretion to the safety of work on terra firma before their precarious vocation brings them to a sticky end.
>
> I have tried to analyse the exact movements of the climb, but have been unable to fix what actually happens. But as far as I can make out the climber places himself inside a loop of cotton rope which has already been passed round the trunk of the tree. Then, with his ankles lashed together to keep his feet from slipping, he heaves in on his legs and moves up the tree like a caterpillar, shifting his loop after each effort until he reaches the top, where brass vessels called *chatties* have been set to collect the sap from incisions in the bark. These he empties into another *chattie* which he brings to the ground. The sap from several trees is then put into a large skin and carried off by the waiting bullock wagon to the nearest town, where it is quickly converted into toddy to gladden the hearts of the locals.

I encouraged Snaffles to paint a sunset watercolour sketch, across one of the little lakes, of the sacred rock at Maula Ali.

It was a delight going for long rides over such beautiful and open country. Riding through the rolling savannah landscape, with its outcrops of rock formations, toddy palm groves, and little blue lakes shining in the sunshine, I sometimes wondered why they paid me to do it. Some people found it too dry and rocky, but dry and rocky appeals to me. I am even a lover of deserts.

But roses have their thorns, and riding over that country had its hazards. I wrote at the time:

> I am now with my own squadron in camp at a little lake called Nagarwaram, only six miles from Bolarum across country. It is a nice little spot and I am enjoying horse soldiering again (after foot-slogging in the Himalayas). We are working at slow paces only, because the grass is several feet high and full of rocks and snags, and we do not want to get a lot of lame horses.
>
> In places the ground is honeycombed with deep, narrow holes out of which the locals have extracted limestone gravel with which to make lime. The holes are often invisible, being completely hidden by grass. Yesterday we had a man and a horse down one of these. They dropped about twenty feet, but neither was killed. We got the man out without much trouble, but it took a good hour and a half of digging, and then some hefty work on the end of picketing ropes, to extract the horse, which suffered little from the fall but got galled by the ropes.

Being in camp with our horses tethered nearby was to me particularly agreeable. I liked to listen to them at night, occasionally stamping, champing, shaking their head and heel ropes; and there was a curious thing which I never understood. Sometimes at night what I can only call a shiver would run the full length of the horse lines as though there were some unseen spirit passing down. There appeared to be no cause which could have suddenly startled or frightened the horses.

The people in the south of India were, as I have already mentioned, smaller and darker than the northerners whom we recruited. They were very cheerful and friendly, and conspicuously clean, washing themselves and their clothes several times daily. The girls did not wear burkhas or veils. They wore attractive clothes, with full skirts and tight bodices, had bare waists and flowers in their hair, and were all smiles and laughter.

The administration was essentially feudal. The feudal lords, the nawabs, owned enormous estates. The most colourful of them was the

Nawab Wali-ud-Dowla. He was said to have won the mile at Eton, but he had long since lost that shape, and was a portly bon vivant in middle age. Exceptionally affable and urbane, he often came to watch the polo, and he had a large cocktail cabinet in the boot of his Rolls-Royce from which he dispensed generous hospitality.

We wanted to get at him on one occasion for reasons that I forget – perhaps to give away prizes, or some such function. Our channel of communication to him was a French major in the Nizam's forces, Major Shamiret. We could get no response, and eventually twisted Shamiret's arm to find out what the problem was. He then admitted that he couldn't help. 'The problem is that he's been in his harem for three weeks, and they won't let him go. We just can't get at him.'

After we had left Bolarum and gone north again some years later, we learnt that his harem had persuaded Wali-ud-Dowla to do the pilgrimage to Mecca. Dutiful to his ladies' wishes, he took a ship to Jeddah. When he landed there, he was asked what was in the packing cases he was taking to Mecca. He had to confess that it was whisky and champagne, but was told that he must leave them behind. So the poor man completed his pilgrimage journey to Mecca without his usual comforts and very sadly died there.

We, the British in India, were always very concerned not to upset anyone's religious susceptibilities, and it so happened that there was a small religious shrine in my squadron lines in Bolarum. It had nothing to do with the Army. It had, I suppose, been there since time immemorial, and we did not want to do anything to disturb it. Its guardian was an elderly fakir who wore little beyond a piece of string and cloth round his waist, had long matted hair and a long greying unkempt beard, and his naked body and hair were always covered in ashes. We did, of course, have to have some control over his activities, but he was very friendly and gave no trouble.

One morning after stables, when I went to my squadron office, my squadron clerk, who prided himself on his English, which he preferred to air rather than talk Hindustani, greeted me by saying: 'Sir. There is an *araz*.' An *araz* is a request, or petition, usually for favours.

'Yes,' I said, feeling automatically a little on the defensive. 'What is it?'

'Sir, there is an *araz* that he should be allowed to keep another goat, from our good friend and neighbour, the clergyman.'

I hope I kept a straight face.

One weekend when I was out shooting, I camped under a tree not far from a fairly large village. I was relaxing, having my supper, when a man came out of the village and said that he had noticed that I was alone, and might like some company to while away the time with a little conversation. He told me who he was – a man of some education; the village schoolmaster perhaps.

Among other subjects, we got onto a comparison of conditions in British India and in a native state like Hyderabad. I said that one thing that surprised me was how cheerful everyone there seemed to be. Surely it must be intolerable living in these medieval feudal baronies. 'Would you not rather be living in British India, where we have a proper regard for law and order and justice?'

He replied, 'No. Not at all. You mention law and order. Here', he said, 'we know exactly where we stand in matters of law and order. If we are taken to court, we know just how much justice we can get for one rupee, five rupees, or twenty-five rupees. But if you come before a British magistrate in British India, you can't arrange anything. You don't know what may happen. You may get a stiff sentence, or you may get off scot-free even if you have committed the crime.'

The dilemma for simple people who are accustomed to other systems is illustrated by the story of the Indian lady whose husband was murdered. She knew who had done it, so she engaged a hired assassin to murder the murderer, which he did, but he bungled it and got arrested. He then had great expense and trouble arranging for false witnesses, false alibis, and so on. Anyway, he managed so to confuse the evidence that the magistrate acquitted him. He then went back to the lady and demanded his money for disposing of her husband's muderer.

'No fear,' she said. 'The judge sahib say you didn't do it.'

The Horse Artillery battery in our brigade was 'G' Battery. Bob Herman of The Royals and I were attached to it for a fortnight's train-ing during its 'practice camp' – its annual exercise carried out with live ammunition.

Among those attending the exercise was a major from Army Head-quarters in Delhi representing the Master-General of the Ordnance. One evening at dinner in the mess, he and the Gunner officers had a ballistics discussion about what happens to the base of a high-velocity shell when it explodes. Does the velocity of the shell carry it forward, or does the explosion send it backwards?

Bob and I were allowed to go where we liked during the firing, and next morning we and the Ordnance representative decided to stay with the guns – which were in a little toddy palm grove full of prickly pear cactus – rather than go to the observation post on a hill some way off from where the firing was being directed. We were standing behind the guns while they were being given some very rapid switches between shots. Suddenly there was an appalling crash. The Master-General's man lost his topee and sank to the ground between Bob and me with blood pouring down his face.

When the guns were switched to a new alignment, the No.1 gunner was supposed to look 'up the spout' to make sure that there was no obstruction to the next shot. Something had clearly gone wrong with that bit of drill, and the next shell from one of the guns must have hit one of the large bits of cactus and exploded twenty yards ahead of us. Bob and I dragged the Ordnance man into the shade, mopped up the blood and found that he had a long but shallow scalp wound on the left side of his head. It was still in the days when we all imagined that if we were in the sun for five minutes without a topee we would get sunstroke, so I went to fetch the wounded man's topee and there, embedded in its cloth layers, was the base of the shell. That concluded the argument. The Master-General's man got away with a slight wound and slight concussion, and the generous 'G' Battery officers presented him with his trophy mounted in silver.

January 1, Proclamation Day, was the principal British Indian cere-monial day, and in 1932 at Bolarum we must have had one of the last great cavalry spectacles. The Bolarum cavalry brigade, the Nizam of Hyderabad's cavalry brigade, 'G' Battery Royal Horse Artillery, and two Royal Artillery field batteries paraded together – 4,000 horses. Colonel Sir Terence Keyes, the British Resident in Hyderabad, took the salute. The whole parade marched past three times in line of squadrons, first at a walk, then at a trot, then at full gallop. You don't salute at the gallop. Commanding a squadron in a parade of that size, at that pace, is a mind-quickening experience, and wheeling 90 degrees into line at a gallop to pass the saluting base is a time not to make a mistake. But it was one of the things that made our regimental soldiering what it was and why we preferred it to office jobs or being ADCs.

Some of us did occasionally get landed with office jobs. Hugh McKil-lop of the Scinde Horse was forced, reluctantly and temporarily, into the staff captain's chair at Brigade Headquarters while the permanent incumbent was on leave. I think I had a slight, and undeserved, reputa-tion for being a little more academically interested than many officers. At all events Hugh had been wrestling with some of those old archaic

Deccan Contingent accounts, and he said to me one day, 'Do you by any chance know what a usufruct is?' I said, 'Yes, but it may depend on the context.' He replied, 'It's one of those beastly accounts. Southern Command Headquarters have asked what we do with the usufruct.' I said, 'It's Latin – to enjoy the fruit of – so I suppose they mean the interest on the account.' 'In that case', he said, 'they won't enjoy my answer.' 'What did you say?' I asked. 'I wrote them a nice little letter,' he replied, 'saying, "When the weather gets hot, we take the wheels off, and put it in a bottle."' As far as he was concerned it turned out to be a not unsatisfactory reply, because he was promptly returned to his more accustomed seat in the saddle.

Of some of the effects of the 1929 worldwide economic slump on us in India I wrote this:

> We, of course, get it in the neck the same as everyone else, but it is not quite as bad as it looked at first. All import duties go up from 10% to 25%, and income tax goes up, while our pay is cut by 10%. It will make a difference to me of about £50 per year [£1,500 or so now] but, for a bachelor, it is not serious. It might come to giving up shooting, and cutting down on polo, but it is going to be the devil for young married captains with families.

And later:

> We have all shut down in this country. The Commander-in-Chief sent round a circular expressing his sympathies for everyone, especially the junior ranks, at these cuts in pay, and suggested that, for the present, all entertaining, mess guest nights, etc. should be stopped, so that officers will not be called upon to make expenditure over which they have no control. So far as I know, the whole country is adopting these suggestions. We can therefore cut out the unnecessary expenses, and so continue to play polo, shoot, etc.
>
> I personally think these drastic cuts in pay are quite correct. We have been living too well.

In the event, I think we adjusted ourselves to such stringency as may have been necessary without much difficulty or disruption of our normal lives. Social life was important in India. We were all separated for years at a time from our wider family lives at home, and we needed to build close and friendly associations in India. Our regiments and other groupings needed to acquire the character of extended families. We did not have to be lavish, but we did need some outlay on entertainment of one another. We did continue to give a ball in the ballroom in our mess at Bolarum. As nearly all the men were Army officers, in their many different mess kits, it was a very colourful affair. Cavalry officers, and officers of the rank of major (field officers) and above, wore box spurs with their mess kit, but we removed them for dancing so that they would not catch in the ladies' long ball dresses.

Some of the mess kits had dark blue jackets with scarlet facings and scarlet cuffs, and scarlet waistcoats covered in gold braid. One regiment had a yellow jacket with black facings, another had a green jacket with white facings, and there were a variety of other colour combinations, all with waistcoats heavily decorated with gold braid.

10

Home Leave

By the training season of the winter of 1931–32 I had been in India more than three years, and I had felt that I ought to try to get some home leave. I was very keen to see home again and my parents and family, and I also had it in mind that I must get the medical attention which I seemed to need. In a letter to my sister Mollie after I had come down from the High Himalayas, I had said: 'My inside is not what it ought to be. If it is not recovered before I come home, I shall see a good doctor.' I was two stone below my proper weight. I was concerned, however, to wait till after the training season and it was in March 1932 that I sailed for home.

There was another factor in the decision about when I should start my leave, which makes the life we led at the time look particularly dated. The Army, quite rightly, did not like officers going on leave in the winter training season, but it was not impossible to get permission to do so. Our brigadier, however, who was an Indian cavalryman, said that he would not grant winter leave home to any officer who did not undertake to buy a horse – it may have been two horses – when he got home and spend the winter hunting. Hunting was doubtless a suitable recreation for cavalrymen, but I thought the stipulation an impertinence and would not have been prepared to go on leave on such a condition. Leave was my own affair, to do with as I liked.

There being no air services, we went on home leave by sea. Rather than go P & O, it shortened the journey to go by the Italian line Lloyd Triestino, and then take the train across Europe. Home leave usually consisted of the annual allowance of sixty days' privilege leave, plus six months' furlough.

It sounds a generous ration of leave, and in a way it was, but that needs qualifying. During the whole of our Indian service of say thirty-five years, the Indian government allowed us three free first-class passages home and back to India. We could spin that out to, I think, five passages by travelling tourist class. In the event, I got home for the third time after eighteen years' service. No one would tolerate that sort of thing today. We had no option. But we were lucky compared with our predecessors, who got precious little furlough and no free passages.

At all events, in the spring of 1932 I sailed for Italy on the Lloyd Triestino SS *Ganges*. On the journey I made friends with a delightful Gurkha officer, Major Robert Bruce, 5th Royal Gurkha Rifles (Frontier Force), and together we made friends with a most amusing, effervescent Greek whose full name was too much for us, so we simply called him 'Taxi'.

Having passed through the Red Sea, the ship was due to dock at Suez early in the morning. It would take all day going through the Suez Canal, and sail again from Port Said into the Mediterranean at six o'clock in the evening. Taxi said that he knew Egypt like the back of his hand and, if Robert Bruce and I were prepared to put ourselves in his charge, we could get off the ship as soon as it reached Suez, hire the first taxi we could find, dash the 100 miles to Cairo, see the sights, and then dash the 100 miles back to Port Said to catch the ship in the evening. We had judged that there was a man of substance under Taxi's frothy cheerfulness, and we also thought that we might never again get a chance to see Cairo, so we agreed.

Taxi spoke Arabic, of which I also had a smattering, and he soon commandeered a taxi. We had a hair-raising drive at top speed across the desert road to Cairo, the taxi driver apparently placing a good deal more faith in Allah to look after us all than seemed to me warranted. When we neared Cairo, Taxi suggested that it would be a good idea to have a wash and brush up and a cup of coffee before we started the sightseeing. He knew a nice little place. He took us to the Semiramis Hotel. Not knowing Cairo, the significance of that did not strike me until, when we went into the coffee room, I saw Lord Derby sitting in the corner reading a newspaper. As he was reputed to be one of the richest men in England, I judged that the coffee was going to cost a bob or two. It did, but what matter? It was excellent. We were living free on the ship and Taxi, knowing the Egyptian ropes, saw that we were not robbed all day.

We went to the museum and so revelled in the marvellous and elegant treasures of Ancient Egypt that Taxi almost literally had to drag us away if we were to see anything else; and both he and we were determined to see the Pyramids, which are some way out of Cairo.

When we got there, one of the dragomen who was hanging about said that if we would give him so much money, he would go to the top of the Great Pyramid in x minutes. Taxi thought it was reasonable. I said to the dragoman, 'I have a better idea. I'll race you to the top and, if you win, I'll double the fee.' That was agreed. We stood back perhaps twenty yards from the foot of the pyramid. Someone said 'Go!' and we were off.

I beat him to the pyramid and was on first, but I did not know the best way and had to let him pass me to give a lead, with the hope that I could overtake him in the last few feet. However, it proved impossible, and we arrived more or less together, panting, on the top. I said, 'Did we do it in x minutes?' He answered, through his gasps for breath, 'I think we did it in half that.' I offered to race him down again, but he rightly said it would be too dangerous.

We spent some time looking at some of the very interesting things in the vicinity of the Pyramids and then returned to Cairo, visited the bazaar and bought some souvenirs to take home; and Taxi, true to his word, got us to Port Said safely in time to catch the ship before she sailed.

My strongest recollection of the train journey across Europe, once we had landed in Venice, was that, after three and a half years of living with my eyes screwed up against the glare of India, I could open them fully again and enjoy the gentler light of our own more northern latitudes.

On arrival back in Britain, I had to give some attention to my health. By the time I got home I had little doubt that I had something serious the matter with me. I could hardly digest solid food. I was fortunate to have enormous stamina, and was thus able, and very concerned, to get all the interest and enjoyment out of life that I could, and not be inhibited by health problems.

I spent the summer intermittently fishing in Ireland, where our family home still was, and in the hands of military doctors in London. They were unable to diagnose my complaint. All sorts of medicaments and nostrums were tried, but without effect. I suppose that the scientific aids to diagnosis were then, seventy years ago, much less efficient than they are now.

My father knew everyone in Ireland and eventually suggested that I should seek a different opinion from the Millbank Hospital military doctors in London. He proposed that I should see a certain Dr Abrahams in Dublin, which I did. He carried out all the tests he could, and had me X-rayed, but still could not make a diagnosis. He then said to me, 'I can try other courses of medication, diet and so on, from what you have had, but I can give no guarantee of success. There is, however, another possibility, but it must be for you to decide. That is that we open you up and have a look inside.' I answered, 'I can't wait. My own feeling is that I have got some sort of a blockage that needs to be removed.' I had, and the operation proved to be successful.

11

An Extra-Mural Interlude

On my return to India from home leave, I had decided to get down to it and work for my promotion exam to captain, which I did, and was relieved to pass with distinction in a number of subjects.

One of my experiences at that time was the machine-gun course at the Machine-Gun School at Ahmadnegar, on the plateau 120 miles east of Bombay. One weekend, somewhere in the vicinity of Ahmadnegar, I was doing what I so often did in India – spending a day or two living under a tree somewhere out in the country, perhaps shooting or fishing or just exploring the countryside. While I was supping alone, an educated man from a local village came to see me. He was carrying a musical instrument like a small mandolin. He said that, as I was alone, he had thought that perhaps I might like to listen to a little music.

I thanked him very much for his kindness but said that Indian music was so unlike our Western music that I did not understand it. He replied that that was no problem: he would play descriptive, representational music, and would explain to me what it was describing, and he was sure that I would have no difficulty in understanding it. And so he played – a love scene, a battle, a hunt, a boy herding goats, and so on. To my surprise I found it not only comprehensible but also very agreeable, because hitherto Oriental music had seemed to me not only very alien but also not at all to my liking.

In the Indian Army it was obligatory for us to pass an Urdu examination graded as the Higher Standard. As soon as I joined Sam Browne's Cavalry in Rawalpindi, I began seriously to work for it. I obtained the services of an elderly Indian schoolmaster out of the bazaar, who had a lot of experience of coaching officers. He was a veritable Oriental Mr Chips with a delicious air of partial dottiness; but he was a born and superb teacher. I was a commissioned officer in His Majesty's Armed Forces, but not to him. In his eyes I was a pupil, and he always addressed me in the Urdu equivalent of 'my son'. For my part I addressed him with the courtesies due in Urdu to one's elders and betters. In the Orient the teaching profession is held in high esteem, and the sacred master and pupil relationship is securely and jealously safeguarded.

The old Munshi Sahib did not simply have the innate gift of holding his pupil's interest and imparting knowledge. He was also a cunning logician in the art of defeating the examiners.

He asked me: 'Will you work hard?'

I replied: 'Yes.'

He then asked: 'Have you a good memory?'

I answered: 'Yes. I'm Irish. We all have good memories.'

'Good,' he said. 'Then I can guarantee that you have already, in effect, passed the Higher Standard exam with distinction.'

He then went on to say that he had minutely examined all the Higher Standard papers for the past ten years and had extracted the whole of the vocabulary, some 1,500 words I think. He said, 'You must learn the whole of that vocabulary. Does that daunt you?'

'No. I shall enjoy it.'

'You are unlikely to get more than a word or two in the exam that is not in that vocabulary, and you will most likely be able to guess them. As you learn the vocabulary, you and I will spend the coming weeks stringing it all together to make the Urdu language.'

I much enjoyed working with him. He was courteous and courtly and dignified, and at the same time he had a deliciously impish sense of humour; and he was firm as a teacher. He pressed me about as hard as I could go, but not beyond. Eventually the day came when I sat the exam and, as he had forecast, passed with credit. He came to congratulate me, and then said: 'You are promising at this sort of thing. Would you now like to have some fun?'

'What do you mean?' I asked.

'Learn Persian. It's a lovely language, with a rich literature that is more than enough for a lifetime.'

'Who will teach me?'

'I will,' he replied.

So I began to study Persian with him and by the time the Regiment left Rawalpindi, I was able to converse in Persian with the not infrequent itinerant Persian carpet vendors. When I got to Bolarum, I discovered that Persian was still the court language at the Nizam of Hyderabad's court – and the carpet sellers came there too. Then, the year after I returned from home leave, a three-month Persian course was advertised to be held in the Language Section of the Military Training Branch at Army Headquarters – as GHQ was then known – at Simla in the hills, where it and the Government of India moved from Delhi in the summer months. It so happened that our new

Commandant (from another regiment) had commanded a levy raised in Persia, the South Persia Rifles, in the First World War, and was himself a Persian speaker. He thoroughly approved of my efforts to learn the language and willingly gave me permission to apply for the Simla course, for which I was accepted.

Jack Gannon, our old Commandant, had retired while I was on home leave. His successor was Lieutenant-Colonel W. A. K. Fraser, CBE, DSO, MVO, MC, from the Central India Horse (CIH). When I got back to the Regiment and found 'Wak' Fraser in command, I asked Branny Branfoot, who had become second in command, what sort of a man he appeared to be. Branny was a born field soldier, with a scathing disrespect for what he regarded as the field ineptitude of most senior officers. It was therefore high praise for Wak Fraser that Branny gave me his view that 'He seems to have more sense in the field than most of them'.

More equivocal were Branny's other two comments. The first: 'He's an extraordinary chap. He doesn't dance, but he loves going to dances, and just sitting out with the girls and chatting with them; and she [Mrs Fraser] seems quite content to have him off her hands for a bit.' The second: 'He doesn't understand us. He can't understand why we don't take our polo more seriously. He says that, if we won't play polo seriously, we had better join the S&T [Supply and Transport Service].'

Three or four of the twenty-one Indian Cavalry regiments made polo so much their principal recreation that they had spare time, and spare resources, for little else. They achieved astonishingly high standards, sometimes having regimental teams of international calibre. Wak Fraser's regiment, the CIH, was one such. We, however, and I dare say other regiments, saw things differently. We enjoyed polo, and played it to a standard at which we might win occasional local tournaments, but we never aspired to being in the big league – competing, for instance, for the coveted Inter-Regimental trophy. The long and the short of it was that we found that India offered such a wide variety of sports, recreations and interests that we were not prepared to devote all our spare time and resources to the ten acres of a polo ground. I am not making any invidious comparisons. We were all free to choose how best to occupy our spare time within the compass of our own individual inclinations. At all events, the unfortunate Wak Fraser was destined to have a series of accidents which virtually put an end to his own polo playing days.

Those wishing to attend the course in Simla were warned that, at the end of it, they would be expected to pass the Higher Standard Persian exam. That meant really hard work even for someone like me who had already acquired a fair smattering of Persian.

There was only one other officer on the course. I did not like him, though I hope he never realised it. He was self-opinionated, and highly critical of everyone, and everything, except himself. He was academically quite bright, but socially crass. He feigned to despise Colonel C. A. Boyle, Probyn's Horse, the man under whom we worked, although we had a Persian teacher.

Colonel Boyle, a large man with an infectious laugh, had the title Adviser in Languages and Secretary to the Board of Examiners. He had an awkward gait, as he had been shot through both knees in the First World War. He was a brilliant Oriental linguist, Persian, Urdu and Arabic being his principal languages. He subsequently held the chair in Oriental Languages at Oxford University.

The language faculty was a section of the Department of Military Training and one morning Colonel Boyle brought the Director of Military Training, Colonel Lord Gort, to see me and my associate in the little room where we worked.

Lord Gort was one of the most distinguished officers in the Army and a very nice man. He thanked us for giving up time to learn a foreign language and added: 'The Army needs all the qualified linguists it can get.'

'In that case', retorted my associate aggressively, 'you'll have to pay for them', and then launched into a tirade on the inadequacy of awards and allowances for linguists.

I was altogether taken aback, looking on in uncomfortable silence as Lord Gort made some courteous response and withdrew. Colonel Boyle afterwards returned and remonstrated quietly with my associate and said that he had been much embarrassed. I endorsed this and said I hoped that Colonel Boyle might find an opportunity to tell Lord Gort that the linguistic fraternity in general did not share my associate's views. Quite apart from its other shortcomings, the outburst was misdirected. Complaints about the language faculty should have been addressed in the first place to Colonel Boyle.

I enjoyed Simla. The climate at 7,000 feet was delightful in the months I was there – April, May, June. There is nothing much to climb but there are lovely mountain walks, and I was able to look with longing at the Himalayan ranges fifty miles to the north, particularly when, on a Sunday afternoon, I would walk the ten or a dozen miles out to Fargu and lie in the grass in the sunshine on the top of the hill there, with an uninterrupted view of the snows across the deep Sutlej valley, and listen to the shepherd boys playing their little pipes among their flocks.

I became a member of the United Services Club and lived there in some comfort, with my own bed-sitting room in which I could work in peace. The place was a sealed pattern late Victorian or Edwardian club, exemplified by the deepest imaginable red or brown leather-upholstered chairs in the smoking room. No ladies, of course. It also had a Canadian tennis court –an excellent game which I learnt to play; a kind of poor relation to real tennis, but by no means to be despised.

I enjoyed the interest of working in the Training Branch at Headquarters, and of getting to know staff officers and something of their work. Senior people, too, were very kind and hospitable to me, and I have a particularly warm recollection of the interest that the Director of Military Operations, Colonel Alan Hartley, of Probyn's Horse, took in me. He and his charming wife had me to dine on a number of occasions. There was a serious Frontier war going on at the time against the Mohmand tribe, and Colonel Hartley was good enough to enlighten me on what was happening, and on the problems of handling the operation at his own senior staff level. I was glad of this renewed – albeit second-hand – involvement in Frontier affairs because, as my letters home reveal, I was becoming disenchanted, away from the Frontier in southern India, with fighting sham battles which grew to have little relationship to reality.

Hospitality in India was remarkable but even so, as a junior officer only temporarily in Simla on a language course, I was surprised to receive an invitation to one of the Viceregal Garden Parties. How did they even know of my existence? I went, and was duly impressed. One of the ADCs had been at Sandhurst with me. We talked and I sensed he wasn't very happy. He asked me to be sure and see him whenever I could while I was in Simla. The brotherhood of regimental life with other like-minded young men was, for most of us, a fundamental part of soldiering, and the ADC's job didn't accord with it.

I worked hard at the Persian. It is a rewarding language; and I had no trouble at the end of the three months in acquiring the Higher Standard certificate. That made me eligible to be selected to go to Persia for language study with a view to becoming a Persian interpreter. In the first week of February 1935 I had a letter from Army Headquarters telling me to get ready to go to Persia and, a week later, instructions to 'proceed' there at the beginning of March.

12
Persia

I left Bolarum for Shiraz in south Persia in the second week of March 1935 and, as I had expected, went by sea from Bombay to Bushire on the south coast of Persia, in the Persian Gulf, calling at Karachi. The ship was one of the small British Indian Steam Navigation Company ships plying regularly between Bombay and Basra in Iraq, calling en route at various small ports.

When we sailed from Karachi, I was the only first class passenger, so I had the ship's officers for company and got to know them well. One singular piece of nautical talk that I recall was that the First Officer told me that he had at one time sailed with a Master who ascribed his never-failing robust good health to the fact that, except in harbour, he drank a pint of fresh sea water, straight from the sea, first thing every morning.

At Bushire the customs official appeared to be in an irritable mood so I greeted him with the most extravagant Persian greeting I could muster. His demeanour changed at once and, after a superficial examination of my baggage, I was told that I was free to enter Iran, and to come and go throughout its length and breadth as I wished.

I was to be the guest, at Sabz-Abad, of Colonel Sir Trenchard and Lady Fowle, the British Consul-General and Resident, and his wife, who had kindly asked me to stay. It was a relief to find that the Persian I had learnt in India was intelligible: I found I could converse freely with the gardeners, the *ferashes* (messengers), and other servants whom I met.

Seen from the sea, Bushire was a pile of mud-coloured houses rising out of the desert, punctuated with numerous 'wind-towers' to catch the sea breezes and provide some cool in the very hot summer months. The heat there was proverbial, and there was a Persian story of a wicked resident who died and went to hell. A week or so later, a friend was very surprised to meet him hurrying down the street. The friend asked what he was doing, when everyone supposed him to be with the Devil. 'It's so cold down there,' he explained, 'that I've come back for my overcoat.'

My interest in Bushire was to find a modern successor to the famous *charwadars* – muleteers – of the past. I found one, a smart young fellow who had recently completed his military service and who now had a new high-powered American car in which he was only too ready to take me to Shiraz. A bargain was struck which required the journey to be made in one day, over the 'Road of Many Passes'. And, as things turned out, I could not have wished for a better or more comfortable car, nor a more efficient driver than Mohammed Ali. He proved to be a cheerful, pleasant and informative travelling companion.

The surface of the road was frightful and it took me eleven hours to do the 180 miles in a new well-sprung Ford car, an average speed of a little over 16 m.p.h. It was not really a road at all, but a glorified mule track destroyed by motor traffic. At least the Shah had established a system of road guards to make the journey safer for travellers. In the old days you were liable to be attacked and robbed by the tribes who lived in the mountains. Now every few miles there was a blockhouse in which there were a dozen or so well-armed road guards, the Ammiyeh, and these blockhouses were connected by telephone and had either a motor cycle or motorcar for communication should the telephone system break down.

It was sundown when Mohammed Ali and I reached Shiraz, and my first impression of the little old medieval town that was to be my home for a year remains vividly in my mind. Coming in from the awful road from Bushire, we entered Shiraz by the wide Khyaban-i-Zend – the Zend Avenue – which is outside the Old City. I was intrigued as we joined the avenue to see the Persians enjoying their evening equivalent of the Spanish *paseo*. The men were neatly dressed, wearing *kepis* – circular, hard, peaked caps; their womenfolk wore black, or dark blue, *chadurs* (veils) which completely hid them, all but their eyes, hands and feet. Persia was a rigid dictatorship under Rize Shah Pahlavi, and the peaked cap – known as the Pahlavi cap – was compulsory for all men.

I had come from the tropics. It was spring in Persia. Shiraz is 5,200 feet above sea level, and there was still snow on the surrounding mountains up to 8,000 feet, and a chill on the evening air. I was glad to reach the hospitable warmth of the British Consulate, where I had been invited to stay for a few days until I had fixed up my own accommodation.

While I was there, there was another visitor, Teviot-Kerr of the Anglo-Persian Oil Company. He and I and Harold Hoyland, the consul, were sitting talking one evening after supper when Hoyland, a large and florid man, suddenly went puce in the face and fell forward in a fit. We ripped off his tie and undid his shirt. Teviot-Kerr was not very mobile as he had lost a leg in the First World War, so I ran to the Church Missionary Society hospital which was not far away, and fetched a doctor. We put Hoyland to bed – his wife was away – and by the next morning he seemed to have recovered. Certainly he had no more fits in the year I was in Shiraz.

Hoyland's predecessor in Shiraz was typical of the old Levant Consular Service officers, some of whom spent almost the whole of their working life in one place and became a much respected, and even revered, part of the local scene. 'Mr Chick' – 'Aga-i-Chick' – lived his bachelor life in Shiraz for thirty-two years. The Consulate and its beautiful garden, which he tended with loving care, were the most imposing premises in the neighbourhood. The British Consul, too, represented the whole might and majesty of the British Empire. But it was not on those circumstances and qualities that, even in his lifetime, the legend of Chick rested. Indeed it was almost the opposite. It was because he was a simple man who went about doing good. He loved Shiraz and became an avuncular figure to everyone in the town, universally respected and the confidant of many. He was a fine Persian and Arabic scholar and, of course, spoke fluent vernacular Persian.

He was religious and it was his habit after lunch to kneel at a low lectern in his sitting room with the Bible, the Book of Common Prayer, or some other religious work, and to study it. In his later years he frequently fell asleep while performing this office. His servants then had to keep his frequent Persian visitors at bay, and quiet, saying: 'He's praying – *Nimaz meekhonad.*'

He was a devoted and expert gardener. Although, of course, he knew that the day must come when he must part from Shiraz and his garden, it almost broke his heart to do so. It had been a love affair lasting half a lifetime. His final act was to kiss every tree farewell.

Next door to the Consulate, in the Khyaban-i-Zend, was a large walled garden named the Bhag-i-Sheikh (The Sheikh's Garden). It contained three or four small single-storey houses, and had formerly belonged to the Eastern Telegraph Company. I do not recall who owned it in my time, but a Persian family, whom I got to know well, lived in one house, and possibly the Consulate had a lien on the others for language students. Both Foreign Office and Army students were sent to Shiraz because the purest Persian was supposed to be spoken there. I rented one of the houses and my daily routine was to put in two hours' work before breakfast, have a teacher for three hours, and then work by myself for the rest of the day. I would try to practise my Persian as much as possible in conversation with the local people.

There was a garden in front of the house which I didn't claim as I couldn't run to keeping a gardener. It had one of the little artificial ponds which all Persian gardens contained, known as the *höz*. This was full of goldfish, a sanitary idea as they ate up mosquito larvae and also, as the *höz* was probably built as a place where household utensils could be washed, the goldfish could eat all the bits of food and prevent the water becoming putrid.

On 21 March, which was the festival of *Noruz* (meaning 'new day'), which is the Persian New Year's Day and really corresponds to our Christmas in importance, I went out after breakfast for a walk. On the way home I met a young Persian dressed in uniform. He greeted me politely and we walked back together. He told me that he was a cadet and hoped to get an Army commission shortly. He then invited me to his home for lunch. There I met a number of his relations, his father, two brothers who were on *Noruz* vacation from the University of Teheran, and a number of his friends.

When I told the old father that I was an Irishman, he was delighted. He said that the Irish and French are really of Persian descent, while the Scotch and English are Mongols. Where he gleaned this information I do not know, but he thought it sufficient grounds to ask me to stay to lunch. He then did me the honour of introducing me to his two wives, both unveiled, charming and very good-looking.

When we were ushered into lunch I found that a table had been prepared for me while the family were to feed, Eastern fashion, sitting on the floor. I protested that as I was descended from the Persians, I must throw off my Western veneer and behave as a true Persian, and I therefore declined to use the table and sat myself on the floor as well.

After lunch I had a long chat with the old man while he smoked, and it was almost four in the afternoon when I managed to terminate what had started as my morning walk. I asked the sons to tea with me the next day, and I hoped to get the old man along before too long. He was a big man in those parts and an important landowner He claimed to spend the whole of his income on enjoying himself and entertaining his friends and relations, as he said it would be no use to him when he passed on to the next world.

The town of Shiraz was built in a long and wide cultivated plain surrounded by mountains which, at their highest points, rose some 3,000 feet above the plain. It was just like the plains away up on the roof of the world on the Tibet plateau except for the cultivation. The mountains were the same bare pink rock and, as the air was clear and the sun very bright, there were the same delicate tints of colour. Large areas of vines were planted at the foot of the mountains

The Shirazis all seemed to love flowers, and most of them who could afford it had some sort of a garden. I suppose the real reason for this pride in their flowers and gardens was a feeling of satisfaction at having produced them from what would otherwise have been a desert. There is the little fable of the Persian who had two pennies. One he spent on bread to nourish his body; the other on a hyacinth to nourish his soul. I once saw a Persian who had grown about a square yard of green grass on the little patch of hard baked earth and rock beside his house. He was on his knees clipping it with a pair of nail scissors.

Persia was trying to modernise itself but was much hampered by lack of what today would be termed infrastructure. Road communications were poor, but this was a huge country, half of it desert, and half the other half mountainous wilderness, with the major towns – and they were not much larger than market towns – two or three hundred miles or more apart; so the cost of building a good road system would have been prohibitive. The reality was a network of rutted and corrugated dirt and dust tracks.

Education was being energetically thrust on the people and there seemed no doubt that many Persians of all classes would reap the benefit in the next generation. I remember attending a large parade of schoolchildren of Shiraz at which the Minister of Education distributed prizes and diplomas. One feature which appealed to me was that teachers whose pupils had attained a high standard were presented with prizes and medals. Had my masters been able to look forward at the end of term to a box of good cigars, a magnum of champagne, or even a copy of the Bible bound in calf, I wonder whether I should have left school with a more profound knowledge of the classics and sciences.

There were some 4,000 boys in the parade. I was unable to compute the number of girls, who for the most part were in their long black veils and were some way apart from the main parade. There were several speeches, including a considerable feat of rhetoric from the Minister for Education in which he outlined the educational programme that had been adopted by the Persian Government. A reply was read by a young schoolboy which was so full of Arabic honorifics to the everlasting glory of Persia and her King that I couldn't understand half of it. Then, I believe for the first time in the history of Persia, a girl was permitted to stand before the parade, unveiled, and read an address. The Shah favoured the emancipation of women.

When this fine-featured young lady had read her speech, which was received with great acclamation, the schoolboys marched past the Minister. There then followed a display by the Boy Scouts, of whom there must have been be nearly a thousand, which included some excellent gymnastics and good close order drill. I was most impressed with the whole ceremony.

While I was in Persia, the autocratic monarch, Reza Shah, decided to grasp the nettle and force both men and women to modernise – that is to say Westernise – their dress. The Pahlavi cap – the peaked *kepi* which the men wore – was abolished by decree, and men were ordered to wear trilby hats. My hat came in for such widespread inspection from my Persian friends and acquaintances that it was almost worn out with handling, and I was forced into being a hat consultant. I was at a loss one day, while out for a walk, when I saw a man coming towards me with his head flashing most curiously in the sunlight. He had ingeniously made himself a trilby-shaped hat out of an old kerosene oil tin. It must have been excruciatingly uncomfortable.

The Shah's other innovation was a much more delicate one, and was handled with as much tact and skill as could be contrived. That was the abolition of the veil (an urban phenomenon – the tribeswomen and the women in the remoter rural areas had never been veiled). He invited his ministers to a garden party, on the stipulation that their wives must come with them unveiled. It was not compulsory. They were given an alternative. They could resign.

That having succeeded, ministers were ordered to give similar parties for their senior staffs, and so the procedure was pushed further and further downwards until the veil had been effectively abolished among the women in official circles. Many of the younger women were, of course, delighted. They wanted to be free to enjoy the fruits of the modern world. But older women were inclined to be more conservative.

At all events, the veil largely disappeared in a remarkably short space of time. But a residue of veils remained on the streets, and the Shah wanted to get rid of them. Whether the next move was officially inspired, or was fortuitous, I do not know, but a rumour reached Shiraz that it had been decreed that in future all ladies of easy virtue must wear the veil. Veils disappeared overnight.

Although the removal of the veil may have taken the women of Persia another step away from medievalism, Shiraz itself nevertheless still remained a small, sleepy medieval town and, on bright starlit nights in summer, lying in bed in my garden, I would listen to the Arabian Nights magic of the booming bell of the leading camel miles away, and then the smaller tinkling bells of the others, as the long camel trains wound their way in from the surrounding desert and wilderness of mountains to the traditional hospitality of the town.

British students of Persian always engaged a reader – some Persian with whom they read, and became familiar with, Persian literature. My reader was a charming man named Rouine. He owned a small stationer's shop in Shiraz. He had read all Shakespeare's plays in English, but he would not risk talking English. He had also made a considerable study of Arabic literature. He was an opium addict – a *wafuri*.

Opium was then a Persian Government monopoly and was freely and legally available. At any time opium addicts could be seen smoking outside *chai-khanas* – cafés – and, particularly in the evenings, the sickly smell was common in the streets. But not many people seemed to become addicted. Rouine was the only one among my acquaintances. Other Persians told me that they used opium just as we might use aspirin, to relieve a headache, or help disperse a cold, but that they were in no danger of becoming addicted. It was, however, Rouine's view that if a person was physiologically predisposed to drug addiction – or alcohol addiction – nothing would save him if he lived in a country where it was freely and legally available.

He said that he had been very strictly brought up by his parents not to touch opium. One day, however, when he was picnicking with friends, he was taken ill, and was given opium to relieve him. He claimed that something similar happened on a number of occasions, and he got hooked. Whatever the truth, there is nothing good to be said for opium addiction. I remember going out with Rouine and some others for several days in the mountains, and one evening he was deprived for an hour or two of his opium which he smoked at regular intervals five times a day. Our transport was delayed and so, therefore, was his evening sundown smoke. He went into a near trance. His eyes rolled about, and he turned deathly pale. Opium could be a killer, and greatly shorten the lives of those unfortunate enough to become addicted.

Although Persia was a Muslim country, wine, beer, and brandy were produced locally, which similarly had its hazards. I did get to know one alcoholic, though only one. He was a well-to-do young man with a fair artistic talent who painted conventional western-type pictures, both portraits and landscapes, in oils. Although he was innately polite, he was a far-gone alcoholic who was often not in a fit condition for company.

Some forty miles north of Shiraz, on the road to Isfahan, are the wonderful ruins of Persepolis – the *Takht-i-Jamsheed* (Jamsheed's throne) – which I visited a number of times. The earliest buildings there, palaces, and perhaps temples, were probably built by Darius I in the sixth century BC, other buildings being added by later kings of his dynasty, the Achaemenid kings of Persia. The vast complex of buildings was partly destroyed by Alexander the Great in about 330 BC, then finally destroyed in the eleventh century AD by the Seljuk Turks. Many of the remaining stone columns have since been brought down by earthquakes, particularly the terrible nineteenth-century earthquakes which razed villages throughout the area.

The masonry at Persepolis is carved with superb delicacy out of a beautiful pale grey limestone. Shortly before I arrived in Shiraz, however, it came under the hand of the modernisers of Persia. Persepolis stands on the skirt of a hill overlooking a wide plain, the Merv Dasht. It was decided to straighten and improve the road across it. To that end the beautiful fallen fluted columns of the Persepolis palace were broken up and used as hard-core and road metal.

Near Persepolis are the huge rock tombs of Darius I and other Achaemenid kings carved out of a mountain cliff face with elaborate subsidiary carvings and decoration. Also carved from the cliff face is a huge bas relief showing the submission of the Roman Emperor Valerian to the Persian King Shapur I, who captured him. Shapur was an able ruler of the Sassanid dynasty which ruled over Persia for 400 years until finally overwhelmed by the Arabs. The whole of this complex of tombs and carvings is known as the Naksh-i-Rustam, meaning 'the picture of Rustam', because some of the carvings, believed to be of Sassanid origin, are thought to represent the legend of that mythical Persian hero.

In May 1935, two months after I reached Persia, British people throughout the world celebrated the twenty-fifth anniversary of George V's accession to the throne. The Church Missionary Society in Shiraz held a special service in their chapel; the British Consul gave a garden party where I spent most of the afternoon with the missionary parson and an old Persian with no teeth, who was for many years in the British consular service in Persia, and who was given the title of Khan Sahib by the Indian Government for good and loyal service.

The Khan Sahib's successor as senior clerical person in the Shiraz Consulate was an Indian and was always known by his Indian Government title of Khan Bahadur. He was a very dignified person in middle life, courtly and serious. He had spent nearly all his service in Persia and was an excellent liaison man with the Persians. When I was in Shiraz, his wife having died, he had recently married a seventeen-year-old Persian girl and was, poor man, reaping the consequences. She was very ladylike, but also very flighty. They used to invite me to tea, but the tea parties were staid imitations of a Victorian parlour; everyone on their best behaviour; no flightiness!

The Church Missionary Society had a substantial organisation in Persia. They were very discreet in evangelical activity. They were sensible, middle of the road Anglicans, there to do good, and they made a really fine medical and educational contribution to the country's requirements. I got to know the CMS people very well. One of the women doctors told me that she operated on an elderly tribesman one morning for a hernia. She went home to lunch. When she returned she found him at the hospital gate, about to climb onto his horse to ride back to the tribe. She sent him back to bed.

Another of the doctors told me that on one occasion when there was an inter-tribal battle going on in the vicinity of Shiraz, a casualty was brought to the hospital. Seemingly some tribesman had run out of ball with which to load his muzzle-loading gun, so he had stuffed his ramrod down the spout and fired it at the enemy. At all events, the casualty who was brought into the hospital was in a medically impossible condition because he was conscious and talking but had a ramrod through his head and sticking out at the back. However, when they operated on him they found that he had an amazing groove in his skull – possibly the only man in the world with such a conformation, and perhaps the only one to have been hit in the head with a ramrod, which had run down the groove and only inflicted a skin-deep scalp wound.

Not many weeks after I reached Shiraz, a young Foreign Service vice-consul, Lance Pyman, also arrived there, and took over one of the other houses in the Bagh-i-Sheikh garden complex. On Fridays he and I used to go for picnics with Persian friends, including their wives and lady friends, which were always light-hearted and great fun. I gradually found myself getting better at the slang, and better able to enjoy the female wit. Persian women talk terribly fast. One of my Persian friends said, 'I call my wife my *mitrailleuse*'; and indeed they all talked together and seldom finished their sentences. Because I did not drink, they used to call me 'Mullah Magan'.

Having been in Shiraz in south Persia for eight months, I thought it time both to take a rest from my formal studies and to see something else of the country. I decided that I must see Isfahan, and that I ought to visit the capital, Teheran. I hoped, too, that I might manage to visit the Caspian Sea.

I left Shiraz on 19 November 1935, early morning, with Lance Pyman. We stopped at Persepolis, and breakfasted with a German friend who was one of the archaeologists working on the ruins, then carried on to Isfahan. It was pouring with rain for about the first 200 of the 300 miles, but we had a closed car and at least we were spared a dusty road. We had some difficulty crossing flooded rivers, but arrived in Isfahan in the evening. It is supposed to be the most beautiful of all Persian cities, and is called by the Persians *Half the world* (Nisf-i-Jahan) which rhymes with Isfahan. We stayed one day there and then went on to Teheran.

This time we had a beautiful day for our journey. The rain had passed away, and it was a bright crisp frosty morning, with the snow-covered mountains which surround the great arid Persian plains glowing pink in the dawn. About a hundred miles south of Teheran is the sacred city of Qum. Coming over a rise, we saw below us, some miles away, the gold dome of the mosque of Masumé shining in the sun, while away to the north, another hundred miles or so, towered the snow peaks of the Elburz range, with the volcanic Demavand rising in solitary grandeur to a height of nearly 19,000 feet. We ate a hurried lunch at Qum, and I fed a donkey on apples, much to the amusement of the Persians who were watching, and then we set off again for Teheran which we reached at sunset.

I was distressed to see the miserable conditions of the people in the villages through which we passed. They looked ill and hungry and in want. Round Shiraz they were poor, but well fed; it was not, I fear, the case elsewhere.

In Teheran I stayed in the Legation. One of the secretaries in the Diplomatic Service was Patrick Reilly, later to become Ambassador to Russia and to France. The acting Minister, Victor Mallet (later Ambassador in Rome), and his wife Peggy were both very kind to me. They took me one evening to a sort of glorified cocktail party and supper and we ended up in a night club. In the party were English, Germans,

Danes, Turks and Persians. Nearly everyone spoke English. Indeed, Persian, French and English were all the languages needed for everybody to speak with everybody else because everyone knew at least two of them.

The two clever daughters of the Turkish Minister sang part songs in English unaccompanied, which I thought rather a wonderful performance.

One young English-educated Persian brought with him a cousin, a sweet and most vivacious little seventeen-year-old girl, who was thoroughly enjoying an evening away from a strict parent. Her father, she told me, was a very strict Mohammedan and said his prayers and did his ablutions regularly five times a day, and made her do the same. She had not been allowed to discard the veil, and thus it was something of a novelty for her to be introduced to a party of this sort and taken to a night club to see a cabaret. I fancied she would modernise the old father before she had finished.

One evening the Mallets took me to the home of some Persian aristocrats. The old – as she seemed to me – grandmother was there. She sat by the corner of the fireside smoking her hubble-bubble. She did not speak French or English which other people were talking, so I sat with her and we talked in Persian. She was all against young girls having a fling before they got married. She told me that she was married when she was eleven, and had two children before she was fifteen.

I wanted to visit the Caspian Sea and the province of Marzanderan, and was lucky to find a companion in Wing Commander Wood, who had come up to the Legation from Baghdad as courier with the diplomatic bag from London. We hired a car and did a three-day trip to the Caspian, during which we motored over a thousand kilometres. The road over the Elburz range was one of the finest mountain roads in the world, crossing a pass some 10,000 feet high; but it was still blocked with snow and we had to take a lower and longer road over the Firuz Koh pass. The new railway line which was then being constructed from the Caspian to Teheran, and which would eventually be linked up with the Persian Gulf ports, passed through the same valley. A Danish engineer who was working on the railway said that this railway, as a mountain railway, was unequalled by anything in Europe, and it certainly looked a wonderful job.

When we had dropped down over the Elburz mountains we were in a new world. Instead of the usual desert scenery of Persia, we entered a land of green and forests, fresh turf and streams and rivers. Between the sea and the Elburz range to the south was a low-lying plain varying from fifty to two miles in width. It was exactly like central Ireland. It was all swamp and marshy meadows, alive with wildfowl. The fields were divided by fences and banks, and the people lived in whitewashed mud cabins, with thatched roofs. They appeared to be very sporting and shot quantities of wild duck which could be seen hanging up for sale in the shops in all the villages.

An interesting feature of this landscape was that in a distance of less than twenty miles from north to south, as the crow flies, the landscape dropped from perpetual snow on Mount Demavand to tropical forest, 92 feet below sea level. At the top were snow leopards, at the bottom tigers – or there used to be; and, at every altitude in that short distance, in effect, were examples of the whole spectrum of the world's land flora and fauna.

The climate was bad. In the winter it was temperate and wet, and in the summer hot and damp. All the people had malaria, and looked ill and pale. They bred a good type of horse, their cattle looked quite sturdy, their sheep were small. There appeared to be no industries except the canning of caviar, and I saw one soap factory.

We spent one night at Chalus, about the centre of the south Caspian coast, where there was a quite well-appointed modern hotel richly carpeted with Persian carpets. The second night we spent fifty miles further along the coast at Ab-i-Garm ('Hot Water') where there were hot springs, and there was a hot sulphur bath for visitors which was said to be very beneficial for the health. Wood and I had a bath and much enjoyed it – without being able to pronounce on its secret properties.

I was glad to have done the trip. Persia had cast its spell over me. In recent years, from a Western point of view, the image of Persia has been temporarily tarnished. There is at the same time an interesting parallel with the historic past. Nearly 1,000 years ago, mischief came out of Persia which is mirrored by that of today. In the eleventh century three brilliant Persian students became close friends when studying under the renowned teacher, Imam Mowaffak, of Nishapur in the province of Khorassan in north-east Persia. They felt assured that at least one of them must reach a position of eminence, so they made a pact that the one who did so would share his good fortune with the others. One of the three was Omar Khayyám, known in Western Europe as a poet, but better known in Persia as a mathematician, astronomer and scientist who devised an astonishingly accurate calendar – more accurate, according to Gibbon, than the Julian. Another, the most worldly successful, became the Wazir – Chief Minister – to two successive Persian kings, both men of great renown. The third student was Hassan-Ibn-Sabbah who, having failed to make a success of his life, approached the Wazir for preferment. Omar Khayyám asked only for facilities to help his scientific work on behalf of the nation, but Hassan sought high honours. The Wazir gave him a place in government, only to find he immersed himself in court intrigues, and even tried to supplant his benefactor. Eventually, disgraced, he left the court.

He then set himself up in the fortress of Alamut in the Elburz Mountains, north west of what is Teheran today. He was a Shia Mohammedan and surrounded himself with other fanatical Shias. From a forward base in Syria he and his fanatical followers set about destabilising the Middle East by acts of terrorism, particularly the murder of prominent Middle East 'political' leaders, include two caliphs of Baghdad and also his own erstwhile benefactor, the Grand Wazir of Persia. It was even supposed that he was responsible for acts of terrorism in Europe. His devotees, drugged with hashish, were prepared for suicidal endeavours to carry out their missions. Hassan had the self-styled title of Sheikh-al-Jebal – Lord of the Mountains – but the Crusaders, who were part of his target, called him The Old Man of the Mountains. Either from his name, Hassan, or from the world *hashishin* – hashish eaters – derives the word *assassin*.

The Persians are an ingenious people and anyone associating with them must be prepared for surprises. Let me give an example.

At the court of the Great Mogul Emperor in India, ambassadors who were granted an audience had to bow down when they came into the presence of the Emperor. But the Persian ambassador refused to do so. He was the personal representative of the King of Kings and would bow to no one. So the Emperor's courtiers thought of a clever means to force the Persian ambassador to bow. They erected a waist-high wicket gateway through which ambassadors must go and thus be forced to bow. They told the Persian ambassador this and he raised no objection.

When his time came to have an audience of the Emperor, he approached the wicket. He did bow down to go through it but he went through backside first. The Emperor must have longed to kick him – or it.

I returned to Shiraz for a couple of months before going back to India in February 1936. On my journey back to India I was delayed for a week in Bushire by the non-arrival of the ship. The Resident and his wife, Sir Trenchard and Lady Fowle, hospitably put me up.

One of their customs was a golf tournament every Saturday morning. I do not play golf, but was invited nevertheless to take part. I drew Lady Fowle as my partner, and elected to play with only one club and a putter. It was a nine-hole course, laid out in an enormous dried-out ancient oyster bed. The fairways had been partly cleared of oyster shells. The greens were 'browns' of baked earth. Lady Fowle played with consummate skill, and I fluked my way round. She and I won, and for years after I treasured my little trophy – a teaspoon with a handle shaped like a golf club.

The Resident, Sir Trenchard, asked if I would like him to give me a run-down on the Persian Gulf. He had enormous influence with all the Rulers in the Gulf States, who for their part greatly appreciated the protection they received from the British presence in the Gulf. We sat in front of a large wall map in his study and he gave me a lucid exposition. Finally, of his own job, he said, 'I know what 100% is of what I would like to achieve. I prudently aim to get 80%; but, for the most part, I have to be satisfied with 60% if I am not to go mad.'

After a week's delay, I boarded the B & I SS *Varela*, bound for Karachi and Bombay where I proposed to disembark. There was only one other cabin passenger, a quiet, elderly American travelling alone. The fact that he was travelling to India naturally interested me, and I wondered whether I could be of any service to him, so I asked him what his plans were.

He said he was on a world cruise. He had joined his cruise ship in Boston, Massachusetts, and sailed across the Atlantic to Gibraltar. There he had left the ship and come across Europe and through the Middle East to Basra, where he had boarded our little cargo ship. He was going to Bombay, and then across India by train, and then through Burma and Malaya to Singapore, where he was going to pick up his cruise liner again.

I said, 'It sounds an astonishing sort of cruise to me. You cross the Atlantic Ocean on your liner. Then you get off and come half way across the world by yourself, almost all by land, before you pick it up again.'

Shaking his head rather sadly, he replied, ' I guess you'd have done the same. There are three hundred and seventy-five widows on that ship.'

Two or three months after my return to India, I had an amusing letter from the vice-consul who had succeeded Lance Pyman in Shiraz, Bill Young. He gave me detailed local news which was of course of interest to me, and concluded his letter as follows:

> The *chadur* – the veil – has almost vanished, and now the women have discovered lipstick, but have not discovered how to use it. It is laid on with a heavy hand, and a very bad aim.
>
> All Persians are most solicitous for your welfare and, when other conversation fails, they always return to: '*Az Mistr Magan che khabar darid*?' ('What news have you of Mr Magan?') – so I tell them you're hunting elephants, stalking tigers, and climbing Everest.

13
Jubblepore

Jubblepore is in the very centre of India, 450 miles north of Bolarum and in what was then known as the Central Provinces of India. It was Thug country, and it was impossible to be there without recalling the Thugs.

The word 'Thug' derives from Sanskrit, having the implication of secrecy and giving rise to the word for a robber. The Thugs were indeed a highly secret sect with several thousand members who carried on a practice of systematic murder and robbery, mainly in the Central Provinces jungles, probably since at least the fifteenth century. Typical of their methods was to meet up with parties of travelling merchants, ingratiate themselves with them and obtain their confidence, and then, when passing through remote jungle areas, strangle and rob them. It was part of their technique that there should be no survivors who might give information. People just vanished without trace. They were expeditiously and expertly buried in hidden graves. Their method of killing their victims was to garrotte them with a handkerchief-like scarf. There was a religious element to their practices related to the worship of the Hindu goddess of destruction, Kali.

Early in the nineteenth century the British authorities made a determined attempt to get rid of this scourge, and entrusted the task to Captain William Sleeman. It proved to be a life's work dependent on meticulous, diligent and dogged intelligence gathering which led to the total annihilation of the Thugs by the middle of the nineteenth century. Between 3,000 and 4,000 were apprehended, of whom several hundred were executed. The remainder were detained for life in concentration camps, one of which was at Saugor, not far from Jubblepore. Just as one can hardly enter the Tower of London without thoughts of the execution of Anne Boleyn, so it would have been hard in the forests of the Central Provinces not to be conscious of the legacy of the Thugs, or of the memory of Sir William Sleeman, the official who, after forty-seven years of continuous service to India without home leave, died on the homeward voyage.

By the time I reached Jubblepore, the Regiment had been there for six months. As I was in Persia when the Regiment moved there, I was naturally delighted to receive Branfoot's Christmas regimental newsletter, as he was acting-Commandant of the Regiment at the time. I quote extracts from it, as it contains an authentic whiff of the old Indian station and regimental atmosphere:

> Our greetings now go to you from Jubblepore where we arrived from Bolarum on 17 October. In many ways Jubblepore is a great improvement on Bolarum. The climate at this time of the year is as near perfect as possible, there is a friendly atmosphere about the place and there are innumerable diversions to relieve the monotony of regimental peace-time soldiering. The country here cannot be called good from a training point of view but it is pleasant, and a day spent out shooting, pigsticking or even training is a pleasure after four years of blistering Deccan sun and barren Deccan rocks.
>
> We are now in the middle of Jubblepore week, which is a week of concentrated gaiety and sport, the young and strong dancing most of the night; rising at 4.30 a.m. to hunt with the Nerbudda Vale Hounds, playing polo or riding races in the afternoon. I fear training is at present at an absolute standstill and this will have to be made good in the near future.
>
> Before leaving Bolarum we had a very thorough individual training inspection, and administrative inspection. The Brigadier's remarks were, 'I am very pleased to see the high standard of training reached both as regards horses and men. This is the result of hard work and excellent esprit de corps. You thoroughly deserve the good report I am giving you.' In August, Sir George Jeffreys, on giving up command of the Southern Command, held a ceremonial parade of the 4th Cavalry Brigade. Sir George described the gallop-past of 'A' Squadron of the Regiment as the best he had ever seen during the whole of his service. (This from a Guardsman appears to be a very high compliment.) One lady was so impressed that she sprang to her feet and clapped, and was rebuked by her stern soldier-husband with the remark that, 'This is a parade of troops and not a race meeting'.
>
> The men are all in good heart, healthy and cheerful and the horses we handed over were all in excellent condition. The horses we have taken over are just as good except the remounts which do not seem to acclimatise here as quickly as in Bolarum.

This comment on the horses acclimatising relates to the fact that they were imported from Australia. As Australia is in the southern hemisphere and India in the northern, acclimatisation meant a major change for the horses. For instance, they grew their coat in the winter; that meant June to September in Australia, and November to February in India. Nature miraculously made the change in one season when the animals reached India, and they grew their coats in the Indian winter months.

One of my earliest concerns on return to India was to get my Persian exam out of the way. It was held in Calcutta. The oral exam was held first, and old Colonel C. A. Boyle, the language specialist, invigilated.

In Persia, because of the great distance between towns, people are identified by their home town. Thus you are a Shirazi, or an Isfahani with the appropriate accent, or a Yezdi with, by general consensus, a deplorable accent. I had become acknowledged as a Shirazi.

For the oral exam, Colonel Boyle produced an elderly Persian to examine me. He was a Shirazi and he was so interested to meet another Shirazi, and to get an up-to-date account of Shiraz and what was going on there, that he and I just talked our heads off in Persian for half an hour. Time was then up, and the exam, *qua* exam, had been a non-event which I passed with the warmest regards of the examiner.

I had studied the set curriculum and, indeed, had gone a good long way beyond it, so the written papers presented no problem. Persian is written in the Arabic script and, written in the careless handwriting that the Persians use, known as *shikasta* – the broken hand, it can be written very fast. I could write it faster than I can write English. At all events, I qualified as an Interpreter First Class and was subsequently appointed Persian Interpreter to the Government of India, a job which I combined with continuing service in my Regiment.

Stimulated by that success, I gave my Urdu a good polishing and took the Urdu interpretership exam later in the year.

14
Elephants and Tigers

In his Christmas newsletter in 1935, Branfoot had mentioned that he had shot a rogue elephant about which he wrote to me when I was in Persia:

I had a terrible three months at that awful seat of learning, the Senior Officers' School. When the beastly show was over, I got a month's leave and went into the Kanara jungles after elephant.

There was a brute of a single tusker which had been terrorising the villagers for years, refusing to be drawn off crops by night, and chasing villagers back to their villages if they tried.

I first had to try to get him by electric light. He was pulling down banana trees about 100 yards outside a village, so I got to within about fifty yards of him and turned on the torch. However, there was so much undergrowth that the beam of light did not have a clear passage, and all I could see was a large grey mass. The old brute looked at the light for a few seconds, and then gave a squeal, and a short rush towards me, so I turned out the light, and he went back to his banana trees.

I tried it again, and the same thing happened, and I came to the conclusion that elephant shooting in the dark is for braver men than I am.

If I had wounded him, and had been chased, I don't think I would have had a chance in the dark.

I waited till dawn, and he cleared off an hour before, and I tried to track him but, beyond getting on his approach tracks, and going about two miles before I discovered I was running heel, I could make nothing of it.

I next came on him by daylight across a forest track, but the wind was dead wrong, and away he went.

The third time was when Wrookie [Hall] was with me, and the elephant was with a herd – he was usually solitary. I suppose being among a lot of cows he became unwary and, after a very exciting stalk, Wrookie doing gun bearer, I got a head shot and down he went. Wrookie was very thrilled, and I was glad to have him with me with the second rifle.

Branfoot, being a bachelor, took only such leave as suited him. He took home leave in the winter only, if he could get it then, bought two or three hunters, settled down at a favourite pub, and hunted with the Blackmoor Vale. His only relative was a married sister, and neither domestic family life nor urban dwelling came easily to him.

One year he took two or three months off and went big game hunting in East Africa. He shot only dangerous game, never deer or antelope, and never hunted the mountain animals. One incident during his African safari made a particular impression on him as a hunter of dangerous game when a native boy in Kenya was had up before the courts and fined for killing an elephant without a licence. It was a rogue elephant, terrorising the local people, and doing great damage to their meagre crops. The boy had gone for it and killed it with a spear. Branfoot said that if he had been the magistrate, instead of fining the boy he would have recommended him for the VC.

I once asked Branfoot how he had come to acquire his taste for big game hunting. He said it had come upon him early, when he was a boy at school at Rugby. Bored one OTC field day, lying behind a hedge waiting for something to happen, he had cut the top inch-and-a-half off a pencil, stuffed it up the breech of his rifle, put a blank cartridge behind it, and fired it at a cow which, to his immense satisfaction and then appalling horror, dropped stone dead. That sowed the seed in the breast of the future hunter.

Branfoot and I hunted tigers and leopards together, but I never hunted elephant. All big game hunting for dangerous animals is, by definition, dangerous. The danger is negligible, however, except to the extent that it is self-created, by wounding animals. Once wounded, they take cover and will attack anyone who comes near them. They must therefore be followed up and finished off. The immediate killing target area is small: the brain, the heart, some parts of the neck. If you miss by half an inch, you may have inflicted a mortal wound, but you nevertheless have a wounded animal to worry about for anything from perhaps half an hour to several hours or even days before it dies. I had two close friends killed by tigers, another badly mauled, and yet another badly mauled by a leopard.

Tigers are nocturnal animals. They kill and eat usually after sundown, and rest in the day. Unlike lions, which live in the open and move in packs, they are solitary and live in thick forest. You needed somehow to locate them on their 'kill'; and as random kills were impossible to predict, the most usual way of trying to shoot tigers was to tie up an animal, usually a well-grown buffalo calf, on a path in the jungle that a tiger might be expected to use. You would first have built a platform in a nearby tree, known as a machan, into which you climbed, just before dark, to await events.

With any luck the tiger would come along, kill the calf, and start eating it. Because it was dark, you couldn't see your target properly. So you had a torch on your rifle which you switched on at the given moment, and shot as best you could along the beam of light. The result was not always a clean kill. In which case the dangerous business of following up the wounded tiger would come with daylight.

Bill Birnie, in my Regiment, calculated that there would be advantages in sitting up on the ground instead of in a tree. The angle of fire would be easier at ground level. He tried it, and got badly mauled. Branfoot, on the other hand, was prepared to shoot from machans but seldom, if ever, did so. He had a preference for stalking tigers on or near their kill in the early morning.

On one occasion I joined him in the thick Malabar jungle along the south-west coast of India. The Malabar coast is lovely. The jungle grows down to the sea shore, which is an endless chain of beautiful bays of white surf and golden sand bordered with palm trees and woods of casuarina pine. We once tried to fish – at certain times of the year when the rouse, or Indian salmon, visits the coast, the fishing is excellent – but the sun was too strong for it to be any pleasure. So we would bathe for about an hour every morning at dawn, and again at sunset. When we went for our early morning swim we would find the fresh foot marks of panthers and elephants in the wet sand. The sea was so warm that one could stay in the water till overcome by fatigue which, in that enervating climate, was easily brought on by any physical exertion. We used to swim out beyond the breakers, and then slowly up and down the shoreline. Branfoot said he did not think it very safe to go far out to sea: although the natives said that no one was ever eaten by sharks there, he did one day see one quite close to the shore.

After some days on the coast we returned to the jungle. Branfoot was camped in a forest bungalow at the foot of the ghats, overlooking a large river. The jungle there was very thick and stretched unbroken, north and south, for hundreds of miles. The bamboos, often over forty feet tall, were the largest I have ever seen, and there was an endless variety of timber, including much valuable teak. The undergrowth was never quite the impenetrable wall of the Congo and Amazon forests, but it was often impossible to see more than a few yards.

We learned from the natives that a cheetal, the spotted deer of the Indian forests, had been killed nearby three or four days before, probably by a panther. Branfoot thought this might be a black panther which had been seen in the neighbourhood. He therefore decided to tie up a goat one night near the place where the cheetal had been taken.

Early next morning, when we reached the spot, there was no goat, nothing but its stomach lying on the ground. We carefully examined the immediate area to try to find which way the kill had been dragged, but the ground was too hard to show any pug marks. We still thought we were dealing with a panther. We moved carefully off along a jungle path, having a good look into all the bushes. Branfoot was leading; I was doing what we called 'gun-bearer'. The plan was that he was No.1 gun, and it was up to him to do the shooting if the stalk was successful. It was up to me to back up the operation in any way that might become necessary.

Branfoot, just ahead of me, crept past without seeing what turned out to be a very large tiger sleeping under a bush right on the edge of the path. I saw it for an instant before it woke. It jumped up and opened its mouth with a fierce snarl, right in my face, and then turned and dashed off into the jungle. I thought for a second that Branfoot was going to fire as he had the heavy weapon, but he refrained. It all happened so quickly that the chance of a fatal shot was small, whereas he could hardly have failed to wound the creature at a range of less than ten yards. We would then have had the unpleasant and exceedingly dangerous job of following up a very cross wounded tiger in thick jungle. Branfoot thought that we had had danger enough, and that we had been lucky that the tiger, woken from a deep, gorged sleep, had not gone for one or other of us. We went after it, but got no further trace of it.

There were other wild life excitements at Malabar. One day we saw a herd of Indian jungle bison, black with snow-white markings. They are large, standing about 16 hands (5'4") at the withers, and very graceful. They make the finest domestic cattle look coarse.

It was not a very good time of year for shooting as the ground was strewn with dead crinkly teak leaves, which crackled extravagantly when walked on. Also, there were constant fires. What caused them I don't know; but all the dead fallen trees seemed to catch fire spontaneously – even the roots were quite burnt out – and much of the undergrowth. It appeared to do very little damage to live standing timber but it felled many dead trees by burning through the base of the trunks. The heat of the fires would explode the hollow green bamboo trunks, which were about eight inches in diameter, and when a bamboo thicket was burning it made a noise like a battle.

If tigers can find secluded enough places, they like to lie in water during the day in hot weather, to keep cool. Once Branfoot and I were in the jungle in May when it was very hot. The country was very rocky and because it was before the arrival of the monsoon, and there had been no rain for months, the stream and river beds were dry except for trickles and pools. There was one small river bed which Branfoot particularly fancied as a possible tiger lying-up place. It had long shelves of broken rock with numerous small bath-like pools. He decided that we should wait till the sun was well up, and hot enough to drive tigers to the water, and then stalk this river bed in rubber-soled shoes – with me No.1 gun this time.

We crept very slowly over the rocks going downstream. Suddenly Branfoot caught me by the elbow and pointed ahead of us. I could see nothing, but he kept pointing and then I saw it: about twenty-five yards ahead of us, two little white spots projecting above a piece of rock and occasionally moving – the two white spots on the back of a tiger's ears. He was lying in a little bath of water, totally obscured from us by the rock formation except for his ears which he twitched occasionally.

Branfoot signalled to me to creep forward, which I did. When I had gone perhaps another five yards, the tiger sensed our presence. He was obviously not asleep, as he showed no signs of sudden alarm. He stood up and started to move off right handed at a smart walk. He was broadside on, twenty-five yards away, and I decided on a heart shot and fired. He staggered, but didn't fall. He raced across the rest of the dry river bed, and dropped over a big rock into the edge of the jungle.

Clearly I had hit him, but missed his heart. I was unlikely to have missed it by much and had almost certainly hit him in the lungs. Our rule, in such a case, was to wait twenty minutes; give him time to die; and then begin the follow up. I did not want to involve Branfoot in my mess, and suggested that I should do the follow up alone. We had no jungle natives with us. He insisted, however, that we were in it together and that, in any event, two rifles were better than one; but I could continue to lead as the No.1 gun.

I confidently expected to find the tiger dead on the far side of the large rock over which he had disappeared; so, when the twenty minutes were up, I approached it with due caution. There was nothing there and, curiously, no blood trail and no evidence of where he had gone. We spent the rest of the day cautiously hunting the surrounding jungle but found nothing, and no trace. I felt sure that he was dead somewhere in the area we were searching. We didn't want to leave him out wounded but, come sundown, we could do no more, and returned to the camp. Next day he was found dead by some natives further down the river bank.

On another occasion Branfoot and I spent ten days in a block of jungle in the Central Provinces tiger forest. We were among the lovely jungle people there, the Gonds, an aboriginal tribe. Those of them who live in or on the edge of the forest exist in ways that can have changed little in thousands of years. They were very keen for us to shoot tigers, which, apart from raiding their cattle, were sometimes a danger to the tribesmen themselves.

We pitched our camp in a little clearing on the edge of the forest where the ripe fruit falling from the *mohur* trees was rapidly fermenting in the hot sun, and the sloth bears were getting drunk on it. There I had what I suppose must have been a very unusual tiger experience.

There was a natural kill. We had not organised it. A young bullock belonging to the Gonds had strayed into the forest and been killed on a jungle path, beside which it was lying. Because it was so sited that an early morning stalk would not be feasible, we decided on a platform, a machan, to shoot from and we built it in a nearby tree. The decision was for me to man it.

We knew the path well because it led to the Waingunga river, two or three miles away, where we went daily to bathe. At that time of year, the month of May, the river was little more than a trickle running through a very rocky bed overhung on both banks by the jungle. There were large areas of dry sand, and large pools, one of which was our bathing place. We shared it with two crocodiles (we had satisfied ourselves that there were only two). They preferred the far bank; we were content with our own shore. They liked to lie in the water with their beady eyes just above the surface. So long as the beady eyes were visible, we remained immersed in the only partly refreshing tepid water. If the beady eyes disappeared, we withdrew onto the hot rocks.

Because tigers are solitary animals, the population density is very low; so there can be broad areas of forest where, at any given time, not one is to be found. But when there is a tiger in a particular area of forest, it is impossible not to be aware of it. It is an eerie experience to be alone at night in an area of jungle when one starts to move. The tension becomes palpable. The jungle creatures are on edge, and there are recognisable danger signals – from a barking deer, or a cheetal with its high-pitched whistle. All around there is a constant background hum of crickets and other insects, and if you are sitting not very comfortably in your machan in some forest tree, you have an intense sense of being alone and isolated in the midst of primordial nature.

On the night in question, just before sundown, I climbed into the machan. It was in a large tree right on the jungle path about twenty yards from the kill, and I settled into it to start my vigil. Darkness fell; there were just a few stars visible through the leaves and branches of the tree. The moon would rise later. The jungle was very tense and, soon after it became dark, a tiger roared, perhaps a mile away. Then silence. Then it roared again, no nearer, but behind me, and further to the right. It roared once or twice again, and then no more.

At about midnight, by which time the moon was high in the sky and shining on the kill which was beyond the shadow of my tree, a deer gave a frightened bark not far away. Then, a little later, I heard the shuffling of leaves just behind me under my tree. Then silence. Then a sudden awful petrifying cough immediately below me, and I realised that there must be a tiger there, unless it was a sloth bear.

I waited, alert. Nothing happened for perhaps twenty minutes. Then, to my right, I saw something moving in the shadow very cautiously. Its head and shoulders then emerged into the moonlight not far from the kill – a young tiger, an almost full-grown cub. As I watched it, my eye caught a movement in the shadow to my left, and there emerged another tiger cub, the same size. They seemed very nervous. They approached the kill cautiously, sniffed it for a short while, but ate nothing. Meanwhile, I was conscious that there was still something under my tree, which I thought must be the tigress, their mother; but she would not venture into the moonlight or go near the kill.

The cubs withdrew into the shadows and I could hear them below me under the tree. Then more shuffling of leaves behind me, followed by a long silence. It seemed clear that they had withdrawn along the path behind me.

Thereafter the jungle fell quiet. Eventually dawn came, and it was soon daylight. Clearly that was the end of that night's *shikar*. I laid my rifle down beside me, and felt free to move and stretch my stiffened limbs. All I had to do was to await the local jungle village men to get me out of the tree with their home-made ladder.

Then suddenly a terrified cheetal crashed through the undergrowth quite close to me with a screaming whistle and, moments later, around the corner of the jungle path straight in front of me a huge male tiger came striding briskly towards me. I could not move to pick up my rifle or he would have seen me instantly. I must wait until he was eating the kill. But he merely gave it a cursory sniff and strode resolutely on, straight under my tree, and off down the path behind me. He had other things on his mind, as I was to discover later.

When the men arrived with the ladder, they asked what had happened. They had been following a tiger's fresh pug marks. Why hadn't I got it? I told them the tale and went back to our camp for breakfast with Branfoot.

We decided after breakfast to follow up the tigers. They had kept to the path down to the river bed, and the pug marks of all four tigers were plain in the dust of the path – a large tiger, the tigress, and two full-grown cubs.

The path petered out into one of the sandy areas in the river bed, and there in the sand were the marks of a major scuffle and conflict. The sand was freshly churned up for yards around, and we were instantly aware that we had been witness to something much more interesting than shooting tigers.

Dunbar Brander, a one-time Indian Service forest officer, in his masterly book on Indian tigers, recorded that the cubs stay with their mother until they are almost full-grown, and are still with her when she comes into season again. A mature male tiger then gets interested but, in order to claim the tigress, he has first to drive off the cubs which are by this time pretty formidable and reluctant to leave their mother; but, in accordance with the laws of nature, he succeeds, and the cubs are forced to part from their mother and go their own way, while he goes off with the tigress.

So, looking at the churned up sand, we were witnessing the scene of the contest between the tiger and the cubs. There was no blood so it must have been mainly a contest of threats and demonstrations. I searched for evidence of the outcome, and found it. Downstream went the pug marks of the two cubs. Upstream went the pug marks of the tiger and tigress.

I have mentioned that I had two close friends killed by tigers. When I was in Persia I learnt of the death of one of them, Anthony Gilliat of The Royals, whom I admired and with whom I had a very close rapport. He had wounded a tiger and was following it up when it attacked him from a thick area of jungle. I still mourn his loss.

There was a story that when King George V went to India, he was given a tiger shoot by a Maharajah. That was a very different sort of shoot from ours. The distinguished gun was placed in a comfortable machan in a tree with an open space in front of him and jungle beyond. The tigers were fed to make sure they would be there. Then, with elephants, beaters and stops they were gently driven towards the gun in such a way as to ensure that they would emerge into the open where expected at walking pace. And so it went with King George, who was a brilliant shot, and he dropped his fine male tiger stone dead. He was then taken down from his machan and led over to see the noble beast, the king of the forest, and found, to his horror, that it had gilded claws.

15
Saugor

On return to my Regiment from Persia, I was told that I had been selected to go on the next Long Equitation Course at the Cavalry School at Saugor in September of that year, 1936, which would last until May of the following year. To go to Saugor, or to the Cavalry School in England at Weedon, was every cavalryman's dream.

When I got there, I found that there were two old friends on the course. 'The rest are strangers,' I wrote home, 'but not for long, I hope.' I described the place as 'nice-looking', but littered with jumps, riding schools, and so on. Jubblepore, where my Regiment was, was only 120 miles away, and I had brought eight horses with me. I would be issued with another three by the Cavalry School, so would have eleven horses in my stable.

Parades started at the usual Indian early hour – 6.30 – which meant one mounted at about 6 a.m. as it was some way to the parade ground. Then we worked straight through till 1.45 p.m. with an hour off for breakfast. I engaged a man to teach me Urdu from 2.30 till 4.45. (This was to bring me up to the standard for the Interpretership exam.) Then I had my own eight horses to exercise which would take me till 7 p.m. After that it might take an hour or so to write up the day's notes, do any necessary reading, etc. Then a bath, dinner and bed. Sleep came easily.

The purpose of the Cavalry Schools at Saugor and Weedon was not to teach us to ride, or horsemastership. If you were not already an expert horseman, you did not get there. The purpose was to ensure, and maintain, a common high standard of horsemanship, and horse-mastership, throughout the Armed Forces. In those days the Army had many thousands of horses, and many thousands of soldiers whose usefulness depended on their horsemanship and horsemastership. There are many different theories on these subjects and, left to themselves, regiments would have adopted a variety of different policies and practices. It was therefore essential that there should be a source of common policy and practice to be followed throughout the Armed Forces. Ideas on these matters did not stand still. New ideas and new theories evolved, and the Cavalry Schools at any given time were propagating the most up-to-date policies and practices that seemed applicable to the Armed Forces' needs. It was, therefore, to enable us both to ensure common standards, and to bring the latest thinking back to our regiments, that we went on these courses. And for us, as cavalrymen, because we spent a large part of our time in the saddle, among congenial and like-minded companions, the courses were very agreeable.

The length of the course, nine months, largely reflected the length of time that, under our system, it took to train a totally unbroken horse up to the point where it was fully trained and battleworthy. It had to be able and willing to do everything that might be asked of a troop horse; finally it had to be trained to a point where it would go quietly as one of four horses being led to shelter from the field of battle by a single mounted man, jumping (all four horses together) obstacles on the way if necessary.

To that end, at the beginning of the course each of us was issued with an unbroken remount – as raw army horses were known – which, under supervision, we had to put through the whole of its training according, in the most minute detail, to the practices and policies favoured at that time by the Cavalry School. For all our work we were divided into two 'rides' of ten officers each under an instructor, and there were comparable rides of Indian officers, Indian NCOs and British NCOs.

I still have my Saugor notes. My notes on training a young horse run to seventy-five handwritten pages. I will quote very briefly from them as I think they could be of interest to the general reader who knows nothing about horses:

> Duration of training. We would like two years to train a horse; the French like four years; but we seldom get more than one year.
>
> The trainee must work to a system. The system is a collection of principles based on experience and justified by results.
>
> The Army system is not the only one, nor is it necessarily the best, or most successful, but it is a proved system, and has been proved the best for the type of horse and rider with whom we have to deal in the Army. It is elastic and can be lengthened indefinitely, or shortened considerably. We can adjust it to suit ourselves and a timed programme.

> Here are a few notes on the elementary training of a young horse:

> Good manners are the basic essential of all horse training.

Lunging on a long rein provides the opportunity to force obedience on the horse calmly and effectively. The horse soon realises that he has no freedom, and must obey the trainer.

It is essential to understand that the mind of the horse conforms to, and reacts to, the mental attitude of the trainer. If the trainer is bored and idle, the horse will also be bored and idle. An angry trainer will mean a frightened horse; a nervous trainer will produce a nervous horse.

When a horse is at fault, the exercise must be repeated again and again until done correctly.

Never overlook a fault, optimistically hoping that the future will correct or eliminate it. Correct it at once.

Never let a horse disobey. Make him obey. Commonsense and tact enable the trainer to reduce the possibility of the horse wishing to disobey to a minimum. The rule is never to ask him to do anything that is too difficult for him at his particular stage of training.

On account of differing characteristics, all horses are different to rule, and different to train. Equitation is an art, not a science.

A horse has a very small brain, but remarkable power of observation and imagination. The latter is the source of all fear, and perhaps the cause of most.

He has a wonderful memory which is exploited in training by working on the association of ideas. By constant repetition of sensations, which are partly mental (voice) and partly physical (legs, hands and body) applied to different parts of the horse's body, his education is brought about.

Go slow, and repeat until perfection is reached.

Ask little, but ask it often, and reward at once for obedience. Reward must be immediate. It may be merely a relaxation, it may be a caress, a word, or a handful of grain.

My remount was a very nervous six-year-old bay Australian Waler. He was a difficult horse – mature, strong, very hot and totally untrained. I did not mind that. Difficult horses were interesting. But it spelt a bit of trouble for me. The very first of my notes on the training of young horses is this:

'Never let a remount get loose. If he does he will be a damn nuisance, as he will think he can always do it. Hang on at all costs!'

1 January 1932: 4,000 horses on ceremonial parade at Bolarum

'G' Battery, Royal Horse Artillery

The author, Rawalpindi, c. 1932

ABOVE Dankar village, Spiti. BELOW Thakru and coolie in Spiti valley.

The Tibet frontier with India; the end of the Hindustan-Tibet road

Miles Smeeton (left) and the author rock-climbing in Baluchistan

Horse lines in camp: Hodson's Horse in Baluchistan

Hodson's Horse cavalry patrol, North West Frontier, 1938

Tribesman, Baluchistan

Boat dwellers, Mancha Lake

The Loralai Brigade: a picket, Baluchistan

'B' Squadron, Hodson's Horse, watering horses: Baluchistan 1938

The author as Master of the South Westmeath Hunt, 1938/39

We were in India, not England. We did not have nice green turf on which to train our horses. Our parade ground was an enormous flat area with a hard gravelly surface. There, very early on in his training, my remount took fright at something – or pretended to take fright – and bolted. I whipped the lunging rein round my wrist, and went after him, stumbled and fell, and was dragged on my back across the gravelly surface. He didn't get away, but I had on only a thin khaki shirt, and my back and arms were badly lacerated. It was thought best that I should go and get tidied up at our little Cavalry School hospital which was presided over by an Irish doctor named Slaughter.

Having examined me, he said, 'There'd be a power of horses down there on the parade ground, wouldn't there?' I agreed that there had been 'a power of horses' using the parade ground for donkey's years. 'In that case', he said, 'I think we ought to give you an anti-tetanus injection.' To my amazement, he went to the trouble of getting an old rag and some surgical spirit and disinfecting my arm – an altogether unexpected refinement. Then, in silent contemplation, he selected a large syringe and plunged it into a nondescript cobwebby bottle that he took out of a cupboard. He then advanced upon me with this weapon and, as he was about to dig it into my arm, he broke his silence. In an almost gleeful voice, he imparted to me a piece of clinical enlightenment that he had so far withheld. 'Do you know,' he said, 'this injection has a very queer effect on some people. I was givin' it to a feller one day, and he was dead before I had the needle out of him.' And, with that, in went the rather blunt implement.

Sure enough, I did not feel very well for twenty-four hours, but I was luckier. I survived.

Training a young horse was only one element in a very comprehensive course. We studied and discussed very aspect of horsemastership – stabling in and out of doors, grooming, feeding, shoeing, saddling, bitting, watering, equestrian gear and so on. My notebook on horsemastership is twice the size of my notes on training a young horse.

We did not, of course, train our own personal and private horse entirely in accordance with the practices of troop-horse training. Equitation being an art, we each had our own ideas. It was my view, for instance – and some might have thought it wrong – that horses are all the better for being jacks of all trades. Mine, at all events, had to do everything. A polo pony would not just play polo: he would race, show jump, pig-stick, perform well at haute école, tent-peg, hunt, hack, and do anything else that suited both me and him, and I think horses enjoyed that varied life.

In addition to all our equestrian work at Saugor, we also did a very comprehensive veterinary course – another very full notebook. And on top of all that, we practised every form of equitation. The instructors demonstrated what was accepted practice at that time and we, even if we had reservations, did our best to emulate them.

In the midst of all this activity, three weeks after the course had begun, a terrible blow fell.

On 4 October 1936 I wrote this home:

> We have just had a terrible shock. The Regiment is virtually about to be disbanded, though it may not be as bad as it looks at the moment. In order that you may understand the situation I must tell you something of the Indian Cavalry system. There are twenty-one regiments of Indian Cavalry, divided into seven groups of three regiments each. Each group has a group centre regiment for a period of about four years every twelve years. Each regiment trains its own recruits and remounts and, when the army mobilises for war, the group centre regiment remains in India, takes over all the untrained and half-trained recruits and remounts from the other two regiments, and drafts its own trained men and horses to those regiments to make them up to war strength. The system is, of course, most unsatisfactory as no regiment can be efficient going off to war with a large number of men and horses it does not know, which have been drafted in from another regiment a few days before; and the group centre regiment becomes a training depot and is at first a rabble of untrained men and horses with a very small trained staff.
>
> For a long time, there has been talk of changing the system, and at last the change is to come and, in its advent, it wipes us out, and two other regiments.
>
> The system now to be adopted is to establish three training depots to train all remounts and recruits for the Indian Cavalry, and to relieve regiments of this work. Thus, all regiments will be up to strength always in trained men and horses and ready to mobilise at once, and it will increase efficiency greatly. However, it was found impossible for financial reasons to make these three depots supernumerary to the existing number of Indian Cavalry

regiments, so it has been decided to convert three regiments into depot regiments and we, Sam Browne's Cavalry, and the 15th Lancers, and the 20th Lancers have been selected. Eighteen Indian Cavalry regiments will remain, divided into three groups of six regiments each, and each group will be served by one depot. Our depot is to be at Ferozepore in the Punjab, and the regiments in our group will be Hodson's Horse (4th), Probyn's Horse (5th), P.A.V.O. (11th Frontier Force), Guide's Cavalry (10th Frontier Force), 13th Lancers and the Scinde Horse (14th).

Some of us will be kept on at the depot, which will still retain the name of Sam Browne's Cavalry, and the rest of us will have to go to one or other of the above six regiments. However, that is really the beginning of the end, as we cannot be kept for ever at a depot and in a few years we shall all be sent to other regiments, and the depot will be run by officers seconded for terms of duty from the six regiments which it serves.

The C-in-C, I believe, wrote a very sympathetic letter to the C.O. expressing his deep regret and reluctance at taking this step which, however, he found it impossible to avoid in his efforts to increase the efficiency of the forces under his command; but he assured us that our name would remain, and that we should keep our identity. That may be so, but the Regiment we know, and have worked for, ceases to exist, and it is a very sad moment for us.

I first heard this news last Tuesday night from a bloke in the 15th Lancers who arrived here that day, having arrived late for the course, as he was in hospital. I have never had a worse shock, as there had been no rumours about it at all beforehand. Next day at polo my orderly asked me if I had heard about the fate of the Regiment. I said I had, but that I was not sure that it was really true. I asked him how he'd heard and he said that the orderly of the Sahib in the 15th Lancers had told him. He said, 'I couldn't eat last night, and couldn't sleep all night after hearing such sad news.' 'Well,' I said, 'you're not the only one; I feel just the same, and I can't really make myself believe it's true, and I expect there are a good many like us.' He has been with me nearly all the time I have been in the Regiment.

During the whole of the time that I have been with the Regiment we, the officers, have lived in greater harmony than any family. There has never been a quarrel amongst us. We all work, and none shirk. We have an extraordinary diversity of interests, but yet we are all much attached to each other, and I think this is why none of us go off seconded on 'jobs', and only go away for short periods when the pocket or some other reason demands a change. We each, I think, feel that we have had a share in building up the Regiment to the efficient machine it is today.

The same friendly spirit exists between us and the men. We have taken great pains to know them well, and to do all we can for them and they, in return, have trusted us and worked hard and willingly. It is very seldom that we have any crime, and it is an uncommon thing to see a man up before his Squadron Commander for any offence. The men and the Indian officers are as cut up over the end of all this labour and friendship as we are. I feel that it is terribly hard on many of them. There are many men in whom I have a close personal interest, whom I have trained and promoted and set on the path to higher rank. Some of those who are endowed with unusual qualities I had hoped as time went on to be able to help on to the highest ranks they could reach. There, I have no doubt, they would have had an opportunity to prove their full worth. Many of them will now I suppose have to go, and all the faithful work they have done for me will bring them little reward, and I am sure that their disappointment will be as keen as mine.

I don't suppose we ever before quite realised how much a home the Regiment was to us. We often talked in mess of the fact of Regimental soldiering becoming boring, and the necessity for change, and we have all planned at one time or another to go off to the Frontier or elsewhere but, in the end, we have always agreed that life in the Regiment is best, and so we have stayed, and we now have no one seconded except one staff college graduate doing his tour of staff duty. This is not so in other regiments where officers often take the first opportunity to get away on a job. I gather that the others now feel as I do, homeless in India – with no centre, no real comfortable home where all are old and faithful friends down to the lowest of the humblest followers.

I have just motored from Saugor to Jubblepore, in my old 30/98 Vauxhall, in torrents of rain and stayed the night with Branfoot. The Regiment were all in good form, but of course all very cut up about the reorganisation.

They move to Ferozepore in the Punjab near Lahore in April and then the depot will be formed and the show will, I suppose, break up during the summer. This will be a big job as it will entail a terrific amount of work on paper. I shall get to Ferozepore in the middle of May or early June and, if the work looks very heavy, I shall cancel my leave again and lend a hand. However, that's a good long way off yet.

I am now in Calcutta for my Urdu interpretership exam. The rain through which I had driven to Jubblepore had persisted for a week and was widespread and had caused extensive flooding. The whole country is flooded. It is caused by a huge cyclone which has been raging in the Arabian Sea for the last week, and I dare say it fits in with the terrible storms round the U.K. and in the Atlantic Ocean, which are recorded in the newspapers.

It is strange to think what a great difference financially a few days' rain out of season in a country like this can made. Whether in this case the difference will be loss or profit, I am not in a position to say. In the Central Provinces the crops are just sown, and in two days the young green shoots, just appearing from the ground, grew several inches. The farmers say that they think the crop is ruined as the roots will be too weak to bear this rapid growth and, when the sun comes out, everything will wither and die. The next few days will prove them right or wrong; however, their loss will not amount to the total loss of a ripe crop, as there is still time to sow again, and the loss will be the price of the seed.

Here in Bengal everything is different. Coming along in the train this morning I came through miles and miles of rice crops; rice, nothing but rice, as far as the eye could see. It is, I think, the most beautiful of all crops, and I had not seen it since I left Bolarum. It is ripening now and, although some of it had been damaged by the rain, most of it was standing and looked good. I don't think the rain has been so heavy in Bengal, and here in Calcutta itself there has been none. The heat is awful and the humidity very high, and everyone is praying for rain to lower the temperature, or sunshine to disperse the clouds and dry up the air a bit.

The Urdu interpretership exam in Calcutta involved an amusing incident. There were only two candidates, myself and an Indian, a Hindu.

Interpretership exams covered more than the language. There were questions on relevant history, religion, customs and so on, and all questions had to be answered in the language of the exam.

The oral exam took place before the written exam. The first candidate was the Hindu and, when he had finished his oral, I followed. Old

Colonel Boyle invigilated, and an Indian *munshi* (teacher) did the examining. In one question I was asked to describe one of the annual Hindu festivals. Although I was aware of its annual occurrence, I happened to know singularly little about it, and so gave a somewhat indifferent answer to the question.

When my oral was over, I rejoined the other candidate in the ante-room, and he asked me how I had got on. I told him that I had been somewhat stumped by that question. Surprisingly, he said, 'So was I.'

When Colonel Boyle came and joined us before the written exam, I said to him jokingly that I thought it an unfair question. If Mahado Singh (or whatever his name was), a good Hindu, didn't know the answer, how could I, a poor Christian, be expected to do so?

Colonel Boyle said, 'All right; consider that question expunged and I'll ask you another, and you can answer in any language you like – English, French, German, Italian, Latin, Greek, Hindustani, Persian, Arabic. What do you know of the Epiphany?'

'All right,' I said, 'you win.'

Anyway, both Mahado Singh and I made up for it in the written exam and received our qualification.

Starting work at Saugor, as we did, very early in the morning, and working through to a late lunch with a breakfast break, and then working again in the evening after dark at the academic aspects of our studies, I suppose we worked about an eight-hour day, five days a week. The weekends were free. The afternoons were traditionally, in the Army in India, a time for recreation. It both kept people physically fit, and helped to prevent the boredom that can result from repetitive peacetime training. I think that, during the nine months of the course, we also got a couple of spells of a week or ten days' leave.

In addition to the work at Saugor, therefore, we also had a lot of fun. Racing, both flat races and steeplechases, pig-sticking, polo, small game shooting, tiger shooting – I recall at least one tiger, because it came back to Saugor in the back of my motor car. I also – and I recruited some others – revived my Sandhurst idea of being ready to play any game, against any opponents, at any time, at the drop of a hat. I recall, for instance, playing in a soccer match – I think I had not played since I was at my prep school. Our star performer was a former member of the Eton XI who had now, however, grown somewhat bandy-legged from years in the saddle.

I had now been officially posted to Hodson's Horse but not yet transferred. This was very satisfactory as it was the regiment I wanted to go to, and it would be on the North West Frontier. There were still three months of the course remaining, after which I hankered for the Himalayas again if I could get some leave.

Such of my letters as have survived reflect little of the developing situation in Europe but in February 1937 I thanked my mother for a leading article in the *Irish Times* she had sent me about Hitler, and I commented: 'The voting of £1,500 million for defence purposes in Britain must have made Hitler & Co. sit up. It should help to keep the peace of the world for a good few years to come, and it puts us in our right place again.' A year earlier I could not see why there was so much fuss over Hitler's activities.

I suppose I could have been regarded as a reasonable, run-of-the-mill, young military officer who kept himself adequately aware of current affairs. I belonged to both the Royal United Services Institute and the United Service Institute of India, and read their journals, and other civil and military journals, the *Spectator*, for instance, and the *Army Quarterly*, but nevertheless it seems clear from my comment on the £1,500 million defence expenditure that I underestimated the threat of war. I was not alone.

One Sunday morning at Saugor we went pig-sticking. The pig were known to be on a long, rocky, thick and thorny ridge which the beaters would beat. We had three heats of three spears each, lined along the foot of the ridge. The three spears in the left-hand heat, from left to right, were Dennis Voelcker of The Deccan Horse, David Garforth-Bles of the Guides Cavalry, and myself.

The beat had not been long started when a boar came off our end of the ridge going very fast, and we were on it immediately going full gallop. It was a lunatic country to be riding in at that pace; absolutely blind, long grass up to our withers, thorn bushes, and hidden rocks galore. Sometimes we could see the pig; sometimes we could see only the swathe of grass moving in front of us as he galloped through it. I had him for a few moments on the right of the line. Then he jinked left across our front and Dennis Voelcker picked him up and went off to the left with David Garforth-Bles after him on his right. Then I lost them altogether. All I knew was that they had gone off somewhere to the left, and I wondered if they had gone into a hidden *nullah*. I cast about looking for them, and then I found them – pig and all – in a well. The going was so thick that even the pig hadn't seen it in time, but had gone in head first, with Dennis Voelcker and his horse on top of him.

The well was open and circular, perhaps fifteen feet in diameter, and lined with rough blocks of rock. The water was only six or eight feet below ground level. Dennis Voelcker, who was wearing a short-sleeved khaki shirt, had hit the far wall of the well with his left elbow which was smashed with a compound break, the broken bones sticking out through the flesh. The horse was alive, and little damaged except for a large graze on its rump. The pig was swimming.

The moment David found them, he plunged into the well and speared the pig. There were some rough lumps of rock sticking out of the lining of the well which served as steps down to the water. David tethered the horse's head with its reins to one of these. By the time I got there, he was trying to get Voelcker out of the well. That we succeeded in doing, and I went to rustle up some help and to get someone to go back to the horse-lines for a horse sling to pull the horse out of the well. Help came, we got the sling, and we sent Dennis Voelcker back to the little Saugor hospital.

We were a hardy lot, hard on ourselves, not soft on each other, and not interested in, or impressed by, heroics. Had we been, I suppose David Garforth-Bles would have been a hero. But as it was, he was told that the sling had arrived and, as he was already wet, he had better go in again and do the job. So in he went, and dived under the horse and fitted the sling. We probably gave him a *shahbash* and that was all. I suppose we ought to have recommended him for an Albert Medal. Meanwhile we pulled the horse out without much trouble, and it proved not to be much damaged beyond the grazed rump. And, last of all, we got out the pig.

The small Saugor hospital could not deal with a wound like Dennis Voelcker's. They dressed it as well as they could, and he was then put in a motor car and driven to the nearest general military hospital which was at Jubblepore, 120 miles away. There he arrived at lunch time. The two young doctors on duty at the hospital found his arm going gangrenous already. They decided to amputate it, put him on the operating table and gave him an anaesthetic but at the same time sent a message to the medical colonel in charge of the hospital who was out at a Sunday lunch party. He, good man, leaving his curry on his plate, went post-haste to the hospital and asked the young doctors what they were proposing to do. They said there was only one thing they could do – amputate the arm, or he would die. The colonel said that if they did that without warning him, it would very likely kill him. He had had one hell of a shock already. He would hardly survive another like waking up to find his arm gone. They must let him come round again and tell him what they proposed.

They did, but Dennis refused to have his arm off. He would risk dying with it, but was not prepared to live without it. So they had to do their best with scraping and cleaning and removing bits, and disinfecting and dressing. To the great credit of the hospital both Dennis and his arm survived, but the arm was permanently bent and stiff thereafter, though it didn't put an end to his equestrian or military life.

We had our own racecourse at Saugor, and we rode both flat races and steeplechases. That, of course, was only amateur racing, but there was also a flourishing professional racing industry in India, in which some Indian Cavalry officers rode as amateurs. Branfoot was one of them, and he knew many of the professional racing fraternity well. One was a former trooper in one of the British cavalry regiments who bought himself out of the Army, and set up as a racehorse trainer. He had a very good understanding of horses, and succeeded. Let us call him Jack. Branfoot got to know him, and one evening Jack and his wife asked Branfoot back to supper in their bungalow. The conversation naturally centred on horses and racing.

Branfoot said to Jack, 'That little chestnut mare, Golden Bough, that you had at one time was something of a disappointment. She was well bred, and a nice-looking horse, but never seemed to do any good.'

'No,' Jack replied, 'her trouble was that she was temperament.'

His wife, who was better educated than he was, corrected him. 'You mean temperamental, Jack.'

'What I mean', said Jack, 'was that you never knew what the hell the bloody little bitch was going to do next.'

One of the Saugor tests was the cross-country ride. We were taken by train to some outlying place with our horses, and arrived after dark. Next morning, armed with map and compass, we were sent off individually, at several minutes' interval, to find our way back to Saugor. We were in full battle order and had a long way to go. Marks were given for the length of time we took – the shorter the time, the higher the marks – and then for our own condition, the condition of our equipment and, above all, the condition of our horses on arrival. We took a variety of routes home, and some of us were more fortunate than others in the state of the route we chose.

I think, as in pig-sticking, it was the horse, not the rider, which gained the honours; and not long ago I was reminded of what I had long forgotten, that my horse won. It was superb across country, and wonderfully economical of its own strength and energy. It never fussed, and would never have let anyone drive it too hard. I have little doubt that it must have ended the cross-country test looking as fresh as a daisy, and honoured me by carting me along with it.

About six weeks before the end of the Cavalry School course, I had a polo accident which resulted in a very badly dislocated right shoulder, and I was kept in bed in the Saugor hospital for a few days. Daphne Vigors, the wife of the Commandant, Colonel Mervyn Vigors, came to see me. She was a sweet person, and one of the best of the many good influences at Saugor.

'You're a disgrace,' she said to me.

'Why me?' I asked. 'What have I done? I'm no worse than anyone else.'

'I don't mean just you. I mean all of you. Every course there has ever been has always put on some entertainment for us all – a concert or pantomime or something. From what I hear – or don't hear – your lot aren't doing a thing.'

She knew that, as I was given to freelance writing, here was something to take my mind off a period of forced inactivity which was really irksome to someone used to the vigorously active life that we led at the Cavalry School. I began then and there to write with my unaccustomed left hand the whole of the libretto for songs, recitations, sketches, jokes and so on for a topical pantomime, largely laughing at ourselves and our instructors.

Improbably, I found quite a wealth of talent among our bunch of cavalry cowboys. Ruling the chorus with a rod of iron was our pianist, the diminutive wife of the commanding officer of a local Indian infantry regiment. She was half the size of the smallest of us; but a martinet when it came to rebuking us for a wrong note or faulty timing.

The programme was deliberately opera bouffe and could hardly fail to be a success with a captive audience that enjoyed being burlesqued. The King's Shropshire Light Infantry (KSLI) who were at Kamtee, not far away, and whom I had known well in Rawalpindi, kindly lent me their dance band of eight musicians for a week, under the command of their band corporal. He and I arranged to have an ensemble overture of popular tunes before the beginning of the programme, and again during the interval, and one solo in each of the two parts of the programme. Daphne Vigors was good enough to say that the whole performance exceeded her wildest expectations.

On 15 April 1937 I wrote home to report that, because I had not had privilege leave for three years, I had been granted three months' leave. I had intended to spend it tiger hunting in the jungle but, as I could not shoot with my right arm in a sling, I would walk in the Himalayas instead.

The course over, I wrote to our Chief Instructor to thank him for all he had done for us. He sent me a charming acknowledgement. His name was 'Lakri' Wood, a Gunner major, a marvellous horseman, enormously vital and intelligent, and the best of good company. (Anyone named Wood in India was liable to become 'Lakri', the Hindustani word for 'wood'.) Less than four months later he was dead – killed by a tiger. Many of us lost a good and cherished friend, and the country lost a potentially fine general.

16
Bound for the Mountains

For my Himalayan leave I had planned a 1,000-mile walk from Simla to Srinagar in Kashmir. I proposed to take the so-called Hindustan-Tibet Road – for the most part an excellent mule track – from Simla north-eastwards to the Tibet border – some 200 miles; and then to turn north into Spiti and Ladakh up to the point where the Indus river crosses the Tibet border, and then to follow the line of the Indus westwards into Kashmir. That would take me through some of the highest and most barren country in the Himalayas, and would be a very agreeable three-months' walk with enough difficulties and problems to make it interesting and worthwhile. I proposed also to take with me Jane, a four-month-old Alsatian puppy.

I wrote to Thakru, my Kulu valley henchman on my former Himalayan trip, and asked him to come with me. This was his reply. He was illiterate. He had got someone to write the letter for him in English, and he had signed it with his thumb print:

> Village Aleo P.O. Manali
> Kulu. 18 April 1937

Sir,

    I received your letter from the Postmaster Manali yesterday and I am very pleased to hear that you are kind enough to engage me again for which I thank you greatly. Yes I shall be in Simla on the 15th May if you will please tell me when and where I am to come and report to you. As regards mule arrangements I suggest that if we took Kulu pack ponies and engage them at or near Simla it will be very cheap and good because I hear that the mule hire near Simla is something like Rs.3/- per stage. While I can get much cheaper pack from this side and we can then proceed towards Spiti or wherever you may wish to go. Therefore will you please let me know before the 15th how many ponies or mules would be required for the trip. If you remember a young mule man called Ashgar Ali who took him from Manali to Losar that young man is very strong reliable and very cheerful I hear he is going to Simla to visit his brother and on his way he could be engaged by you for the trip and I can speak to him on my way to Simla. It is very kind of you to bring me new boots for which I am very grateful and thank you very much. Also will you kindly send me some money to pay for my trip to Simla and buy few things here for the journey.

I am dear Sir.

Your most obedient Servant.

Thakru Shikari

'Rs.' is an abbreviation for rupees. The value of a rupee at that time was about one shilling and sixpence. In today's currency it would perhaps be £3.00, but would have up to three times that purchasing value in India.

In order to go into the High Himalayas, I had to get a pass to cross the so-called 'Inner Line' which in effect included the high passes nearest to the remainder of the Indian subcontinent. Licences and passes were also needed for other purposes. On my earlier visit to Kulu, I applied to the Kulu district officer's office for a licence to fish for trout in the Beas river. That resulted in my receiving the following letter from a typically considerate and diligent Indian subordinate in the sub-district officer's office:

Kulu, 9 August 1930

Sir,

When still I was in my bed today morning My Dear God reminded me that you forgot to sign on the fishing license and also forgot to write the word *Esquire*. I at once awoke up and saw the office copy and found the mistake. I regret very much it was due to a great botheration in the day time. Trust you will not mind it.

I am enclosing a duplicate license to avoid inconvenience.

I beg to remain,

Sir,

Your most obedient servant,

Namak Chand

S.D.O's Office

Kulu

There is surely nothing unkind in having a laugh at other people's efforts with English. I hope others have had a laugh at my efforts with their language. One of my favourites is that of the retired man from the

East who annually had an exchange of correspondence at Christmas time with his former faithful servant whose mother had been the family washerwoman.

One of the old servant's letters began sadly:

Respected master,
    Before I impart to you any more about my news, you will I faithfully believe, be grieved to learn that the hand that rocked the cradle has now kicked the bucket ...'

I reached Simla on 17 May 1937. Bill Birnie, in my Regiment, who was doing a job in Army Headquarters, and his wife, Sally, kindly put me up in their flat.

In the Simla bazaar we were able to get all the stores we wanted. I decided to stick to the same rather dull and monotonous fare as on the last trip because, although we had lost weight, we all remained healthy, and the things we took with us did not go bad and stood up to a fair amount of wetting and other hazards. The staple elements were sacks of onions, dried apple rings, potatoes and rice. We also had raisins and a small quantity of delicacies to relieve the total boredom of the diet. Two additional important elements were wholemeal flour, which we had to do our best to keep dry, and this time considerably more well-salted meat than the last time as I was not going to be able to shoot with a heavy rifle with my dislocated shoulder.

I chose to start my journey into the Himalayan hinterland by the Hindustan-Tibet Road both because it took me to where I wanted to go – to the southern end of the Western Tibet border with India – and because there is a beckoning romance about the Hindustan-Tibet Road like, for instance, the Trans-Siberian Railway. It somehow compels you to experience it if you can.

The gifted Charlotte Canning, an evocative watercolourist of India and wife of Lord Canning, Viceroy of India at the time (1860), decided to trek part of the way up the Hindustan-Tibet road. She marvelled at the great peaks of the Himalayas when she got among them, and only regretted that she had not done more to record them with her brush. She wrote a very long letter to her friend Queen Victoria with a detailed account of her trek. The Queen wrote on it 'Very dangerous'. Mountains are always dangerous, but the Hindustan-Tibet Road hardly deserved the Queen's verdict when I traversed it in 1937, though it remained no less dramatic and interesting.

The road followed the River Sutlej which runs for almost the whole of its course through a deep gorge flanked by precipitous mountains. This made for fine scenery but an almost total absence of suitable camping sites; and such flat ground as there was which was not under cultivation was soiled by the flocks of goats and sheep which moved up the Road in the early summer.

Transport animals were very hard to find and exceedingly expensive. As there was practically no grazing for them, you had to buy their fodder in the villages. Water was very scarce and supplies almost unobtainable, though a little milk and a few eggs could be bought at some villages. The one commodity that was plentiful was firewood.

I had excellent weather except for a little rain during the first thirty miles from Simla, which at least kept us cool. The average shade temperature at 5 p.m. was over 70°F; the lowest night temperature was 50°F. The highest day shade temperature was 100°F, at Rampur.

A journey up the Hindustan-Tibet Road is without doubt one of the easiest and most pleasant ways of seeing almost every type of Himalayan scenery. The road divides itself into three phases. From Simla to Narkunda – forty miles – the country is typical of the outer Himalayas, the 'Hills'. The saddle in the ridge at Narkunda is really the gateway to the major ranges of the Himalayas, then, a hundred miles further on, at Chini, the Sutlej bursts through the granite core of the outer ranges and the densely forested snow-capped peaks give way to the barren rock-strewn wastes of the Tibet plateau.

To get the best of this journey, the traveller should not go to the very end of the road at Shipki La, the pass on the Tibet border. He should stop at Namgia, a few miles short of Shipki, and cross to the north bank of the Sutlej. He should then go two days' march up the Spiti river to Chango. These two marches are superb. Then, not forgetting his camera, he should climb, in the dark hours of the early morning, the 5,000 feet or so to the snow line above Chango. That view alone will compensate him for all the hardships he may have endured on the journey from Simla.

After two days in Simla, we started our march early on the morning of 18 May 1937, with a baggage train of ten mountain ponies. The first three days' marching took us through, and well beyond, the barrier at Narkunda. Up until then, I hardly felt that I was properly in the mountains. Fine as the scenery was, it was not the High Himalayas, and the influence of Simla could be felt everywhere. However, as soon as we reached the ridge at Narkunda and looked out across the Sutlej valley

5,000 feet below, to the massive snow mountains which shone as clear as crystal in the morning sun, I felt that we were on the threshold of the land of *Om mani padme hum.*

From Narkunda we marched steadily downhill through a fairyland of deodar forests, huge sweet-smelling pines, growing thick on the precipitous mountainside. Thakru and I walked all the way together and he told me of his adventures during the past six years. His Hindustani had improved enough for us to be able to converse fluently. He had been shooting and trekking with all sorts of people; and I was glad to hear that most of the officers who had employed him were tough enough to cope with these mountain regions.

Jane the puppy was doing well. I thought she would soon tire of running along behind me, and that I should have to put her up on top of the baggage. However, she showed no signs of distress and, after a meal and a good sleep, was soon up and rampaging round the camp. One evening when a large and very fierce-looking dog appeared, about three-quarters Tibetan mastiff, Jane went for him with all hackles up and showed him quite definitely where he got off. I assisted him in making up his mind with a well-aimed chunk of rock; and he took the hint and cleared off.

At Thanedar, a march beyond Narkunda, Thakru and I were waiting for the transport to catch up with us, and to pitch camp. We were chatting with a group of men there, and I asked if there was any influential man in the village. They replied that the most important man in those parts was an American who had settled down in the village and owned a good deal of property in the vicinity; 'and this', they said, pointing to a small boy dressed as a Hindu gentleman, 'is his son.' 'He has presumably married a local lady?' I said. 'Yes,' they replied, he had.

I started talking to the boy, who was aged about twelve, bright and forthcoming, and far more intelligent than the remainder of the onlookers. He knew no English, he said, though he could make fair headway with reading it; his Urdu, however, spoken with a Punjab or Pahari (hill) accent, was delightful.

He was interested in Jane, and asked me whether I'd like to come to his house to see his Alsatian puppy. So when our transport had arrived and I had put on clean clothes, I was glad of the opportunity to have a look at the American who had had so Indian a son, even with the help of an Indian lady. Having climbed the hill, I found the boy playing with his dog outside the back of his house. He took me inside and introduced me to his father.

I had half expected to find a hearty backwoodsman in check shirt and corduroy trousers, so it was with considerable surprise that I found myself greeted by a small, neat, scholarly-looking man, dressed like his son in the clothes usually worn by a Hindu gentleman of good estate. His voice was pleasant and cultured. The room into which I was shown was low and beamed, with crowded bookshelves from ceiling to floor. There were only two chairs, one in which he sat with his back to the window and the other in which he asked me to be seated, facing him, and from which I could get a view of the snow mountains through the window behind him.

I soon managed to discover his interests, chiefly philosophy – currently principally the Vedic Philosophy – and history, and so the conversation ran along through Marcus Aurelius and the Sufi philosophers to the Sanskrit and the Pahlavi languages and the Arian origin, to modern Persian nationalism and thus to the awakening of a national spirit in India. When we reached the subject of Indian nationalism, of course we also touched on the matter of British imperialism and our rule of India.

At this point he launched into a strong criticism of the police, and told me a story of an unfortunate local girl of uncertain moral character who was married to a young farmer. They found it difficult to agree, so they decided to part. In these mountain districts, in a case of incompatibility, the two parties could agree to differ, dissolve the marriage and go their separate ways. In this case the girl returned home and lived with her parents. However, after some months it appeared that she was pregnant with a child which could not be her husband's. The girl was anyway quite neurotic and this calamity and shame, coming close upon the disturbing affair of parting from her husband, caused her one day to slip unnoticed from the house, drop down the mountain into the valley below and throw herself into the Sutlej where she was drowned.

For several days her relations looked vainly for her and eventually her body was discovered some miles down the river lying just awash among some stones on the river bank. The place was such that there was no chance of performing the full Hindu funeral rites of burning the body, and committing the ashes to the river, so her relations burned some grass and twigs over her and then placed the body back in the water and covered it with stones.

When the police came to hear of the tragedy, they arrested the girl's father and mother and three other male members of the family and charged them with murder. They were all still in gaol and, even if they were acquitted, the family would be financially ruined. Stokes had himself put in a plea with the police on the grounds that there was no motive for the murder. Illegitimate children, he said, were not uncommon in the hills, and brought no dishonour to the family; only to the girl herself. In Pathan country and certain strict parts of Rajputana such an occasion could be a pretext for murder, but not there in Pahari country where morals were less strict, and no doubt influenced by polyandry which was practised in some parts of the Himalayas.

Meanwhile I learned from him something of his activities. He had come to India thirty-three years before and settled here in the mountains. He had been born in Philadelphia but had not been back for the past twenty-one years; I should say he was now a man of about sixty. He told me of his political activities, and how he was a great friend of Gandhi.

He then said that he knew for a fact that many men in Indian gaols were innocent and that he had had a good opportunity to study their cases while himself serving a sentence of six months' imprisonment as a political prisoner in Lahore Central Gaol.

He rambled on about Gandhi and other Indian politicians and the necessity for, and possibility of, 'reform'. But I had soon had enough of political theory, so I made my farewells and returned to the company of the rougher men with whom my dealings for the next couple of months would be considerably more practical than theoretical. I subsequently learnt that his name was Stokes, although he had later taken a Hindu name. Despite his seemingly quiet even demeanour and civilised manner, he was a man riven with paradoxes: a Christian missionary who had turned Hindu; a British forces recruiting officer during the First World War who had then joined the pacifist anti-British Congress Party; an intellectual living in the wilds; a socialist who had become a large landowner. His time in gaol explained his anti-police prejudice.

The fourth march out of Simla, a good day in which we covered twenty miles, took us to the little town of Rampur. On the Simla side of the town was a state rest house, erected and maintained for the use of travellers by the Rajah of Basahar, the state of which Rampur was the capital. Not only was it most convenient for me to use the place, but I thought that it would actually be discourteous not to. So I wrote to the Diwan and asked if I might have permission from the Rajah to avail myself of the hospitality of the rest house. I also asked if I might have the pleasure of calling on him and His Highness. The reply came back welcoming me to the rest house and appointing the hour of 9.30 for me to see H.H.

At 9.30 a.m. I duly attended the Rajah's court. I was met by his secretary who took me in to where H.H. sat behind a table on a raised dais. He greeted me and beckoned me to be seated in a chair beside him. He was an old and very kindly-looking man with a simple manner, though a little nervous. He spoke no English, so we conversed in Hindustani. He asked me about my journey, and where I proposed to go, and for how long I should travel. He told me something of his state, and offered me any assistance I might require while travelling through it. After a short conversation I thanked him for the hospitality he had afforded me and took my leave.

I judged the moving spirit in the state to be the Diwan, whom I visited next. His court was similar to that of the Rajah, but the man himself contrasted sharply with the kindly simplicity of his master. He was obviously highly intelligent, still in early middle life, and alert and active. He spoke perfect English and had been educated at Lahore University. He was not busy he said, so I sat and talked with him for a while. He was interested in everything and spoke with some knowledge of international affairs. He was not a member of the state, but had been delegated from the Punjab Government. He told me many interesting things about the state, not least about the Baspa valley which he thought was perhaps the most beautiful valley in the world. It was overlooked by huge snow mountains and by one peak in particular named Castle Rock which changed colour throughout the day in such a way that it might be made of pure crystal.

I had returned to the rest house when about a dozen prisoners from the state prison, shackled with heavy iron shackles, arrived and did some gardening. They scratched effortlessly at the ground for an hour or so and then went away again. It struck me that if they were never required to work much harder than that their lot was not a bad one. They were very pleasant-looking, some of them boys not much more than seventeen years of age. They came again in the afternoon and sat under a pear tree for a long time and talked and laughed before going off to cut some of the grass and weeds growing in the garden, which they fed to the chowkidar's (caretaker's) cattle. They then withdrew once more, clanking their pitiful way back along the road to gaol. I wonder what crime they had committed.

We set out from Rampur early the following day. On the second day out we crossed several *nullahs*, all dropping so steeply from the snow mountains above that they were white foam all the way. Much of the road ran along precipitous cliffs, hanging almost sheer over the Sutlej 1,500 feet below, and some of the scenery was as impressive as any I have ever seen. The transport men wanted to camp at a place where two big thundering torrents met, but it was too hot, and all the ground had been fouled by goats, and anyway I wanted to get a bit further. We went on a mile or so and I met an Indian Public Works Department subordinate who was passing through. He told me to carry on for about a mile and a half and I'd find a place with plenty of room to camp and plenty of shade. He opened up a map which not only showed the various heights of places along the road but also, rather disturbingly, recorded the places where fatal accidents had occurred to Englishmen travelling along it. I noticed that two miles beyond where we had camped the previous night it said 'Sir A. Lawrence killed here in 1864' (a bridge collapsed).

The following day we dropped very steeply down into the Sutlej valley and crossed the river to the north bank by the bridge at Wungtu. I have never seen a more turbulent torrent than the Sutlej where it bursts through the Wungtu gorge. It is still a huge river which drops 2,000 feet in twenty miles, and our march that day was a wonderful experience. Thakru thought that surely the world must become inundated with all these rivers year after year flowing down to cover it.

Lawrence of Arabia, in one of his letters home from Syria, when he was doing archaeological work before the First World War, wrote: 'I wish someone would find an occupation for flies; they have too much leisure.' It was hard not to agree. At our height of eight to nine thousand feet they were still a curse, and I looked forward to getting above the fly line as we gradually ascended to fourteen and fifteen thousand.

The day following the march along the bank of the torrential Sutlej, we were in a place with plenty of grazing and we gave the ponies a day's rest. I had a number of sick people who came for relief, but I could do very little for most of them. Their case was really pitiable: there were no doctors, and no dispensary nearer than Rampur sixty-five miles away across the mountains, and most of these people were simply too poor to undertake the journey there. There was no relief and no cure for the sick unless nature could overcome the illness.

The following day we marched again. After ten miles we passed through the village of Rigi, which we had been told further down the road was famous for its *sharab* (wine), made from the grapes which grow there. Thakru spent an hour and a half buying two bottles of this *sharab* which appeared to be a very strong brandy of some sort. One of the bottles he palmed off on me and the other he kept for himself to use as medicine when he got back to Kulu. I hoped I should not have to use mine. It burnt well with a pale blue flame, but then so does methylated spirits.

This was perhaps the most spectacular part of the whole Hindustan-Tibet Road. The path was cut along the face of a cliff several thousand feet above the Sutlej; while opposite, across the river, the peaks of the Great Himalaya Range rose sheer out of the river to over 21,000 feet. Their lower slopes were thickly wooded and their summits crowned with hanging glaciers of blue ice hundreds of feet thick. In the spring you can sometimes see one of the ice avalanches which drop from these peaks, shaking the whole valley with a noise like a huge explosion.

Three miles beyond the Rigi cliffs the country opened out into the little granite-strewn plain of Chini. In the mid-nineteenth century it was proposed to establish the summer capital of India at Chini. A house for the Governor-General had been built there, and its remains and the parade ground for his bodyguard could still be seen. I believe it was abandoned because of the distance from the 'Plains' and the difficulties of getting there. Also there was hardly sufficient space to house the summer capital of the Government of India.

From now on the scenery and influence would be Tibetan. On the following day we saw the first of our *mani panni* walls and Tibetan stupas or *chortans*, archways with a tomb above them supposed to hold all that remained of some saint or holy man. The day after that we wiped another fifteen miles off the slate and I was well satisfied. We were now through the Great Himalaya Range. At 9,000 feet, the air was invigorating and marching no longer a hardship.

The influence of India was beginning to fade: we were in the land of scant beards and slant eyes, long felt boots and unwashed bodies, drums, trumpets, prayer wheels and yaks' tails; copper urns, salted tea and few women. Although we were still among pine trees, they were growing thinner; and soon we would be in country where there was no scarcity of stones, wind and water but very little else, country with a fascination all of its own.

Another two days took us to Namgia, the last village before the Tibet border. We had now left the trees behind. There were a few in the vicinity of the widely scattered villages, oases in a desert of barren mountains.

About a mile downstream of Namgia, the Spiti river joined the Sutlej coming in from the north. Its entry was magnificent, not rudely bounding down the mountainside like any common stream, but making its entrance majestically through portals of sheer rock rising 500 feet above its bed. This, you felt, was the gateway to forbidden lands.

We had now reached the end of the Hindustan-Tibet Road, but to get the full flavour of the country we were in, we decided on an additional two days' march northwards up the Tibet border. Here we no longer had a mule track – some sheep paths if we were lucky. Of the first of those days we dropped steeply from Namgia to the Sutlej, which was much smaller above the mouth of the Spiti river, and crossed by a wooden bridge built onto and off a huge rock in the middle of the river.

I really enjoyed myself travelling in wild country over real rough going. The track we came by was not seriously dangerous, but it was about as stiff as I liked from the point of view of safety. We covered only about ten miles in a day's march of just over twelve hours. The transport men worked splendidly, as they always seemed to when things got difficult. It was a good day, too, as far as the pot was concerned as I collected quantities of wild rhubarb, and also managed to get a blue rock pigeon and a chukor (red-legged partridge) with the .22 rifle which, as it had no recoil, I could manage to shoot off my right shoulder even though my right arm was still in a sling from my Saugor accident.

On the second of the two days into the Western Tibet border hinterland, we reached the village of Chango, a little green patch in the wilderness of rocks. It was just like an armchair with a seat about a mile in each direction. The seat was green with young crops, and the arms and back were brown rock. If a giant were to have sat in it, he would have rested his back against mountains going up above the snow to 18,000 feet, with his arms on lower mountains and his legs in the Spiti valley below.

I decided to spend a day or two at Chango as I did not want to weary the men and animals with continual marching. Also, kit needs repair and rearranging, and there was washing and cleaning to be done. Thakru and I felt we could leave the men to it and, with an old Tibetan out of the village who had attached himself to us, we decided to climb the mountains behind the camp – the back of the armchair.

We started at 3 a.m., and we got fairly hot, scrambling up the first thousand feet by the light of a dying moon. It was lovely, and I thoroughly enjoyed it. My wind seemed to be very good and I had no difficulty in leaving Thakru and the very nice Tibetan puffing far below. I think we must have climbed about 5,000 feet, and we got to the bottom of the snowline. I could see over Tibet, for we were on the border or very near it (if there was any real border), and I had a fine view of the huge snow range which lies along the north edge of Spiti and which I had crossed on my last expedition.

It was very cold in the wind, and in the shade, so we sought sunny slopes and as a result got very sun-scorched. We saw large flocks of burhal, all females. No doubt there was a party of rams somewhere on the mountain. Then, having spent the whole day out, we got back to camp at about 4.15 p.m. after a scramble down the mountain. Thakru and I ended with a race down about 200 feet of loose shale slope – it was like running down a moving staircase as all the slope moved with us. I managed to fetch up against a big boulder, and he only saved himself by a whisker from going into a very cold and rocky stream.

Anyone who had got as far as Chango could be satisfied that he or she had experienced not all, but a very great deal, that the Himalayas have to offer; they could turn and retrace their steps to Simla, and enjoy it all again on the homeward march. I, however, had to go on, fallen to the siren temptation of the beckoning Himalayan hinterland beyond.

I had wanted to keep going northwards as close as I could to the Western Tibet border, through Hanle, until I struck the Indus valley, but I could not get north along the Pare Chu river valley – a tributary of the Spiti river – without going into Tibet, which I had given an undertaking to the Indian authorities not to do. I was therefore forced to turn westwards up the Spiti river valley until I could find somewhere to cross the enormous mountain range along the north side of that valley. The going was very rough; we covered ten or eleven miles in nine and a half hours. There were two big torrents to cross and a smaller stream, all of which presented serious hazards.

We started by crossing the Chaladdokpo *nullah*. It would have been possible to ford it, but there was also a rickety bridge just wide enough for one animal to cross, though without any sort of protection, which the transport men thought was safe enough. Although it would save a lot of time to use the bridge, it was such an uncertain-looking contrivance that I gave my consent to make use of it with considerable reluctance. It was made of two poles supported on rocks and revetted with rough stones, with pieces of flat stone and strips of wood as its platform. We took the ponies across one by one and it quaked and shook in the most unnerving way under the weight of each animal. But we eventually got them all safely across and we climbed up the steep side of the *nullah* out onto the open mountain slope. The whole exercise took about an hour.

We then dropped steeply into the Pare Chu valley, which reeked of sulphur, an unpleasant though strangely healthy smell. The river was a mad torrent of black water perhaps twenty-five yards wide and quite unfordable. Spanning it was another shaky bridge, in worse condition and longer and more frightening than the one we had just crossed. We decided to unload all the animals, manhandle the loads across and lead the ponies over. As the third pony was nearing the far end of the bridge it slipped and fell off. It dropped some twelve or fifteen feet. Had it fallen into the water we should never have seen it again.

Just below were two large flat-surfaced rocks which converged downwards making a convenient V into which the pony fell – fortunately on its back. There it lay wedged in the V of the rocks with its legs in the air and its quarters in the stream. It was so firmly wedged that even the force of the current couldn't dislodge it. It was saved from a broken back by the fact that it still carried its pack saddle, which consisted of a number of very thick blankets attached to a rough wooden tree.

We got the pony out of its bed of rock. Its back was badly cut, and it was very shaken, but no bones were broken. It was one of two ponies I had taken on some ten marches back, to help us over what I thought would be difficult going. As our loads were now much lighter, I decided there and then to send both it and its running mate back. I therefore dressed its wounds, paid off its owner, gave him something for the damage it had sustained, and saw it safely back over the bridge and on its way to a less exacting land. Then we loaded up the rest of the ponies, who were now all safely across, and continued our march.

A couple of miles further on we reached another torrent of black water, again unfordable and crossed by a similar bridge. This however was much shorter, not more than ten yards across, but very narrow indeed. There was little danger here except that a fierce gale was blowing up the funnel through which the river ran and I considered that there was every possibility of a man or pony being blown off balance and falling into the torrent. We got the ponies across by one man holding their heads and another their tails, and thus giving support both to themselves and to the ponies. But it was a great relief to see the last man and pony, and Jane, safely on the farther shore. The toll we paid here was Thakru's plush cap, decorated with the feathers of a Monall pheasant's crest. It was swept from his head by a gust of wind and carried, bowling along the rocks, for twenty yards upstream where, after appearing once for a brief moment, it was swallowed up in the black waters. It was a small price to pay for our safe crossing.

Our troubles were by no means at an end. With some difficulty we climbed the steep side of the *nullah* and were then faced with a series of flat polished slabs of rock along which we crawled and slithered, perilously near the precipice overhanging the Spiti river below. There were only a few sheep paths to follow. The transport men were magnificent. They worked like demons and exposed themselves to considerable personal risk in order to get the ponies and kit over all the difficulties. We had one mule in the caravan, nowhere near as sure-footed as the ponies which were both more careful and more courageous.

It seemed that the only way northward out of the Spiti valley was over the Parang La Pass (18,300 feet) which I had used before. En route we would pass through the village of Dankar, the so-called capital of Spiti.

17
Ashes

The worldly hope men set their hearts upon
Turns ashes – or it prospers; and anon,
Like snow upon the Desert's dusty face
Lighting a little hour or two – is gone.

OMAR KHAYYÁM

On 10 June I was up at 5.30 as usual. The sky was very overcast and the weather looked doubtful. I felt unusually cold, but the air temperature was 40°F which is not very cold. I had a spot of breakfast and we were starting to pack up when it began to snow. The clouds were very low and heavy and soon it was snowing hard; so, having learnt from experience on the Shigri glacier that it was as well not to move in these parts in bad weather if you have any alternative, I decided to wait till the weather cleared.

The snow persisted, the clouds grew thicker and I grew colder. I piled on more clothes till I had nothing further with which to cover myself. I studied the air temperature and, as it persisted in registering 40°F, I began to doubt its accuracy; and then suddenly the fever broke. In half an hour I was reduced to a quaking lunatic, and it took four days for me to begin to feel normal again. It was a relapse of malaria, which must have been brought on by a chill. It had been nagging at me for some time. I had had it on me very slightly when I was in Simla, and again a week later for two days, but both times I managed to drug it down. This time I had no real warning and anyway I don't think I could have stopped it. The good fortune was that it snowed that morning and kept me from packing up camp, for had it come on while we were on the march I should have been in a real fix: there might have been nowhere to camp, no water and nothing to burn and it took only a very few minutes for me to be in a condition in which I was unable to move, let alone walk.

I supposed that hill men would be familiar with malaria. It was therefore curious that when the fever was on me and I was lying with my whole body shaking with uncontrollable ague, struggling to breathe (at 13,000 feet), they crowded round the door of my tent seemingly convinced that I was about to die.

I had now completed one third of my journey, but was forced to the reluctant decision that it would be irresponsible to go on. I was too weak to walk and would have to have had some animal to ride at least for several days. The next camp would be at 18,000 feet and very cold and might cause another serious occurrence of malaria. Indeed my temperature never dropped to normal for the next fortnight. To go on, too, meant going into higher and more difficult country. It was not fair on the men to expect them to get me out of that if I became incapacitated with illness. I decided, therefore, to make for the Kulu valley. Even that meant ten days to a fortnight's very rough marching, river fording, two high passes, and the Shigri glacier once more. But in Kulu I would be at only 6,000 feet; it would be warm; and I could get plenty of fresh healthy food.

So after we had broken camp at Dankar on 14 June we marched for several days to Losar at the east end of the Spiti valley. I had a temperature and was feeling ill all the way.

One day Thakru breakfasted with the village *lambadar*, whom he knew, and was given a Tibetan mastiff puppy not more than six weeks old, a sweet little thing, just a ball of yellow wool. They are fine dogs. It is said that one is a match for a wolf, and two will bay up and kill a leopard. They are the dogs that the hill shepherds use to mind their sheep. Thakru's was fearless, as cross as blazes and a most independent little article. He would stop and investigate any smells he fancied without any fear of being left behind, deviate from the path whenever he saw an inviting stream, and swear with wrath whenever my Jane wanted to play with him. He was really a most amazing little animal, with terrific conceit and self-confidence; beside him Jane looked quite the lady, though she often couldn't resist the temptation of pulling his ears just for the fun of hearing his bad language.

We had a day's halt at Losar to prepare for the five or six days' march it would probably take us to get through the rugged Chandra valley where the going was extremely hard over very steep, boulder-strewn mountainsides, with no villages, no supplies to be had, and nothing to burn except sheep and goats' dung. We decided to take wood with us. Most of the wood which was burnt in Spiti was Tibetan gorse. It had to be fetched from great distances to the villages as it was very scarce.

On the following day we crossed the Kunzam pass (14,000 feet) into Lahoule, then, next day, we covered the fifteen miles that brought us into the valley of the Chandra river. There we encamped a mile or two from the Shigri glacier. It was a magnificent bit of country. The mountains of Lahoule for their wild and rugged glory would be hard to surpass. Everywhere there are high snow peaks, many of them about 20,000 feet, and glaciers. The Shigri glacier is superb. This huge river of ice rolls 10,000 feet from the high peaks into the bed of the Chandra river. I believe that a century and a half ago the ice did not reach as low as it does now but was piled up higher up the valley. The pressure of ice eventually became so intense that it suddenly burst away from the rocky mountainsides supporting it. Millions of tons of ice and debris dropped into the Chandra valley, which is nearly half a mile wide, completely blocking the flow of the river. A lake formed and this in its turn burst through the dam of ice which held it and the flood did untold damage further down the valley.

We crossed the Shigri glacier safely. It had altered very noticeably since I was last there, and the course of the Shigri river, which is a river of considerable size which flows from the glacier, had quite changed. The ice had receded a lot and the river had cut its way through the end of the glacier. We were able to take quite a different route from the one we took previously and, instead of going across the ice, kept down along the bed of the Chandra river. We then forded the Shigri river where it divided into a number of streams, the deepest of which was about three feet deep and very rapid. After this we had to cross a shoulder of ice strewn with boulders which, though there was only about 300 yards of it, took an hour and a half.

We had now said goodbye to the Tibetans. They are cheerful people and in many ways attractive. I think they are very honest – you could camp down anywhere near a Tibetan village and leave your kit lying all over the place, go to sleep at night and not a thing would be missing in the morning. A Tibetan could gather firewood, stack it in a heap on the mountainside and leave it there for a month. No one would touch a single twig. Not that a thief could escape detection for long where the population was so small.

In Spiti there were more women than men, but the custom of polyandry was nevertheless practised. The women, however, unlike the women of Lahoule, were not 'queens'. In Spiti they did most of the work, while the men must have drunk a good deal of the proceeds. (I call the people of Spiti Tibetans. Strictly speaking they were Bots, but they wore Tibetan costume, spoke the Tibetan language and had the same religion.)

On 21 June we crossed two streams large enough to cause us diffi-culty. Over both there were now footbridges which did not exist before.

They consisted merely of two or three rough beams of wood with their ends resting on a rock each side of the water and a deck of a few loose flat stones; even a tightrope walker might have been excused a slight feeling of nervousness when crossing them. The day before a Kangra shepherd had come up the valley with a flock of goats and two of his animals lost their footing crossing the Puti Runi footbridge. They fell into the water and were seen no more.

The going in the valley seemed even worse than it was before. There had been a number of fresh avalanches and here and there the mountainside was covered with fresh-fallen blocks of granite which caused us some delay. Nor could we cross the torrent coming down the Hampta *nullah*, but we hoped the water would be low enough to let us cross in the morning because the snow above would have stopped melting during the night. The transport men were very keen to get across that evening as there was some brushwood on the far side, whereas there was nothing to burn where we were. However, we decided that it would be madness to try to ford the stream. About three hundred yards above the camp was a snow bridge over the torrent. It looked rather thin and the transport men queried whether they should risk it or not. I told them I wouldn't hear of it. There was no possible excuse for risking the lives of men or animals just for the sake of a bit of firewood when we could probably ford the river quite safely in the morning. As I was speaking, about half the snow bridge collapsed into the water and was instantly carried away on the flood.

When I awoke the next morning I knew from the thunder of the Hampta river that there was no hope of our fording it. I went and looked at it. It had fallen two or three feet during the night, but anyone trying to ford it would certainly have been drowned. The only thing was to try the snow bridge above. It had lasted during the night, but was obviously on the point of collapse and I am sure it didn't last another day. There was not much of it left, but we inspected it and decided that although there was some risk, it would be unlikely to break before midday when the water in the river would have risen sufficiently to pound it from below and the sun would have softened it on top. It was fairly thick, probably two or three feet in the middle and about eight or ten feet at the edge.

I thought that to cross it was a reasonable risk and the men agreed with me. I said I would go first with a specially heavily laden pony. Feroze Din, my maverick who, in Shakespeare's words, was 'bloody, bold and resolute', insisted on coming with me. I argued that it would be foolish to have his extra weight on the bridge, but said he could come next. When I got to the far side and found that we couldn't get off until we had ramped up the crevice between the snow and the bank, by clawing down rocks off the bank, I called him across, without a pony, to help.

After we had got the whole caravan across, we moved on to a place where we could adjust the animals' loads. I looked back in time to see another lump of the snow bridge break off and disappear into the torrent. It was a wholly wrong decision to cross the snow bridge; a quite unwarrantable ghastly risk, and I can only have taken it because I was sick. The alternative was to go perhaps 5,000 feet up the mountain and cross above the source of melting snow which was causing the torrent. But I was too ill to face the climb. To get the ponies up 5,000 feet of very steep rock-strewn mountainside also presented problems which I may not have felt I could face. But the right course would have been to contrive to get up to the snow and to cross there. Perhaps the moral is that sick men should not be in a decision-making role.

After a long day's march we crossed the Rotang Pass and dropped down into Manali at the head of the Kulu valley. My temperature was 101°. Our worst problem was the absolute impossibility of obtaining supplies. The traveller must live on poor fare and be content to eat monotonous and badly cooked food, because his fires of wet dung will not be hot enough to cook it well. At the same time he is subjected to severe physical strain.

In the outer Himalayas, that is to say those parts to the south of the big snow ranges, the people are for the most part cultivators. In some valleys, such as Kulu, they were rich, and in others, such as the Sutlej valley, they found it a hard struggle to make a livelihood. The chief products of this area are rice, barley, maize, fruit and timber. Of these all are cultivated and marketed privately except the timber, the forests for the most part being either owned or leased by the Indian Government Forest Department. The problem of transporting the timber from this area of steep mountains and deep valleys to the plains was often difficult, but for the most part it was accomplished by a combination of floating down the rivers and hauling down the steep mountainsides by wire ropeways.

The greatest hardship suffered by the people of those mountains was lack of medical comforts and assistance. Although there was acute poverty in some parts, few people were really in want of either food or fuel, but for the sick and diseased there was little hope. Missionaries and private individuals have established dispensaries all over India and have undoubtedly done much in this way to alleviate suffering.

Nevertheless the outer Himalayan people were on the whole cheerful, intelligent and good-natured. They neither overworked nor were unduly idle. I noticed that all the men smoked the *hookah* and I asked if any non-smokers were ever to be found in the hills. I was told that all men smoked whether they liked it or not, and if a man did not smoke a *hookah* he would be regarded with considerable suspicion. I asked why. They said that smoking a *hookah* was a pleasant form of relaxation. If a man did not smoke it, the inference would be that he was so intent on his work that he could find no time to smoke. And if any man was so hard-working himself, he would demand as much if not more work from anyone whom he might employ and thus the vicious circle of overwork would begin. Smoking a *hookah*, it should be mentioned, is a whole time job and cannot be combined with any activity other than talking, coughing and expectorating and, of course, the courteous gesture of loud eructation.

They were very independent and, although friendly and pleasant, would seldom go out of their way to give you any assistance. On the whole they had a pretty good time. They were not much priest-ridden and I think they took good care to have plenty of parties and sprees, with plenty of inferior alcohol to give them a sore head the following day.

Beyond the high mountains were the Tibetans. There was really not much for them to do. All the winter they were snowed up in their villages, so they ate what they had laid up during the summer. They carved religious inscriptions on rocks which they carried out into the country during the summer months to build the sacred walls – the *mani panis*. They prayed a good deal mechanically, and counted their beads and mumbled '*Om mani padme hum.*' They devoted much time to the study of their very complicated religion, and they repeated their old fables and stories. During the summer the men continued this life except that they ate less and drank more. The women tilled the fields and harvested the crop when it was ripe, and they also wandered under male escort far into the hills in search of brushwood, to lay up a store for the winter. They appeared to be healthy, and were all very fat. The men were dyspeptic but the women, who worked hard and didn't drink, were most cheerful and very noisy, chattering and babbling away all day.

In Lahoule there were less women than men, some of them very well off. They were absolute queens; they married as many husbands as they liked, and in the summer sent them off on errands – one to take a flock of goats and sheep to graze in Rupshu, another to do some trading in Leh and another in Kulu, and so on.

In the summer the shepherds travelled with their flocks into the highest and most distant parts of the Himalayas, going as high as 18,000 feet in places and crossing most difficult passes. They were fine hardy men, rather dour on the whole, but clean-living and honourable, the best I think of all the hill people. Year in, year out, they travelled with their sheep, some of them going many hundreds of miles. They started when they were boys about ten years of age, travelling with their fathers, and, from that time on, year after year, they took the flocks up into the mountains away from the heat of the plains to graze in the cool highlands during the summer, returning to their homes in the winter, till at length, too old for the hardships of such journeying, they sent some grandson to take their place. There was so little grazing in the high mountains that the flocks had to keep travelling continually or they would die of starvation.

The shepherd is a man to be studied. He lives a full life. His responsibility is unending. Day and night he must be ever-watchful. He suffers every kind of hardship and privation, and faces every sort of weather, yet he accomplishes all this at a moderate pace. He never hurries; indeed he cannot hurry for he is tied by the slow pace at which his flocks move and graze. He moves slowly and is seldom tired or distressed. I have often been amazed at the distance the shepherds travel in a day, though apparently they hardly move. You will pitch your camp next to a shepherd and his flock at night. Next morning when you wake he has gone. You march and pass him on the way. On you go, marching for all you're worth and eventually, tired by your exertions, you pitch your camp. Late in the evening the shepherd, still moving at his slow pace, by no means exhausted, having rested through the heat of the day, passes your camp and settles himself down for the night a little further on. There is no hurry, no fuss, no worry, no furious working off of nervous energy; yet the result is the same, with this difference, that the shepherd has covered, without exerting himself in any way, the same distance that you have covered in exhausting yourself by averaging three miles an hour up and down hills.

As on my former Himalayan journey, I was fortunate to have Thakru as my companion and henchman – courageous, upright, cheerful, hard-working, tactful and honest. His sense of duty was complete; he had a high moral code of his own. This was a virtuous man. He and I had a very close rapport, and absolute trust in each other.

With a month of my leave left, I decided to remain near the village of Manali at the head of the Kulu valley. It was a delightful place, a wide valley at about 6,000 feet, with the thundering Beas torrent racing through it, fed by crystal-clear mountain streams, the whole sur-rounded by bright snow peaks, and much of it shady woodland with a cushion of pine needles underfoot. Where better could I recuperate – warm sunny days, but not too hot, and cool nights. Feeling guilty, however, of idling and trout fishing in Kulu while Branfoot was try-ing, almost single-handed, to set up the new Depot in Ferozepore, I offered to return and help him. But he urged me to complete my leave in Kulu. The heat in Ferozepore was awful: 'We have forgotten', he said, 'what a Punjab summer is like, having been down country for so long.'

I had my accumulated mail sent to the post office in Manali. It contained an unforgettable letter from a brother officer – one of the shortest I have ever received:

Dear Bill,
    You will be greatly grieved to hear that Daphne has died.
                    Yours,
                    Pat

Lovely and lively Daphne who had needled me into producing the Saugor pantomime – and only thirty-seven years of age. The Indian hot weather had claimed another victim. 'Never the lotus closes, and never the wild fowl wake ...'

The antibiotics of today would have saved her as, too, they might have saved Charlotte Canning who, the year after her Hindustan-Tibet Road trek, died in Calcutta of some undiagnosed fever at the early age of forty-four. Life in India may have been a wonderful, varied and interesting experience, but there were other sides to it, and a study of the epitaphs in British Indian cemeteries tells another story. Hazards to health struck without discrimination.

During the month that I was in Kulu, Miles Smeeton of Hodson's Horse, who had been in the same ride as me at Saugor, turned up with his fiancée. She was an extraordinarily adventurous woman. She had walked across China from Canton to Burma. A British consular official in Canton tried to dissuade her, warning her severely of the threat from voracious Chinese men, to which she replied, 'Oh, don't worry. I far prefer dishonour to death.' But she managed cleverly; whenever she spent the night in a Chinese village, she always put herself in the hands of the women who would see that there was no truck between her and the men. I asked her why she had made the journey. 'To try out their food,' she answered. She also did a similar remarkable journey through the length of Patagonia.

When I met them in Kulu, they were proposing to return to the plains of India by canoe down the Beas river. Neither of them had any experience or knowledge of boats. I found Miles putting together a prefabricated German canoe, made of canvas and bits of wooden ribbing – an extremely flimsy craft called a follboat. I asked him where he proposed to launch it. He said, 'Here.' 'Here' meant on the Beas river in Sultanpore half way down the Kulu valley where the river, fed by the melting snows in summer, is a creaming white torrent.

Having spent my boyhood in boats, I said, 'In that case you won't go twenty yards before you are swamped, and probably drowned.' I took him down to the river's edge, and persuaded him that I was right.

He said they would go down to Mandi instead, where the river was smoother, and launch the canoe there. I said I thought it was lunacy, without a reconnaissance. The map showed that there was an average fall of twenty-five feet per mile for the next ten miles below Mandi; it was an enormously heavy river and that must mean some very rough water.

They wouldn't listen, and they set off. It was not long before they found themselves swept into a gorge and saw rising in front of them a huge wall of white water. The flimsy craft hit it, broke backwards in two pieces and they were carried down deep under water. Beryl was not strapped in. Miles was and, as he went down, had the presence of mind to undo his straps. Eventually he came to the surface, and saw 'B', as she was always known, also on the surface. She was a very strong swimmer and was swimming for the shore. He also managed to make it. He thought he had been carried many feet down under water, and he had a splitting headache for hours afterwards.

I suppose that, at the point where they were wrecked, there was an enormous rock, or ridge of rock, on the bed of the river which caused the upsurge of water. Anyway, thinking to undo his straps was typical

of Miles's resourcefulness. I once said to him that I thought him the
most resourceful person I had ever known. He replied that one of his
former commanding officers had written in his annual confidential
report: 'This officer has a remarkable facility for getting himself out of
scrapes that he should never have got into.'

18
Ferozepore

I stayed a little over a month in Kulu, and then returned to Ferozepore for what were the last moments of Sam Browne's Cavalry as an active regiment. I found everyone in Ferozepore, including our Indian soldiers, weary of the heat. We still had 400 horses for training the recruits. I wrote of them: 'I never remember seeing the whole Regiment sweating, standing doing nothing in their stables, as they were yesterday evening; every horse wringing wet, and they had not been out on exercise.'

On 31 July 1937 I wrote:

Today we really cease to exist as a regiment. We say goodbye to the last of the men this afternoon, and the new staff come in. It is all very sad, but everyone is more or less used to the idea of it by now.

Tonight there is the hiatus between the going away of our men and the arrival of the others. We are very short-handed and every man in the place will be busy looking after the horses and finding line guards.

1 August. Today I got on a horse for the first time since my accident in March. I don't think it will be possible to do much active riding till September as no horse could stand it. Mine dripped with sweat though I was only out for about three-quarters of an hour and only walking with a little very slow trotting.

We were allowed to keep some of our own Indian officers and NCO instructors, and we got an excellent lot of additional Indian officers and instructors from the other six regiments in the Group. At the same time British officers also began to arrive, some of them old friends, some soon to become new friends, and we very quickly began to shake down into a very agreeable and effective entity.

We had one innovation. The Indian Army had never had British Army-type quartermasters – men of ability and long experience who had risen through the ranks, eventually to be commissioned as quartermasters. It was nevertheless decided that the three new Indian Cavalry

Depots should have such quartermasters. For the appointment, I was able to get the services of the Regimental Sergeant-Major at the Cavalry School at Saugor, RSM Watts – a brilliant horseman, a very nice man, and a man of such parts that Lakri Wood, the Chief Instructor at Saugor, said that I had deprived him of his 'guide, philosopher and friend'. 'Bolo' Watts who, with his wife Elsie, were firm friends of mine, once told me this little story about his early days in the Army when he was a young trooper in the 4th Hussars and a boxer.

He was a lightweight. The farrier corporal trained him. Having won his weight in the regimental competition, he was entered for the Alder-shot Command competition. After a number of hard fights, he reached the final in which he had a gruelling scrap which he won. He then had to receive his prize from the Commander-in-Chief, the Duke of Connaught.

Afterwards, the farrier corporal asked him, 'What did the Dook say to you?'

He said, 'Well done, Watts. It's young fellahs like you we want in the Army!'

'What did he give you?' asked the farrier corporal.

'He gave me this medal, and this half-sovereign,' answered Watts, holding them out on the palm of his hand.

'Well,' said the farrier corporal, 'hang that medal on your watch-chain, and be proud of it for the rest of your life; and, as for this half-sovereign', picking it off Watts's hand and slipping it into his own waistcoat pocket, 'it isn't much for all the work I've put into you.'

In getting the new Sam Browne's Depot into an effective working unit, life was not all work. We played polo and had our other usual equestrian interests and recreations, and Johnnie Walker of Hodson's Horse and Aspinall of the Scinde Horse and I were a regular weekend shooting team. The Sutlej river, a vast sedate river of the plains, which ran not far from our lines, had often changed its course, leaving little lakes and *jheels* (swamps) perhaps a mile or more long where we had excellent duck and snipe shooting, and there were also partridge and sand-grouse.

I had gone to Ferozepore for a few days after leaving Saugor and before going to Simla to start my Himalayan trek. I wanted to see the Depot and to drop my kit there. While there, I went fishing on the Sutlej and caught delicious little fish with sea trout flies. But after the rains and the melting snow of the summer months it was a very different river. The fishermen all said that in their opinion the fish cleared out during the summer floods and either dropped back down the river to some place where the water started to get cleaner, or else ran up the side streams towards the mountains.

Malaria persisted. I dosed myself with quinine. Then I decided to see a doctor. He asked, 'How long have you had it?' I told him. He said, 'You're a bloody fool. Malaria is a very serious illness. Always report sick.' He took me into hospital for a few days, but I did not always thereafter take his advice. It was the main killer in India at that time; estimated to account for the lives of five million people annually.

Branfoot, as the last Commandant of the 12th Frontier Force Cavalry (Sam Browne's), and the first Commandant of the new 2nd Cavalry Depot in Ferozepore, and I, the first adjutant of the new Depot, felt that it would be a fitting thing in the autumn of 1937, when the hot weather was over, to hold a final reunion for Sam Browne's pensioners.

We had a number of reasons. We felt that some sort of a farewell to the old Regiment was needed. There were obviously potential problems in welding together personnel from the six regiments of the group and some old Sam Browne's people to run the new Depot, and we thought that a get together of this sort would help smooth things out. Also, the Indian Army always needed the support and goodwill of the villages from which we recruited, and we thought (rightly as it turned out) that this gathering would engender the goodwill of the village greybeards for the new arrangements.

We discussed the idea with the newly attached officers from the other regiments, and with their Indian officers, and they were all in full agreement and entered enthusiastically into the extensive preparations which we had to make.

More than 300 pensioners came, impeccably turned out in the very smart mufti traditional to each of their different communities, and we had three days of junketing, sports, competitions, entertainment and so on, and one afternoon we were 'at home' to the garrison with sports and competitions in which officers and other ranks of other units could take part. Perhaps the highlight was the veterans' tent-pegging competition. Four of the old 1931 team who had won the inter-regimental trophy were among the retired sirdars, and they showed that they had lost none of their skill. In particular old Jemadar Akhbar Shah had the crowd on their feet roaring with delight and encouragement at his beautifully timed lance play. He was the winner.

Our hopes for the outcome of the reunion were more than fulfilled. Not only were the pensioners there, but also the future was not forgotten. As a contemporary press account records: '... mingling with the crowd, in their smart uniforms, were representatives of future generations, boys from the three military schools at Jhelum, Jullundur and Ajmer, sons of Indian officers of Sam Browne's Cavalry and of the other regiments in the new 2nd Cavalry Group.'

One old sirdar said to me that he had had misgivings about attending the reunion after the Regiment had been broken up, thinking to find himself among strangers; but the hospitality and kindness shown to him and all other pensioners by members of the six other regiments now serving with Sam Browne's Cavalry, combined with the spirit with which they all competed in these sports, was sufficient to convince him that the old *Risala* was not dead. Indeed he now saw this new group as a strong tree out of which grew six green and flourishing branches.

19
Loralai

After Christmas 1937 I handed over the adjutancy of the Ferozepore Depot to Randal Plunkett, later Lord Dunsany, of the Guides Cavalry, and went to Loralai in Baluchistan on the North West Frontier to join Hodson's Horse.

As a newcomer to the Regiment they were extremely good to me and gave me charge of 'B' Squadron, the Punjabi Mussulman (PM) Squadron. They were in very good order, and I had first-class Indian officers. Hodson's Horse were a very efficient regiment which had attracted a lot of able and dedicated officers. Like Sam Browne's, they did not make a fetish of polo, but energetically pursued a wide variety of interests.

It was a small, but very agreeable, station in a quiet part of the North West Frontier. 'Of course', I wrote, 'there is no gay [in its old-fashioned meaning!] life here, cinema, girls and so forth.' The scenery, too, was stark: a wide open valley about 5,000 feet above sea level, set in a wilderness of barren mountains. That suited me. There was first-rate rock-climbing on absolutely sound, very hard, igneous rock, on which we could climb in rubbers (gym shoes). Miles Smeeton, who had been at Saugor with me, and who was adjutant, introduced some of the Indian officers to rock climbing, but I felt that they never saw the point and regarded it as one of the curious eccentricities of the *Sahib Log*.

There was good shooting and some of us took a week's leave and went and shot on the Mancha Lake 'down the hill' in the Indus valley in Sind, 100 miles north of Karachi. It is an extraordinary formation at the foot of the south-east Baluchistan mountains. The Indus flows about fifteen miles east of the mountains, and the lake is formed by an overflow from the river during the summer floods. The lake is a sheet of about twenty square miles of water and is only about two and a half feet deep, certainly nowhere over three feet deep, and mirror calm. It is formed by the Indus failing to silt up this bit of the plain. The country to the east of the lake is the flat alluvial plain of the Indus built up of thousands of years of silt. Along the east side of the lake, between it and the river, are wide belts of thick reeds and grasses, and these have acted as a filter to the silt which would otherwise have filled up the lake centuries ago.

There were thousands of duck, chiefly mallard, wigeon, gadwall and pintail, together with other common Indian ducks, and some flocks of greylag geese. Mallard were the bulk of our bag because they stuck to the reeds and, though it was a wonderful sight to see so many, we got only very small numbers. The other duck all kept to the open water and we got only odd ones. On a shoot like that I liked getting small bags, because shooting fifty birds or so a day to your own gun ceased to be a pleasure after a couple of days and degenerated into a slaughter; but to fluke a dozen or two real high ones gave more satisfaction.

It was part of the routine on the North West Frontier to take out columns – say of brigade strength – for a week or a fortnight or more, and march through a stretch of country, mainly to remind the tribes that we had plenty of military strength to deploy if they got restive and started giving trouble. The Loralai Brigade moved out on such a column for several weeks in the spring of 1938. It was an enjoyable exercise. We practised frontier warfare techniques, and operated all the time as though we were in hostile country, meticulously picketing our daily route and so on. I recall that one day I was asked to command the column rearguard, and I had some small units of other regiments under my command. I was astonished at the order-giving technique of some of them. Orders were given, and then had to be repeated back to ensure they were understood. I felt that the enemy would have won the war while all that was going on. I could give my men their orders at the gallop if necessary, and before I had half finished they would know what was wanted and be off and do it.

It was a perfectly legitimate thing to do to take out such a column in Baluchistan, but I thought the most senior person involved in its planning was not very scrupulous, and I believed that he had deliberately chosen the time and route in order to try to provoke one of the major tribes, whose migration season it was from their winter quarters. I believed that our column intentionally trailed its coat across their migration route in the hope that it might lead to hostilities, and some consequent kudos for the man concerned if we won a successful battle. As it turned out we saw very few of the tribespeople, and they had the good sense to keep their fingers off the trigger.

Some mountains attract men's fancy and become the subject of a legend. One such in India of those days was the Takht-i-Suliman

(Solomon's Throne) in Baluchistan although, on account of its remoteness and security difficulties, it was seldom climbed by Europeans. The planned route of our column passed underneath it, and I was determined to climb it if I could get, or create, a suitable opportunity. I asked Miles Smeeton if he would come with me. He was not as mountain-besotted as I was, but he was a keen rock-climber and had done a short trip through some of the hill states in the Himalayas the year before.

The Brigade Commander decided to halt just to the west of the Takht-i-Suliman mountain. The legend the Pathans have about it is that Solomon once got onto his magic carpet and flew to India where he demanded a bride. The lady was produced with due ceremony, and Solomon placed her on the carpet and away they flew. She, however, wept copiously at leaving her native land so Solomon landed his carpet on this mountain and they sat on the *takht* (throne) and the lady looked her last on India.

As we were to have a halt of two days here, Miles and I decided that we must somehow get to the *takht* and see the view which Solomon and his bride saw, so we got permission to take an escort of a couple of levies and go. We were told that we would find it hard to get there and back in the day, but that it had been done before by somebody from this place who did it in thirteen hours. The conformation of the mountain is such that, with a climb to a ridge, then a drop into a valley, and a climb out of that to the summit, there is 10,000 feet of uphill climbing in the day and a round trip of some twenty-five miles.

The need for the two levies was that British officers were not allowed to wander about tribal territory unescorted. They were prime targets for hostile tribesmen, and it was essential that they should not take unnecessary risks. The loss of valuable life was obviously the prime consideration, but there was also the fact that the murder of British officers was politically embarrassing.

A substantial part of the peace-keeping force on the North West Frontier was locally recruited levies, quasi-military bodies commanded by British officers. There was a levy fort where the brigade was encamped, and they were good enough to lend Miles and me a couple of armed levies who were, as it happened, delighted to come with us to the *takht*. The tribesmen enjoy a challenge, and a lark, and a quick nip up to the *takht* and back was in line with their idea of a bit of fun.

The evening before our climb we were faced with a difficult question. Another of our officers asked if he could come with us. Of course he was fit, but he had no mountain experience, and a day in the saddle is not the same as a hard day's mountaineering, even though it was only uphill walking and scrambling, and not technical mountaineering. However, we concluded that his desire to come showed a very good spirit, and we agreed. We were wrong.

We started at 5.10 a.m. We went steadily and very well to the top of the first ridge, doing the 4,000 feet in a little over two hours. Here the third member of our party said he was very puffed and doubted whether he could keep up with us to the top, so we decided to leave him to find his own way back. We asked the levies if they thought this was safe and they said absolutely, as there wasn't a soul in this part of the country. The camp was still in sight away down below us so there appeared to be no possibility of the least experienced person losing his way; he had food and water with him, so we cheerfully left him to go back in his own time. We hastened on into the gorge.

It was a new world up there. Baluchistan is a desert; there is not a tree in the whole country except the few almond trees and willows planted wherever there is a village; but here we were in a beautiful forest of cedars and pines, and wild tulips were growing between the rocks, and birds were singing everywhere. It was a cold sparkling morning and, full of joie de vivre, we ran and jumped down the steep mountainside and the two Pathans sang as they went.

We then started our climb the far side. It was still early in the morning and the high ridge of the *takht* shaded us from the sun. We were in good trim and though we were not hurrying we were climbing very fast. About 2,000 feet from the top we reached snow and it was delightful to be walking once more on a crisp frozen surface. About a thousand feet higher we had our only bit of difficulty. We had to cross a slab of rock which would normally have been quite straightforward, but about twenty feet of it was covered with ice and rather dangerous. We took off our boots and went in our bare feet and got across safely. We then went up a gully full of fine trees standing in the snow, and we were soon on the top, exactly five hours after leaving camp. We were of course miles ahead of the man who had done the round trip in thirteen hours.

The *takht* itself is an extraordinary place. The far side of the mountain, the east side, dropped away below us in an absolutely sheer cliff, for thousands of feet. It might be two thousand, it might be five. About fifteen feet down this cliff, jutting out, was a flat slab of rock about the size of a large sofa which is the throne on which Solomon and his bride are said to have sat. Unless you go over the fearfully exposed face of this cliff and climb down and sit on the ledge, you have not completed the pilgrimage to Solomon's Throne. We dropped down onto it and sat there and had something to eat and quenched our thirst with snow as we had no water with us.

The view was wonderful. Stretching away to the east were the low foothills of the Frontier and then India, just as far as you could see, the hot shimmering plains, till the sky and the earth merged into the heat haze.

We stayed forty minutes on the top and then started back and decided to knock spots off the thirteen-hour record. We raced down the hill and were in the gorge in an hour. We took the climb up the far side steadily, but were still going really strong and did about 1,500 feet in forty-five minutes. Then we stopped on the ridge and had another snack and then came bounding down into the camp, the whole trip having taken nine hours ten minutes, including the halt on the top.

It was 2.20 p.m. when we got in and then we were faced with a problem because the third member of the party had not arrived back. As we were climbing up the last *nullah* bank, I said to Miles, 'How would you like to be told you had got to do that again now?' He answered that it would take something much worse than a bullet to make him start out again.

However, when we found that the other man had not got in, it looked as if we should have to go out again and look for him. We waited an hour and a half, had a good tea and then, feeling somewhat refreshed, started out again to climb the first ridge. We took Charles Trench with us, our signals officer, and a Pathan levy. We climbed for about an hour and a half and then found a path crossing the way we were going, and on this we found a boot mark leading downhill. We concluded that this must be the wanderer's mark and decided to try communication with camp. The levy had a small mirror with him so we flashed it on the camp and were very relieved to be answered a little later by a helio which flashed, 'Come in. *Sahib agia hai*' ('the Sahib has returned'). With some relief we turned about and made for camp. Miles and I received a reprimand for leaving a man out alone and unescorted in tribal territory. So far as I remember nothing was said to the 'loner' and Miles and I continued to think that he had done well to make the attempt. The fact that he got into difficulty serves to show that mountains are dangerous for the inexperienced.

From the Takht-i-Suliman we continued our column back to Loralai without further adventures.

20
Home Leave 1938–39

I had not been home for five years, but although I had been with Hodson's Horse only a few months, the Commandant, Colonel Frank Stevens, kindly granted me leave and furlough home, and I left Loralai in late April 1938.

Language study was still one of my hobbies. There is no end to the study of Persian and its enormous literature and I wanted to concentrate on that. However, Colonel Boyle, 'the language king' as we called him, dissuaded me. He said I knew enough Persian for all official purposes, and that I would be more use to the Army with a similar knowledge of other languages. I already knew a good deal of Arabic, and he asked me to do Arabic and Russian interpreterships next.

Shortly before I went on leave, therefore, and thinking that I would soon get bored, I decided that, after I had done things that I wanted to do, and seen friends and relations, I would go to Riga and study Russian. Also, I would do it on my own resources and not as a sponsored Army language student. In that way I would avoid the pressure of having a deadline to take the exam.

To begin with, however, I went home to Ireland and enjoyed some fishing. Then my mother wanted to do a tour of England in her car to visit family and friends, and asked me to go with her, which I was very glad to do.

After we had started the tour, I received a telegram from Miles Smeeton, saying he was getting married and that he and his wife intended to spend their honeymoon rock-climbing in the Lake District, but they wanted a third person on the rope. Would I join them? (She was the same girl as he had nearly drowned in the follboat on the Beas river in India.) They would be staying at the farm of Mr and Mrs Greenup, who had other spare rooms, so my mother and I joined the honeymoon party on the shores of Lake Wast Water. My mother had spent her girlhood in the Slieve Bloom mountains in Ireland. She loved mountains and was a keen mountain walker, so she came up every day with us. However, she had never rock-climbed, so we didn't suggest it.

Like so many things in Miles's life, his marriage was unusual. Before joining Hodson's Horse, he had been in a British infantry regiment. Rather inappropriately for a subaltern, he fell in love with his commanding officer's wife. She reciprocated. He left the regiment. Hodson's Horse took him in, not as a refugee, but because he was a first-rate officer. Eventually there was a divorce between Beryl and her first husband, and she and Miles could get married.

So here we all were in the Lake District, with our cherished late friend Lakri Wood's wish fulfilled that they would get married, and we climbed many of the good rock-climbs in the area including the famous Needle. A memorable part of the honeymoon was the wonderful Lake District country food which Mrs Greenup produced, and which we devoured with ravenous mountaineering appetites.

While I was in England, I took the opportunity to attend a voluntary course laid on by the War Office for overseas service officers home on leave, to give us an opportunity to catch up with Whitehall thinking. One lecture in particular I recall, from a cavalry general. He said that the civil war in Spain had shown the vulnerability of tanks and armoured fighting vehicles. The dive-bombers which Germany had sent to help General Franco's forces had made 'pepper-boxes' – his word – of the Republican side's armoured vehicles. Moral: we must stick to our horses. Why they should be any less vulnerable to dive-bombing escaped me.

The curious Lake District holidaying had an unexpected consequence for me – a meeting with another mountaineer, which resulted in my having the privilege of being signed on with the Fell and Rock Club for three weeks' climbing in the Alps in Switzerland in the latter part of July and early August that year, 1938. My leave period was dwindling and my Russian course in Riga was getting pushed a bit further away but, after the wonderful Alpine trip when, based on Fafleralp, we climbed all the great peaks in Valais, there occurred something which altogether demolished the Russian project.

My father's youngest sister, my aunt Violet Magan, who had never married and had lived all her life close to Athlone in the centre of Ireland, had for many years been honorary secretary to the local pack of hounds, the South Westmeath Hunt. She told me that they had no master for the coming season; the committee knew I was home on leave, and had asked her to ask me if I could take over the mastership. It was too tempting an opportunity to miss. I could learn Russian anytime, but this was a one-off chance of being able to hunt an Irish pack of hounds. So I accepted, provided I could get the necessary additional leave, which my CO, Frank Stevens, generously granted me. Paddy Massey, who was his adjutant at the time, was surprised that it was not turned down, but the CO said it was good training for a cavalry officer in man management, animal management and financial management.

The South Westmeath Hunt had begun many years before as a pack of harriers, so their uniform was green, with red facings. It was a small pack run on a shoestring by a number of local enthusiasts including sporting shopkeepers out of the town, farmers, of course, and at least one very sporting parish priest. The hounds were uneven but they hunted like demons, and a handful of the leaders were very good.

The hunt had an enormous country on both sides of the Shannon. On the east side, in Westmeath, it was a typical central Irish mix of enormous banks, enormous ditches, fences, walls, wire, open fields, woodland and bog. Some of the coverts were the coverts of my grandfather, Assheton Biddulph, MFH, during the forty years or so that he owned and hunted the King's County Hunt. I taught my horses to jump wire, a novelty locally. Then, on the west side of the Shannon, we had a large area of the County Roscommon, almost all small fields separated by loose stone walls; as one Irishman put it, 'You'd be seasick with leppin'.'

The only hunt staff was a kennelman. The whip, who had been whip for years, Paddy Fitzpatrick, was, like me, a volunteer and provided his own horses and uniform. It was a sort of 'sillidar' arrangement. But, unlike me, he had no duties except to be there on hunting days, when he would meet me at the kennels and we would take the pack to the meet. I had known Paddy all my life. He was one of my Aunt Violet's lifelong local supporters. He was a stage Irishman, full of pungent droll sayings, and a quite brilliant man with horses and hounds.

As I saw it, my first duties were to get the hounds fit and to get to know the country, and in particular the farmers over whose land we might run. For both those duties the best tool seemed to be a bicycle. I was at the kennels every morning at dawn, and then Billie, the kennelman, and I took the hounds out on exercise until breakfast time.

After breakfast I would tour the country seeing farmers, earthstoppers, and other people whom it was necessary or prudent to visit. One or two farmers were known to be sticky, and I was especially concerned either to get their agreement, or to respect their wishes if they did not want the hunt on their land. In these diplomatic matters, Father

Plunkett, our hunting priest, was particularly helpful. I found I also
had a good deal of correspondence, and I wrote to the masters of some
of the bigger packs who were good enough to spare me a few couple
of good hounds.

When we started cubbing, I insisted that we did some of it on foot.
I am a great believer in getting your feet wet. There is a lot you can
learn from the ground that you cannot learn from the back of a horse;
and it is perfectly possible for fit people to follow a pack of foxhounds
on foot. Moreover, we did not have unlimited mounts, and it saved
our horses from possible injury before the hunting season proper
started.

My recollection is that we did not have a blank day, and I enjoyed
every minute of it. The place to be in the hunting field, to get the
maximum enjoyment from it, is the man with the horn. One day
remains in my mind. It was not just raining. It had rained stair-rods all
night, and continued all day. Paddy and I took the hounds to the meet.
None of the field turned up. We had one short hunt, and decided to go
home.

On the way, we passed a pub. Drink was mother's milk to Paddy, so
we stopped. I said to him: 'You keep the hounds out here, and I'll go in
and get you a drink. What would you like, whiskey?'

'Yes please, Master.'

'Would you like water with it?

Paddy replied, 'Haven't I wather enough all day? Aren't my pockets
full of it?'

So he got an undiluted four fingers to warm his cockles.

In September 1938 came Prime Minister Neville Chamberlain's awful
'peace in our time' Munich agreement with Hitler. I felt ashamed of it. I
also felt that we were drifting into war, though it might not be for some
time yet. At all events, before the hunting season was over, I felt it was
time to get back to my Regiment, and I think I missed the last few
meets. Paddy, the whip, was really more capable of hunting the hounds
than I was, and there were members of the hunt willing and capable to
whip in.

My other principal recreations that winter were a certain amount of
mainly snipe shooting with my father, who was one of the best shots in
Ireland, and enlistment with a provincial Irish Rugby football club, the
Shannon Buccaneers. We were an elderly team, average age perhaps
about thirty, but most, if not all, of them had played good standard

Rugby. We had a former Irish international, a former Royal Navy full back, several former members of the Trinity College, Dublin, team, and I think we didn't lose a match. 'Tell it not in Gath', but I ended the season still convinced that rugger is the best game in the world, even better than polo. It must be unusual for an MFH to be an active playing member of a Rugby football club.

21

The Shadow of War

Back in India I rejoined Hodson's Horse in Loralai, Baluchistan, on the North West Frontier, and resumed command of 'B' Squadron, the Punjabi Mussulman Squadron. Baluchistan was a quiet Frontier area. The Baluchis, whose country we were in, did not subscribe to the turbulence of the more northern tribes such as the Wazirs. We did not have to live in a barbed-wire enclosed encampment in Loralai, and we could go shooting and climbing in some areas without military escorts.

Although in our spare time we carried on with such leisure enjoyments, we were all, by the spring of 1939, fully conscious that we were facing a probable major war. This is not the place for a history lesson on the rise of the Nazi Reich, but the danger had grown and arrived. It was therefore with renewed urgency that I, no doubt like every other Indian Cavalry squadron leader, set myself the goal of having under my command the best squadron of cavalry in the Indian Army.

Of one thing I was certain. Despite the cavalry general at Aldershot, warfare was going to be mechanised. Curiously, the Persian poet Firdosi, writing in the tenth century, had foretold it – horseless iron chariots propelled by *naft* (the inflammable oil that seeped out of the ground).

I do not know whether any other officer in my Regiment had studied the construction and workings of an internal combustion engine, and the process of ignition and transmission, but I doubt it. By chance I had. When at home on leave, I had bought an old Riley motor car which I had decided to restore and maintain myself both for economy and interest. Indeed, I dismantled and rebuilt the engine with my own hands.

If, as I was sure, we were going to be mechanised, it seemed to me that we should familiarise ourselves with mechanics. If we were going to have to drive mechanical vehicles, we would need to know something about how they worked. I therefore asked our Commanding Officer if I could run a voluntary course in ignition and transmission for Indian officers and NCOs. I think he thought I might be going off my head, but he agreed. So I worked out a course of lectures, borrowed a cut-down demonstration engine, and other demonstration mechanical parts, from our helpful local Supply and Transport Officer, and the course started. It was well attended, and we coined a few new Urdu words to deal with some of the mysteries. I hope it all proved useful when the Regiment was mechanised the following year. As it happened, the best horsemen turned out to be the best tank drivers. Perhaps, after all, it was a matter of sensitivity – what a cavalryman calls 'hands'.

One day in June 1939, a few months after I had returned to the Regiment from home leave, Frank Stevens called me into his office and told me that I had been detailed by Western Command Headquarters to go on a special intelligence course – me alone, no one else – in Simla, where the military and Government headquarters spent the summer months. Army Headquarters (as GHQ was then known) and the Intelligence Bureau in the Home Department of the Government of India had, some time earlier, agreed that a few Army officers should each be given a familiarisation course of three months in some of the security intelligence responsibilities in which the military and civil departments, particularly the Intelligence Bureau, had common interests, and it was for this that I was required. The Intelligence Bureau was the MI5 and MI6 of India combined.

'Well,' I said to Frank Stevens, 'you can tell them that I'm not going. We shall be at war with the Germans again in no time, and I'm staying with my squadron. It's pointless for me to do this sort of course. I shall never put the knowledge to any use. Some staff officer can do it. I am a regimental officer, and have no intention of doing anything else.'

Of course, one can kick up a polite shindy but, in the end, you have to go. Frank Stevens tried to soften the blow by saying that it would be good for me to miss the hot weather and the malarial months by being in the cool climate of Simla, and it would be useful experience to see the 'monkey house' – as he irreverently referred to Army Headquarters – at work.

The evening before I left, I went down to the horse lines and, leaning against a stall with a straw in our mouths, I and my senior Indian officer had a long talk. I told him all the things I wanted done in the squadron while I was away. At the end, he said, 'Why are you telling me all this?' 'Because,' I replied, 'as you know as well as I do, we are almost certainly going to be at war before the winter, and we have got to have everything absolutely shipshape.' 'Yes,' he said, 'but why are you bothering about it? It will have nothing to do with you. You'll never come back.' 'Of course I'm coming back,' I said. 'this beastly course lasts only three months.' 'No,' he said, 'you wait and see. I'm telling you. You'll never come back. Once they get hold of you, they'll never let you go.'

Up to that time, my army life and outlook were, I think, typical of a lot of soldiers of those times. We really enjoyed regimental soldiering, and all the opportunities for varied and interesting experiences that went with it, and our only ambition – and even that looked a long way off – was one day to command our own regiment, and then retire with still plenty of time to resume the active and sporting interests which we had enjoyed when we were young.

So it came about that one evening in the latter part of June 1939 I set off reluctantly down the hill from Loralai on the hot and dusty road to the rail junction at Sibi, one of the hottest places in India at that time of year, and started the long stifling journey to Kalka, the railhead at the foot of the Simla hills. There, after breakfasting in the station restaurant, I took the narrow gauge railway up the mountains to the deliciously cool air of Simla, where I had a comfortable room in the well-appointed United Services Club, of which I had been a member since I was in Simla in 1933 on the Persian course.

The next day I reported to Army Headquarters where I was given a desk and became in effect a general staff officer, grade III (GSO III), shuffling paper. The Intelligence section in which I found myself seemed to have a rather ill-defined role concerned with military security. It was immersed in political work which was of concern to the civil Intelligence Bureau and, perhaps for that reason and because the work was not strictly confined to military matters, I rather presumptuously thought that what was going on was rather amateurish, but I kept my views to myself.

I was based on that section for the first month of my course, which turned out not to be a course in the usual sense, as I was given no instruction by anyone. I wasted as little of my time as I could there, preferring whenever possible to visit other sections, discovering what they were doing and privately assessing the value of what they were at, because, as a dyed-in-the-wool regimental officer, I suspected the staff of not always being at things which were either very sensible or very useful.

Some did, however, seem to be doing very useful work, and doing it well. Best of all was an old friend from Sandhurst days who had made a corner for himself in some highly recondite and extremely valuable staff work.

The second month of the course was to be spent in the civil Intelligence Bureau. There things were very different. I was among civilians, and it was immediately apparent that I was among professionals. Churchill said that all government business ought to be conducted on paper and, once in the Intelligence Bureau, I began to see and experience that going on. The minutes and memoranda that I saw passing to and fro were of strikingly high intellectual quality and indeed, not infrequently, of high literary quality too, with neat little touches now and again reflecting well-cultivated minds.

This quiet, low-key, Rolls-Royce bureaucratic machine had its own rather sophisticated sense of humour, sometimes expressed in Latin tags, and it spawned some amusing file anecdotes. My favourite was one attributed to Lord Curzon, when he was Viceroy. A file which had done the rounds of the Government of India ended on his desk, and he penned the final minute in his own hand, and in red ink, which was the Viceroy's prerogative: 'I have studied this file with meticulous attention, and find myself wholly in agreement with the gentleman with a signature like a trombone.'

There was also the story of a file that landed on the desk of a former Commander-in-Chief full of Latin tags from the Civil Service. He wrote on it: 'I, too, know Latin, and I consider the suggestion made here to be non sanguineum bonum.'

But, despite occasional levity, all business was carried on at a profound level of serious responsibility. Committees, too, were properly conducted. People came well and fully prepared. The agenda was adhered to. There was no waffling, no going off tangentially. Points were dealt with briskly. Agreements were decisive. Minutes were well, accurately and quickly prepared.

This may not have been a course in the normal sense but there, in the Intelligence Bureau, I really was learning something about the professional handling and conduct of Government business at the highest level, and I felt very privileged to be so readily and freely accepted into so much confidence. Perhaps, too, I learnt for the first time the meaning of consistently hard brainwork.

Moreover, the Bureau did in a sense give me instruction. They made me privy to the whole of their structure and administrative layout, and they gave me the chance to learn on the job. They minuted files to me, particularly any having a direct bearing on armed forces interests, and allowed me to try my own hand at drafting minutes and memoranda. This suited me down to the ground. I am a Celt. I had been writing all my life.

They were, in fact, much more interested in me than Army Head- quarters had been, because the training course which I was undergoing had been initiated and sponsored by their Director – Sir John Ewart. I, too, enjoyed working with them. I liked them personally, and much admired their professionalism.

The third month of my course I was due to spend in the Government Headquarters of one of the provinces. I was sent to Bengal, to Calcutta, where I joined the Central Intelligence Office, which was the Intelli- gence Bureau's local office. It was late August 1939 when I got there, and I had not been there long when, on 3 September, war was declared.

22

War

I very distinctly recall the sickening news that Hitler had plunged the
world into war; the agreeable peaceful life of all of us was now at an
end for an unforeseeable time to come. I expected to be recalled to my
Regiment immediately. But I counted without the fates.

The moment war was declared, Sir John Ewart, appreciating that the
armed forces would now be acutely sensitive to feeling assured that the
civil authorities were not overlooking their needs and interests, invited
the Commander-in-Chief, General Cassels, to place an Army liaison
officer in the Intelligence Bureau. He would have full and unfettered
access to all information in the Bureau, and he would be free to use his
own discretion to pass whatever he liked to the Military Intelligence
Department in Army Headquarters.

The Commander-in-Chief agreed, and Sir John immediately
responded by asking, 'May we keep Bill Magan who has now been with
us for six weeks, knows our staff and our working methods, and knows
his way about our organisation?'

The Commander-in-Chief agreed to that also, so clearly I could not
start bellyaching, but I extracted as firm a half-promise as I could that I
would be relieved after no more than six months and allowed to return
to regimental duty.

But back in Loralai, in the Frontier hills, my squadron had, mistak-
enly I felt, to do without me. I felt I ought to be, and wanted to be, with
my soldiers. An ameliorating fact, certainly, was that the war had not
yet come to India, or indeed anywhere except Poland and on the high
seas and a little in the air, and the Indian Army was not yet therefore
engaged in combat.

A disadvantage of my Intelligence Bureau liaison appointment
was that it had placed me too much in the limelight. I had caught the
eye of the Commander-in-Chief himself, because some of my reports
and memoranda landed on his desk. He thus discovered that I had
not been to the Staff College. I had no intention of going there as I
was firmly resolved to devote myself to regimental soldiering, and to
keep clear of the staff. However, he ordered that I was to go on the

next course when I had handed over the Intelligence Bureau liaison job.

An example of how recreational activity could prove of professional use occurred at that time. Gertie Tuker – then Colonel, and later General Sir Francis – who had been in Loralai when we were there, was now Director of Military Training. He called me into his office one day and said he recalled that I was a climber. He added that, although many units were expert at mountain warfare as we knew it on the Frontier, no training was given in technical rock-climbing or climbing on snow and ice. Did I think this could prove useful and, if so, how could the Army tap in on these techniques? I reminded him of General Wolfe's ascent of the Heights of Abraham in Quebec, which, though not exactly a climbing operation, was somewhat comparable; also of Tamerlane's statement that to have ten men at the right place at the right time was better than 1,000 men in the wrong place; and I proffered such advice as I could, and hoped it was helpful.

Nine months after my liaison appointment had been created, the war situation changed dramatically. During the latter part of 1939 and the early part of 1940 there was no combat warfare anywhere in Europe with the Germans other than in Poland. That period became known as the Phoney War. However, in April 1940 real war came for the rest of us at last. Germany overran Denmark and Norway and in May carried out a massive assault on Western Europe, overrunning Holland, Belgium and France by the latter part of June.

On 10 June Italy declared war on France and Great Britain, and that brought the combat into the Indian sphere because the numerous Italian forces in North Africa were bound to attack Egypt, and those in Ethiopia were similarly likely to attack various British African territories, for instance the Sudan, British Somaliland and Kenya. Indian forces were bound to be used for the protection of those territories which were the outposts of, and the gateway to, India.

By June 1940 I had found a suitable and willing successor to my liaison appointment, Arthur Goring of Probyn's Horse, but I still had the Staff College course ahead of me before I could get back to my squadron. In the event, I neither went to the Staff College nor back to my Regiment.

As soon as the Italians declared war in early June 1940, two Indian divisions were ordered overseas, the 4th Indian Division to Egypt and the 5th Indian Division to East Africa to deal with the Italians in Eritrea. The 5th Indian Division was commanded by Major-General

L. M. Heath, and he asked for me by name to go with him as his divisional Intelligence officer. I had handed over my liaison job to Arthur Goring, and I then had to approach the Commander-in-Chief, on the grounds that I was required for active service, to ask him to rescind his instruction that I was to go to the Staff College. He agreed.

The 5th Indian Division was stationed in Hyderabad State in Southern India and had already started to embark in Bombay. I was ordered to go to Bolarum, near Secunderabad, where 5th Indian Divisional Headquarters still was. I was at the time in Simla where GHQ India (then still known as AHQ, Army Headquarters) was in its summer quarters. I think I allowed myself three days over a weekend to pack up and get to Bolarum, some 1,500 miles' journey by train.

I had packed up in Simla and was on my way to the railway station when a messenger caught up with me telling me to go urgently to see Major Ross Howman of the Military Intelligence Department. Thither I went, to be told that my 5th Indian Division appointment had been cancelled. There had been a crisis in India which was of major concern to both the military and civil authorities, and the Commander-in-Chief himself had ordered that I was to be appointed to investigate it. My squadron senior Indian officer's prediction was beginning to look rather accurate.

My replacement in 5th Indian Division was a charming and capable officer of the Gurkhas, named Oliver, a mountaineer. Sadly, he was killed in the East African campaign against the Italians. Perhaps that one had been meant for me.

The crisis was that the Sikh squadron of an Indian Cavalry regiment, the Central India Horse, which was part of the 5th Indian Division, and which was in Bombay docks awaiting embarkation, had mutinied, and the whole squadron was being sent back to Bolarum to be court-martialled. My assignment was to investigate the cause of the mutiny.

There was plenty of political agitation in India at the time. If that was at the bottom of this mutiny, then I did not feel myself competent to investigate it without police assistance. Through the good offices of the Intelligence Bureau, therefore, I borrowed two inspectors of police from the Punjab, one a Hindu, the other a Sikh, both able and experienced men and very nice colleagues, with plenty of experience of Indian political subversion.

We travelled to Bolarum together, and sat through the court-martial as observers to try to pick out the ringleaders, and any others who might seem especially suspect. There was little else we could do until the court-martial was over, as the case was *sub judice*. It was a particularly painful experience for me to have to watch a squadron of fellow Indian cavalrymen being court-martialled.

Sixteen of the mutineers were condemned to death, and the remainder of the squadron to varying terms of imprisonment. None of those sentenced to imprisonment seemed to me and the police inspectors to be important. Of the sixteen who were condemned to death, we concluded that twelve were relatively unimportant, and we managed to get their sentences commuted. The remaining four we decided to question closely – not an agreeable assignment, questioning men in the condemned cell.

Three of the four were brave men. They accepted that they had as soldiers committed a capital offence, and must pay the penalty. One of them was only eighteen and recently married. In fact none of them were conspirators, but they had taken a particularly prominent part in the mutinous act. I tried to get their sentences commuted. I failed. It has haunted me ever since that I did not fight harder for them. Looking back, I think I grossly underestimated my opportunity, and perhaps my own ability, to influence events. Had I insisted on seeing the Commander-in-Chief personally, I think I would have obtained an interview, and might have had some success.

The fourth man, Bishan Singh, was the only one to plead for mercy. He was also the arch-conspirator. He was a sinister man who had been recruited into the Communist Party of India when the Regiment was stationed in Meerut, where the Communist Party had its headquarters. Although I am personally opposed to capital punishment, for intellectual as well as humanitarian reasons, I made no attempt to get Bishan Singh's sentence commuted. The extreme price was going to be paid by someone as the supreme example, and a plea for Bishan Singh would have weakened my plea for the other three.

In my view, that Sikh squadron was unlucky. The Regiment went to Bombay to embark, but was held up for several days in the docks by bad weather. Sikhs are very active and energetic people, and all of us who have served with them know that if they are not kept fully occupied they are apt to get into trouble. The enforced idleness in Bombay gave Bishan Singh his chance. The lights had gone out in Europe. Italy had joined Germany. The political line, therefore, taken by Indian agitators was: 'The British, now alone, cannot survive against Germany and Italy. Sooner or later, and probably sooner, Britain will be overrun. British rule in India will collapse. In that case, the greatly preponderant

Muslim population in the Punjab will try to overrun the Sikhs. The right place for Sikh soldiers, therefore, is at home in the Punjab, guarding their wives and families, and not fighting Britain's inevitably losing battles against a European enemy in Africa.' The squadron fell for the bait.

That unfortunate episode, too, was the last special association I ever had with the Indian Cavalry. Our marvellous, but by that time anachronistic, life as officers in horsed Indian Cavalry regiments was at an end for ever.

Thinking over my life as a young man, I realise how very fortunate I was to have all the opportunities I had for a widely varied career of enormous interest. The enjoyment of Sandhurst in my day; the privilege of serving for a year in India with one of the Army's most distinguished regiments – the 60th Rifles. Then the Indian Cavalry: the wonderful, companionable Indian soldiers we had, with their extremely efficient, responsible and reliable Indian officers. Horsed cavalry at that. The pleasure and interest of 600 horses, and a ceremonial occasion with 4,000 horses on parade. The unlimited opportunities for sport and games: polo, hockey, squash and even rugger. Stalking the jungle tigers, and the wily Himalayan ibex. Then the beautiful lakes and *jheels* where we shot duck, snipe and even wild geese; and the whole sunburnt plain where we found chukor, partridge, sand grouse and quail. The opportunity to penetrate far into the Himalayan regions that had hardly, indeed perhaps never, been visited before, and to live among the greatest mountains in the world. And the beauty, the pleasure, the wonderful climate, of the lower valleys, and fishing for trout in the crystal-clear, fast-running water of the mountain streams. The opportunity to learn foreign languages up to interpretership standard. The delight in their literature. What a joy to read Saadi and Hafiz in the original Persian. The interest of being the official Persian interpreter to the Government of India. The pleasure of writing Persian in the Arabic script. The fascination of living as a Persian for a year and getting to know so many Persians, including the lovely girls, and speaking nothing but Persian with all of them. And then back to India and our wonderful social life there – more girls, English ones at that. In our Regiment we were a band of brothers, and with their wives and daughters we were an extended family. This compensated for being cut off from our real families at home.

But there were home leaves, few and far between, but wonderful when the time came. The chance to renew an affectionate relationship with family members and old friends. The opportunities, too, for recreation – fishing, shooting, mountain climbing, particularly tackling the highest Alpine peaks. And the chance to become a Master of Foxhounds, and at the same time to join a top class rugger club.

This recitation may make it seem as though life was all fun, and in a way it was; but at the same time we were serious soldiers and, although I say so, first-class soldiers. It was our pride to make our Army the best in the world. We left nothing undone. We were well aware that the peace of the Indian subcontinent, and hundreds of millions of people, depended on us, and we were not going to betray that trust.

As I have mentioned, I was involved in one North West Frontier war against a marauding Afridi tribe. We were 100% ready at all times for service on 'The Frontier', or elsewhere. But we were not there to make war. We were there to keep the peace.

The war changed the lives of many of us and I never got back to my Regiment. I do however remain in touch with Hodson's Horse and had an opportunity to visit them in India recently. They have maintained their excellent traditions and are still as fine a Regiment as they were when we had the honour to belong to them.

Despite my wish to remain a regimental officer I was destined to be a professional Intelligence Officer for the rest of my official career – for the last fifteen years as a Director of MI5, another exceptionally interesting life.

Index